Cooking Light

weeknight
one-dish
meals

ISBN-13: 978-0-8487-36972
ISBN-10: 0-8487-36974

Printed in the United States of America
First printing 2012

Be sure to check with your health-care provider before making any changes in your diet.

Oxmoor House

VP, Publishing Director: Jim Childs
Creative Director: Felicity Keane
Brand Manager: Michelle Turner Aycock
Senior Editor: Heather Averett
Managing Editor: Rebecca Benton

Cooking Light® Weeknight One-Dish Meals

Project Editor: Holly D. Smith
Assistant Designer: Allison Sperando Potter
Director, Test Kitchen: Elizabeth Tyler Austin
Assistant Directors, Test Kitchen: Julie Christopher, Julie Gunter
Test Kitchen Professionals: Wendy Ball, RD; Victoria E. Cox; Margaret Monroe Dickey; Stefanie Maloney; Callie Nash; Catherine Crowell Steele; Leah Van Deren
Recipe Editor: Alyson Moreland Haynes
Photography Director: Jim Bathie
Senior Photo Stylist: Kay E. Clarke
Photo Stylist: Katherine Eckert Coyne
Assistant Photo Stylist: Mary Louise Menendez
Assistant Production Manager: Diane Rose

Contributors:
Project Editor: Laura Hoxworth
Copy Editor: Jacqueline Giovanelli
Proofreaders: Jasmine Hodges, Kate Johnson
Interns: Erin Bishop, Maribeth Browning, Mackenzie Cogle

Time Home Entertainment Inc.

Publisher: Richard Fraiman
VP, Strategy & Business Development: Steven Sandonato
Executive Director, Marketing Services: Carol Pittard
Executive Director, Retail & Special Sales: Tom Mifsud
Director, Bookazine Development & Marketing: Laura Adam
Publishing Director: Joy Butts
Finance Director: Glenn Buonocore
Associate General Counsel: Helen Wan

Cooking Light®

Editor: Scott Mowbray
Creative Director: Carla Frank
Executive Managing Editor: Phillip Rhodes
Executive Editor, Food: Ann Taylor Pittman
Special Publications Editor: Mary Simpson Creel, MS, RD
Senior Food Editors: Timothy Q. Cebula, Julianna Grimes
Senior Editor: Cindy Hatcher
Assistant Editor, Nutrition: Sidney Fry, MS, RD
Assistant Editors: Kimberly Holland, Phoebe Wu
Test Kitchen Director: Vanessa T. Pruett
Assistant Test Kitchen Director: Tiffany Vickers Davis
Recipe Testers and Developers: Robin Bashinsky, Adam Hickman, Deb Wise
Art Directors: Fernande Bondarenko, Shawna Kalish
Associate Art Director: Rachel Cardina Lasserre
Designers: Hagen Stegall, Dréa Zacharenko
Assistant Designer: Nicole Gerrity
Photo Director: Kristen Schaefer
Assistant Photo Editor: Amy Delaune
Senior Photographer: Randy Mayor
Senior Photo Stylist: Cindy Barr
Photo Stylist: Leigh Ann Ross
Chief Food Stylist: Charlotte Autry
Senior Food Stylist: Kellie Gerber Kelley
Food Styling Assistant: Blakeslee Wright
Copy Chief: Maria Parker Hopkins
Assistant Copy Chief: Susan Roberts
Research Editor: Michelle Gibson Daniels
Production Director: Liz Rhoades
Production Editor: Hazel R. Eddins
Assistant Production Editor: Josh Rutledge
Administrative Coordinator: Carol D. Johnson
Cookinglight.com Editor: Allison Long Lowery
Nutrition Editor: Holley Johnson Grainger, MS, RD
Production Assistant: Mallory Brasseale

Cover: Baked Ziti and Summer Veggies, page 88
Back Cover (clockwise from top left): Artichoke and Goat Cheese Strata, page 84; Warm Pasta Salad with Shrimp, page 30; Thai Rice Noodles with Chicken, page 161; Simple Lobster Risotto, page 173; Quick Chicken Noodle Soup, page 277

To order additional publications, call
1-800-765-6400 or 1-800-491-0551.

For more books to enrich your life, visit **oxmoorhouse.com**

To search, savor, and share thousands of recipes, visit **myrecipes.com**

Cooking Light

weeknight one-dish meals

Oxmoor
House®

Fall Vegetable Curry, 12

Chicken and Root Vegetable Potpie, 118

Contents

Baked Mac and Cheese, 193

Superfast Chicken Posole, 279

Chicken Fried Rice with Leeks
and Dried Cranberries, 159

Beer-Braised Beef with Onion,
Carrot, and Turnips, 175

Chickpea Chili, 301

Fall Salad
with Apples,
Walnuts, and
Stilton, 342

Welcome

Quick and easy, yet delicious and comforting, one-dish recipes are some of the best-loved dishes in cuisines around the world. From hearty soups and stews to slow-cooker favorites and savory casseroles, one-dish meals are guaranteed to please every palate. Paired with a simple salad or homemade bread, these dishes bring home-cooked goodness to your table without unnecessary hassle or time.

For a fast and delicious weeknight meal, try our Curried Chicken and Cashews (page 65) to turn up the heat on your average dinnertime experience. Our Mongolian Beef (page 40) will also satisfy your craving for the spicy and savory.

With schedules busier than ever, takeout seems to be the most viable option for simplicity and speed. However, in the time it takes to place your typical takeout order, you can whip up a satisfying casserole to feed the whole family and then some. Both nutritious and cost effective, the recipes found in our Casseroles chapter are ideal for family dinners or your next potluck.

A longtime favorite, Eggplant Parmesan (page 95) is perfect for a Meatless Monday, as are Artichoke and Goat Cheese Strata (page 84) and Vegetarian Moussaka (page 90). We've also included some top-rated recipes, such as Chicken Enchilada Casserole (page 115) and classic Turkey Tetrazzini (page 120).

Dinner will be waiting for you when you get home with slow-cooker recipes like White Chicken Chili (page 326) or Beef Burgundy with Egg Noodles (page 314).

If you want to add a little something extra as an appetizer or side, be sure to check out the last chapter, full of kitchen-tested ideas to complete your meal with flavor and style.

Simple yet superb, the recipes you'll find in Cooking Light *Weeknight One-Dish Meals* will not disappoint.

The *Cooking Light* Editors

Lemongrass Pork, page 43

quick & easy

Vegetarian Country Captain

Traditionally, Country Captain is a mild chicken stew seasoned with curry powder. We've replaced the chicken with edamame and cauliflower for a vegetable-loaded version to help you meet your daily produce goals.

1 tablespoon canola oil
1½ cups finely chopped onion
1½ cups diced peeled Granny Smith apple
  (about ½ pound)
1 tablespoon all-purpose flour
1 tablespoon curry powder
3 garlic cloves, minced
2 cups organic vegetable broth
2 tablespoons mango chutney
2 tablespoons whipping cream

½ teaspoon kosher salt
3 cups cauliflower florets
2 cups frozen shelled edamame (green
  soybeans)
3 cups hot cooked long-grain white rice
¼ cup dried currants
¼ cup sliced almonds, toasted
Chopped fresh cilantro (optional)
Sliced green onions (optional)

1. Heat oil in a large, heavy nonstick skillet over medium heat. Add onion; cook 7 minutes or until tender, stirring frequently. Add apple; cook 5 minutes, stirring frequently. Add flour, curry powder, and garlic; cook 1 minute, stirring constantly. Add broth; bring to a boil. Reduce heat, and simmer 2 minutes or until slightly thick. Stir in chutney, cream, and salt. Add cauliflower and edamame; cook 8 minutes or until cauliflower is tender, stirring occasionally. Serve over rice, and top with currants and almonds. Garnish with cilantro and green onions, if desired. Yield: 4 servings (serving size: ¾ cup cooked rice, 1¼ cups cauliflower mixture, 1 tablespoon currants, and 1 tablespoon almonds).

CALORIES 473; **FAT** 14.9g (sat 3.4g, mono 6g, poly 4.4g); **PROTEIN** 16.7g; **CARB** 70.6g; **FIBER** 5.8g; **CHOL** 10mg; **IRON** 4.4mg; **SODIUM** 641mg; **CALC** 122mg

Fall Vegetable Curry

This superfast vegetarian meal embraces Indian flavors. Serve over hot cooked rice accented by ¼ cup unsalted whole cashews.

1½ teaspoons olive oil
1 cup diced peeled sweet potato
1 cup small cauliflower florets
¼ cup thinly sliced yellow onion
2 teaspoons Madras curry powder
½ cup organic vegetable broth
¼ teaspoon salt

1 (15-ounce) can chickpeas (garbanzo beans), rinsed and drained
1 (14.5-ounce) can no-salt-added diced tomatoes, undrained
2 tablespoons chopped fresh cilantro
½ cup plain 2% reduced-fat Greek yogurt

1. Heat olive oil in a large nonstick skillet over medium-high heat. Add sweet potato to pan; sauté 3 minutes. Reduce heat to medium. Add cauliflower, onion, and curry powder; cook 1 minute, stirring mixture constantly. Add broth and next 3 ingredients (through tomatoes); bring to a boil. Cover, reduce heat, and simmer 10 minutes or until vegetables are tender, stirring occasionally. Sprinkle with cilantro; serve with yogurt. Yield: 4 servings (serving size: 1 cup curry and 2 tablespoons yogurt).

CALORIES 231; **FAT** 3.9g (sat 0.9g, mono 1.6g, poly 0.9g); **PROTEIN** 10.4g; **CARB** 40.8g; **FIBER** 8.6g; **CHOL** 2mg; **IRON** 2.5mg; **SODIUM** 626mg; **CALC** 106mg

SIMPLE SUB: No Madras? Combine 1½ teaspoons regular curry powder and ¼ teaspoon ground red pepper.

Turkish Carrots and Lentils

Slightly sweet and spicy, ground Aleppo pepper brightens the sauce, while carrots and yogurt lighten earthy lentils. Serve with a simple romaine salad.

3 tablespoons extra-virgin olive oil
1½ cups thinly sliced onion
1 garlic clove, minced
1 tablespoon tomato paste
½ teaspoon ground Aleppo pepper
1 pound carrots, halved lengthwise and thinly sliced (about 3 cups)

¾ teaspoon sea salt, divided
3 cups water
1 cup uncooked dried green lentils
¼ teaspoon freshly ground black pepper
¼ cup Greek-style yogurt
Dill sprigs (optional)

1. Heat oil in a large saucepan over medium heat. Add onion to pan; cook 9 minutes or until lightly browned, stirring occasionally. Add garlic; cook 1 minute. Stir in tomato paste and Aleppo pepper; cook 30 seconds. Stir in carrots and ¼ teaspoon salt; cook 1 minute. Remove from heat.

2. Combine 3 cups water and lentils in a large saucepan, and bring to a boil. Cover, reduce heat, and simmer 30 minutes. Uncover, increase heat to medium-high, and stir in onion mixture; cook 2 minutes or until liquid almost evaporates. Stir in remaining ½ teaspoon salt and freshly ground black pepper. Cover with a kitchen towel, and cool to room temperature. Serve with yogurt. Garnish with dill, if desired. Yield: 4 servings (serving size: about 1 cup lentil mixture and 1 tablespoon yogurt).

CALORIES 357; **FAT** 12.2g (sat 2.8g, mono 7.7g, poly 1.2g); **PROTEIN** 17.4g; **CARB** 48.6g; **FIBER** 10.6g; **CHOL** 3mg; **IRON** 5mg; **SODIUM** 549mg; **CALC** 64mg

Quick White Bean, Asparagus, and Mushroom Cassoulet

Cassoulet—a rich, slow-cooked bean stew with meat—is reinvented here as a quick-cooking vegetarian dish, starting with canned beans and using mushrooms to lend a meaty mouthfeel and earthy flavor.

5 cups water
3 cups (2-inch) slices asparagus (about 1 pound)
2 tablespoons extra-virgin olive oil, divided
3 cups sliced chanterelle or oyster mushrooms (about 10 ounces)
1/3 cup finely chopped shallots
6 garlic cloves, minced
1/4 cup dry white wine

1 1/2 cups organic vegetable broth
1/2 teaspoon dried oregano
2 (15-ounce) cans no-salt-added cannellini beans, rinsed and drained
1/4 teaspoon freshly ground black pepper
2 ounces French bread, cut into 1-inch cubes
1 tablespoon butter, cut into small pieces
1/2 cup (2 ounces) grated Parmigiano-Reggiano cheese

1. Bring 5 cups water to a boil in a large stainless-steel skillet, and add asparagus to pan. Cover and cook 2 minutes; drain. Rinse asparagus with cold water; drain well. Set aside.
2. Return pan to medium-high heat. Add 1 tablespoon oil, swirling to coat. Add mushrooms, shallots, and garlic; sauté 8 minutes or until mushrooms are tender. Add wine; cook 3 minutes or until liquid evaporates. Stir in broth, oregano, and beans; bring to a simmer. Reduce heat to medium; cook 12 minutes or until thick and beans are very tender. Stir in black pepper.
3. Preheat broiler.
4. Place bread and butter in a food processor; pulse until coarse crumbs form. Add remaining 1 tablespoon oil and cheese to coarse breadcrumbs; pulse until combined. Stir asparagus into bean mixture; sprinkle coarse breadcrumb mixture evenly over bean mixture. Broil 3 minutes or until crumbs are golden brown. Yield: 4 servings (serving size: about 1¾ cups).

CALORIES 328; **FAT** 14.2g (sat 4.6g, mono 6.5g, poly 1g); **PROTEIN** 15.7g; **CARB** 36.3g; **FIBER** 8.8g; **CHOL** 16mg; **IRON** 5.7mg; **SODIUM** 530mg; **CALC** 198mg

Fettuccine with Mushrooms and Hazelnuts

Look for blanched hazelnuts, which should have most or all of their skins removed.

1 (9-ounce) package refrigerated fettuccine
1 tablespoon butter
¼ cup chopped blanched hazelnuts
1 tablespoon olive oil
4 garlic cloves, thinly sliced
3 (4-ounce) packages presliced exotic
  mushroom blend

½ teaspoon salt, divided
¼ teaspoon freshly ground black pepper
2 teaspoons chopped fresh sage
2 ounces Parmigiano-Reggiano cheese,
  shaved
2 tablespoons finely chopped fresh chives

1. Cook fettuccine according to package directions, omitting salt and fat. Drain in a colander over a bowl, reserving ¾ cup cooking liquid.

2. While water for pasta comes to a boil, melt butter in a large nonstick skillet over medium-high heat. Add hazelnuts to pan; sauté 3 minutes or until toasted and fragrant. Remove from pan with a slotted spoon. Add oil to pan, and swirl to coat. Add garlic and mushrooms to pan; sprinkle with ¼ teaspoon salt and black pepper. Sauté mushroom mixture 5 minutes; stir in sage. Add pasta, reserved cooking liquid, and remaining ¼ teaspoon salt to pan; toss well to combine. Remove from heat; top with shaved cheese, toasted hazelnuts, and chives. Yield: 4 servings (serving size: about 1½ cups pasta mixture, 2 tablespoons cheese, and 1 tablespoon hazelnuts).

CALORIES 364; **FAT** 16.5g (sat 5.7g, mono 7.6g, poly 1.2g); **PROTEIN** 16.8g; **CARB** 40.2g; **FIBER** 3.2g; **CHOL** 56mg; **IRON** 2.4mg; **SODIUM** 563mg; **CALC** 204mg

NUTRITION TIP: Hazelnuts provide protein and vitamin E in this meatless dish. They're also high in monounsaturated fat.

Pasta with Zucchini and Toasted Almonds

Serve with olive tapenade breadsticks: Combine 1 tablespoon extra-virgin olive oil, 1¹/₂ teaspoons minced garlic, 1 teaspoon fresh lemon juice, ¹/₄ teaspoon salt, ¹/₈ teaspoon freshly ground black pepper, and 15 finely chopped pitted kalamata olives in a small bowl. Spread olive mixture over 1 (11-ounce) can refrigerated breadstick dough. Twist each breadstick; bake at 375° for 15 minutes or until browned.

2 cups cherry tomatoes, halved
2 tablespoons minced shallots
1 teaspoon minced fresh thyme
2 teaspoons fresh lemon juice
³/₄ teaspoon kosher salt
¹/₂ teaspoon freshly ground black pepper
¹/₄ teaspoon sugar
5 teaspoons extra-virgin olive oil, divided

1 (9-ounce) package refrigerated linguine
1¹/₂ teaspoons minced garlic
3 cups chopped zucchini (about 1 pound)
³/₄ cup fat-free, lower-sodium chicken broth
3 tablespoons thinly sliced fresh mint, divided
¹/₃ cup (1¹/₂ ounces) grated fresh pecorino Romano cheese
3 tablespoons sliced almonds, toasted

1. Combine first 7 ingredients in a medium bowl. Add 2 teaspoons oil, tossing to coat.

2. Cook pasta according to package directions, omitting salt and fat. Drain well.

3. Heat remaining 1 tablespoon oil in a large nonstick skillet over medium-high heat. Add garlic to pan; sauté 30 seconds. Add zucchini; sauté 3 minutes or until crisp-tender. Add broth; bring to a simmer. Stir in pasta and 1½ tablespoons mint; toss well. Remove from heat; stir in tomato mixture. Place 1½ cups pasta mixture in each of 4 bowls; top evenly with remaining 1½ tablespoons mint. Sprinkle each serving with 4 teaspoons cheese and about 2 teaspoons almonds. Yield: 4 servings.

CALORIES 344; **FAT** 12.7g (sat 3.1g, mono 6.6g, poly 2g); **PROTEIN** 14g; **CARB** 45.5g; **FIBER** 5.3g; **CHOL** 58mg; **IRON** 3.4mg; **SODIUM** 601mg; **CALC** 163mg

Arctic Char and Vegetables in Parchment Hearts

Perfect for when you need just two servings, this recipe also doubles easily for entertaining. You can do the prep work in advance.

1½ tablespoons unsalted butter, softened
1 teaspoon grated lemon rind
1 tablespoon fresh lemon juice
1 teaspoon chopped fresh dill
2 (6-ounce) arctic char fillets (about 1 inch thick)

¼ teaspoon kosher salt
⅛ teaspoon freshly ground black pepper
¼ cup julienne-cut leeks
¼ cup julienne-cut red bell pepper
¼ cup julienne-cut carrot
¼ cup julienne-cut snow peas

1. Preheat oven to 450°.

2. Combine first 4 ingredients in a small bowl; stir until blended.

3. Cut 2 (15 x 24–inch) pieces of parchment paper. Fold in half crosswise. Draw a large heart half on each piece, with the fold of the paper along the center of the heart. Cut out the heart, and open. Sprinkle both sides of fillets with salt and pepper. Place one fillet near fold of each parchment heart. Top each fillet with half the vegetables and half of the butter mixture. Start at the top of the heart and fold edges of parchment, sealing edges with narrow folds. Twist the end tip to secure tightly. Place packets on a baking sheet. Bake at 450° for 15 minutes or until paper is puffy and lightly browned. Place on plates; cut open. Serve immediately. Yield: 2 servings (serving size: 1 fillet, ½ cup vegetables, and about 1 tablespoon sauce).

CALORIES 301; **FAT** 14.6g (sat 6.4g, mono 3.8g, poly 2.7g); **PROTEIN** 34.8g; **CARB** 6g; **FIBER** 1.4g; **CHOL** 111mg; **IRON** 1.8mg; **SODIUM** 369mg; **CALC** 45mg

SIMPLE SUB: If arctic char is not available from your fishmonger, you can substitute fresh or frozen wild Alaskan salmon.

Halibut with White Beans in Tomato-Rosemary Broth

Beans absorb some of the delicious broth. For a special dinner, serve in shallow rimmed bowls; garnish with fresh rosemary. Add a simple salad of arugula tossed with a light vinaigrette; top with shaved Asiago.

1 tablespoon olive oil
4 (6-ounce) halibut fillets
¼ teaspoon salt
¼ teaspoon freshly ground black pepper
2 garlic cloves, minced
2 cups chopped plum tomato (about 4)

1½ cups fat-free, lower-sodium chicken broth
½ cup dry white wine
1 (16-ounce) can cannellini beans or other white beans, rinsed and drained
½ teaspoon chopped fresh rosemary

1. Heat oil in a large nonstick skillet over medium-high heat. Sprinkle fish with salt and pepper. Add fish to pan; cook 5 minutes on each side or until fish flakes easily when tested with a fork or until desired degree of doneness. Remove fish from pan; keep warm. Add garlic to pan; cook 30 seconds, stirring constantly. Stir in plum tomato, broth, wine, and beans; bring to a boil. Reduce heat; simmer 5 minutes. Remove from heat; stir in rosemary. Serve immediately with fish. Yield: 4 servings (serving size: 1 fillet and ¾ cup bean mixture).

CALORIES 299; **FAT** 7.9g (sat 1.1g, mono 3.8g, poly 2g); **PROTEIN** 39.8g; **CARB** 14.9g; **FIBER** 4g; **CHOL** 54mg; **IRON** 3.2mg; **SODIUM** 535mg; **CALC** 117mg

Sesame Halibut en Papillote

En papillote *refers to the method of steaming in the oven, where the food is baked in parchment paper. Steam is trapped inside, keeping the food moist and flavorful. The impressive presentation belies this dish's simple preparation.*

1 tablespoon dark sesame oil, divided
2 garlic cloves, minced
4 cups shredded bok choy
½ teaspoon salt, divided
½ teaspoon sambal oelek (ground fresh chile paste)

4 (6-ounce) halibut fillets (about 1 inch thick)
¼ teaspoon freshly ground black pepper
1 teaspoon sesame seeds, toasted

1. Preheat oven to 400°.

2. Heat 1 teaspoon sesame oil in a large nonstick skillet over medium-high heat. Add garlic; sauté 30 seconds. Add bok choy and ¼ teaspoon salt; sauté 5 minutes or until crisp-tender. Remove from heat; stir in chile paste. Sprinkle fish evenly with remaining ¼ teaspoon salt and pepper.

3. Cut 4 (15-inch) squares of parchment paper. Fold each square in half, and open each. Place ½ cup bok choy near fold; top with 1 fillet. Drizzle each serving with ½ teaspoon oil; sprinkle with ¼ teaspoon sesame seeds. Fold papers; seal edges with narrow folds. Place packets on a baking sheet. Bake at 400° for 18 minutes or until paper is puffy and lightly browned. Place 1 packet on each of 4 plates; cut open. Serve immediately. Yield: 4 servings.

CALORIES 233; **FAT** 7.8g (sat 1.1g, mono 2.8g, poly 2.9g); **PROTEIN** 36.7g; **CARB** 2.3g; **FIBER** 0.9g; **CHOL** 54mg; **IRON** 2.1mg; **SODIUM** 459mg; **CALC** 158mg

Linguine with Clams and Fresh Herbs

Fresh clams are not only sustainable, but they also require no feed and they filter the water in which they live.

8 ounces uncooked linguine
$\frac{1}{3}$ cup finely chopped fresh flat-leaf parsley
1 tablespoon chopped fresh oregano
2 teaspoons grated lemon rind
2 tablespoons olive oil
2 cups vertically sliced red onion
$\frac{1}{4}$ teaspoon crushed red pepper

4 garlic cloves, sliced
$\frac{1}{2}$ cup white wine
$1\frac{1}{2}$ pounds littleneck clams
2 tablespoons butter
$\frac{3}{4}$ teaspoon salt
$\frac{1}{2}$ teaspoon freshly ground black pepper

1. Cook pasta according to package directions, omitting salt and fat, and drain well.
2. Combine parsley, oregano, and rind.
3. Heat oil in a large skillet over medium-high heat. Add onion, red pepper, and garlic; sauté 4 minutes. Add wine and clams; cover and simmer 5 minutes or until shells open. Discard any unopened shells.
4. Combine clam mixture, pasta, butter, salt, and black pepper in a large bowl; toss until butter melts. Sprinkle with parsley mixture; toss well. Yield: 4 servings (serving size: 1½ cups pasta mixture and 6 clams).

CALORIES 373; **FAT** 14.2g (sat 5g, mono 6.6g, poly 1.4g); **PROTEIN** 15g; **CARB** 47.5g; **FIBER** 2.5g; **CHOL** 32mg; **IRON** 9.5mg; **SODIUM** 521mg; **CALC** 61mg

Speedy Cioppino

The bright taste of a lemon-dressed salad goes well with the seafood stew: Combine 1½ tablespoons fresh lemon juice, 1 tablespoon extra-virgin olive oil, ½ teaspoon sugar, ½ teaspoon Dijon mustard, ¼ teaspoon salt, ⅛ teaspoon black pepper, and 1 minced garlic clove, stirring with a whisk. Combine 6 cups gourmet salad greens, 1 cup halved cherry tomatoes, and ½ cup slivered red onion. Drizzle dressing over salad; toss well.

1 tablespoon olive oil
1½ cups (1-inch) cubed red potatoes (about 8 ounces)
1 cup chopped onion (about 1 medium)
½ cup finely chopped fennel bulb
1 tablespoon minced garlic
½ teaspoon dried oregano
⅛ teaspoon saffron threads, crushed

1 cup dry white wine
1 (14.5-ounce) can petite-cut diced tomatoes, undrained
1 (8-ounce) bottle clam juice
1½ pounds mussels (about 40), scrubbed
½ pound peeled and deveined large shrimp
1 (8-ounce) cod fillet
2 tablespoons thinly sliced fresh basil

1. Heat oil in a Dutch oven over medium-high heat. Add potatoes and next 5 ingredients (through saffron); sauté 5 minutes or until vegetables start to soften. Stir in wine, tomatoes, and clam juice; bring to a boil. Cover and cook 15 minutes.
2. Add mussels, shrimp, and cod to pan; cover and cook 6 minutes or until cod is done and mussel shells open. Discard any unopened shells. Stir gently to break cod into chunks. Sprinkle with fresh basil. Yield: 4 servings (serving size: about 1¾ cups stew and about 10 mussels).

CALORIES 311; **FAT** 7.2g (sat 1.2g, mono 3.2g, poly 1.5g); **PROTEIN** 36.5g; **CARB** 24.4g; **FIBER** 3.8g; **CHOL** 140mg; **IRON** 7mg; **SODIUM** 674mg; **CALC** 122mg

Warm Pasta Salad with Shrimp

Toss the pasta with the tangy mustard dressing while it's warm so it will absorb more flavor. If you prefer to serve this salad chilled, make it up to a day ahead, toss, and refrigerate until you're ready to serve.

3 cups uncooked farfalle (bow tie pasta)
¼ cup fresh lemon juice
1½ tablespoons Dijon mustard
1 teaspoon minced fresh garlic
¼ cup olive oil
½ teaspoon kosher salt
½ teaspoon freshly ground black pepper

12 ounces medium shrimp, peeled and deveined
1½ cups chopped fresh spinach
1 cup canned cannellini beans, rinsed and drained
¼ cup minced red onion
2 tablespoons chopped capers

1. Cook pasta according to package directions, omitting salt and fat; drain.
2. Combine lemon juice, mustard, and garlic in a small bowl, stirring well with a whisk. Gradually add olive oil, stirring constantly with a whisk. Stir in salt and black pepper.
3. Heat a large nonstick skillet over medium-high heat. Add shrimp to pan, and cook 2 minutes or until done. Stir in spinach, cannellini beans, red onion, and capers; toss to combine. Add the pasta and juice mixture to shrimp mixture; toss. Yield: 4 servings (serving size: about 2 cups).

CALORIES 487; **FAT** 16.4g (sat 2.4g, mono 10.1g, poly 2g); **PROTEIN** 28.9g; **CARB** 56.2g; **FIBER** 4.9g; **CHOL** 129mg; **IRON** 5.6mg; **SODIUM** 664mg; **CALC** 103mg

FYI: Fresh shrimp elevate a classic Italian trio—beans, greens, and pasta—to a new level. And a few go a long way to stretch your food dollar.

Bombay Shrimp Curry with Coconut Rice

5 teaspoons canola oil, divided
1 pound peeled and deveined shrimp
³/₄ teaspoon salt, divided
¹/₄ teaspoon freshly ground black pepper
1¹/₂ cups prechopped onion
1¹/₂ tablespoons curry powder
1 tablespoon mustard seeds

¹/₄ teaspoon ground cinnamon
¹/₈ teaspoon ground red pepper
1¹/₃ cups hot water
1 cup frozen peas and carrots
1 cup light coconut milk
1 cup uncooked instant rice
1 tablespoon chopped fresh cilantro

1. Heat 2 teaspoons canola oil in a Dutch oven over medium-high heat. Sprinkle shrimp with ⅛ teaspoon salt and black pepper. Add shrimp to pan, and cook 2 minutes on each side or until done. Remove shrimp from pan.

2. Reduce heat to medium. Add remaining 3 teaspoons oil; swirl to coat. Add onion; cook 2 minutes, stirring constantly. Add ½ teaspoon salt, curry powder, and next 3 ingredients (through red pepper); cook 1 minute, stirring constantly. Add hot water and peas and carrots; bring to a boil. Cover and reduce heat to medium-low; simmer 4 minutes. Return shrimp to pan; cook 1 minute.

3. While curry cooks, bring milk to a boil in a saucepan. Stir in remaining ⅛ teaspoon salt and rice. Cover and remove from heat. Let stand 5 minutes or until liquid is absorbed.

4. Place about ⅓ cup rice on each of 4 plates; top each serving with about 1 cup shrimp mixture. Sprinkle each serving with ¾ teaspoon cilantro. Yield: 4 servings.

CALORIES 366; **FAT** 12.5g (sat 3.8g, mono 4.7g, poly 2.7g); **PROTEIN** 28.4g; **CARB** 36.1g; **FIBER** 4g; **CHOL** 172mg; **IRON** 5.9mg; **SODIUM** 660mg; **CALC** 115mg

> **BUYING TIP:** Buy U.S. or Canadian wild-caught or farmed shrimp for the best sustainable option.

Shrimp Korma and Basmati Rice

2 teaspoons butter
1 cup chopped red bell pepper
1/2 cup chopped onion
1 1/2 tablespoons all-purpose flour
1 teaspoon grated peeled fresh ginger
3 garlic cloves, finely chopped
2 teaspoons Madras curry powder
2 teaspoons garam masala
1/2 teaspoon salt, divided

2 cups organic vegetable broth
1/3 cup water
1/3 cup coconut milk
1/4 cup diced tomato
1/4 cup frozen green peas
1 pound peeled and deveined large shrimp
4 cups hot cooked basmati rice
1/4 cup plain fat-free yogurt

1. Melt butter in a Dutch oven over medium-high heat. Add bell pepper and onion to pan; sauté 2 minutes. Add flour, ginger, and garlic; cook 1 minute, stirring constantly. Add curry powder, garam masala, and 1/4 teaspoon salt; cook 30 seconds, stirring constantly. Stir in broth and 1/3 cup water; bring to a boil. Stir in milk and tomato; reduce heat, and simmer 5 minutes. Add peas, shrimp, and remaining 1/4 teaspoon salt; cook 5 minutes or until shrimp are done. Spoon about 2/3 cup rice into each of 6 bowls. Top each serving with about 1 cup shrimp mixture and 2 teaspoons yogurt. Yield: 6 servings.

CALORIES 295; FAT 5.9g (sat 3.5g, mono 0.7g, poly 0.7g); PROTEIN 20.1g; CARB 39.1g; FIBER 2g; CHOL 119mg; IRON 4.3mg; SODIUM 524mg; CALC 71mg

Lowcountry Shrimp Pilaf

Serve this quick dish with a green salad and crusty bread.

1½ tablespoons canola oil
1½ cups prechopped green bell pepper
1 cup prechopped onion
1 tablespoon minced garlic
2 teaspoons Old Bay seasoning
1 pound peeled and deveined large shrimp

½ cup dry white wine
1 (8-ounce) bottle clam juice
1½ cups instant white rice
2 tablespoons chopped fresh thyme, divided
1 (14.5-ounce) can diced tomatoes with
  jalapeño peppers, undrained

1. Heat oil in a large nonstick skillet over medium-high heat. Add bell pepper and onion to pan; sauté 2 minutes. Add garlic and Old Bay seasoning to pan; sauté 1 minute. Add shrimp, wine, and clam juice; bring to a boil. Stir in rice; cover and remove from heat. Let stand 5 minutes or until liquid is absorbed.

2. Place pan over medium-high heat. Stir in 1 tablespoon thyme and tomatoes; cook 2 minutes or until thoroughly heated, stirring occasionally. Sprinkle with remaining 1 tablespoon thyme. Yield: 4 servings (serving size: 1½ cups).

CALORIES 365; **FAT** 8g (sat 0.8g, mono 3.5g, poly 2.4g); **PROTEIN** 27.8g; **CARB** 44.7g; **FIBER** 3.9g; **CHOL** 174mg; **IRON** 6mg; **SODIUM** 756mg; **CALC** 117mg

Spanish Spaghetti with Olives

8 ounces uncooked thin spaghetti
1 tablespoon olive oil
2 cups chopped onion
2 teaspoons minced garlic
1 teaspoon dried oregano
½ teaspoon celery salt
¼ teaspoon crushed red pepper
¼ teaspoon freshly ground black pepper

¼ teaspoon crushed saffron threads (optional)
8 ounces ground beef, extra lean
1²/₃ cups lower-sodium marinara sauce
½ cup sliced pimiento-stuffed olives
¼ cup dry sherry
1 tablespoon capers
¼ cup chopped fresh parsley, divided

1. Cook pasta according to package directions, omitting salt and fat; drain.

2. Heat olive oil in a large skillet over medium-high heat. Add onion to pan; sauté 4 minutes or until tender. Add garlic; sauté 1 minute. Stir in oregano, celery salt, red pepper, black pepper, and saffron, if desired. Crumble beef into pan; cook 5 minutes or until beef is browned, stirring to crumble. Stir in sauce, olives, sherry, capers, and 2 tablespoons parsley. Bring to a boil; reduce heat, and simmer 15 minutes.

3. Add spaghetti to sauce mixture. Cook 2 minutes or until thoroughly heated. Sprinkle with remaining 2 tablespoons parsley. Yield: 4 servings (serving size: about 1¾ cups).

CALORIES 445; **FAT** 12.1g (sat 3g, mono 5.9g, poly 0.8g); **PROTEIN** 22.3g; **CARB** 60.6g; **FIBER** 5.4g; **CHOL** 21mg; **IRON** 5.2mg; **SODIUM** 679mg; **CALC** 72mg

FYI: Supermarket shelves are groaning with jarred marinara sauces. We tasted and compared numerous brands for flavor, consistency, and nutrition. Our lower-sodium pick: McCutcheon's.

Quick Beef Boliche

Boliche *is a Cuban dish that traditionally cooks for a long time. In this twist, we offer similar flavors with a faster preparation.*

Cooking spray
1 (1-pound) top sirloin, cut into (1-inch) pieces
1/2 teaspoon salt
1/4 teaspoon freshly ground black pepper
3 ounces hot chicken Italian sausage
3/4 cup chopped green bell pepper
1/2 cup chopped onion
1/2 cup chopped celery
3 garlic cloves, minced

2 cups refrigerated diced potatoes with onions
1/4 cup sliced pimiento-stuffed olives, divided
1 bay leaf
1 (14.5-ounce) can no-salt-added diced tomatoes, undrained
1 tablespoon fresh lime juice
Lime wedges (optional)

1. Heat a large Dutch oven over high heat. Coat pan with cooking spray. Sprinkle beef with salt and black pepper. Add beef to pan; sauté 3 minutes or until browned. Remove casings from sausage. Add sausage to pan; sauté 1 minute or until browned, stirring to crumble. Stir in green bell pepper, onion, celery, and minced garlic; sauté 2 minutes or until tender. Add potatoes, 2 tablespoons olives, and bay leaf to pan. Pour diced tomatoes evenly over beef mixture. Cover, reduce heat, and simmer 35 minutes or until beef is tender. Discard bay leaf. Stir in remaining 2 tablespoons olives and lime juice. Serve with lime wedges, if desired. Yield: 4 servings (serving size: 1¼ cups).

CALORIES 281; **FAT** 7g (sat 2.4g, mono 2.9g, poly 0.7g); **PROTEIN** 29.8g; **CARB** 24.6g; **FIBER** 4.9g; **CHOL** 62mg; **IRON** 2.6mg; **SODIUM** 684mg; **CALC** 52mg

Mongolian Beef

Serve this slightly spicy dish over wide rice noodles to catch the garlic- and ginger-laced sauce.

2 tablespoons lower-sodium soy sauce
1 teaspoon sugar
1 teaspoon cornstarch
2 teaspoons dry sherry
2 teaspoons hoisin sauce
1 teaspoon rice vinegar
1 teaspoon sambal oelek (ground fresh chile paste)

¼ teaspoon salt
2 teaspoons peanut oil
1 tablespoon minced peeled fresh ginger
1 tablespoon minced garlic
1 pound sirloin steak, thinly sliced across the grain
16 medium green onions, cut into 2-inch pieces

1. Combine first 8 ingredients, stirring until smooth.

2. Heat peanut oil in a large nonstick skillet over medium-high heat. Add ginger, garlic, and beef; sauté 2 minutes or until beef is browned. Add onion pieces; sauté 30 seconds. Add soy sauce mixture; cook 1 minute or until thickened, stirring constantly. Yield: 4 servings (serving size: 1 cup).

CALORIES 237; **FAT** 10.5g (sat 3.5g, mono 4.3g, poly 1.1g); **PROTEIN** 26g; **CARB** 9.1g; **FIBER** 1.7g; **CHOL** 60mg; **IRON** 2.7mg; **SODIUM** 517mg; **CALC** 67mg

---

FYI: Enjoy the sweet, salty, spicy, and sour tastes typical of Asian cuisine. Condiments such as ground fresh chile paste, hoisin sauce, rice vinegar, and lower-sodium soy sauce add big, bold, Far East flavor. They are available in supermarkets and don't require a trip to an ethnic grocery store.

Sour Beans with Minced Pork

Achieving the correct balance of flavor in the beans depends on using two types of vinegar—white vinegar alone will make the beans too tart, while rice vinegar will yield a taste that's too mild.

1 (3½-ounce) bag boil-in-bag long-grain rice
1 cup white vinegar
1 cup rice vinegar
1¼ pounds green beans, trimmed and cut
   diagonally into ½-inch pieces
4 teaspoons peanut oil
1 tablespoon minced peeled fresh ginger
1 tablespoon minced garlic

1 teaspoon crushed red pepper
½ pound lean ground pork
⅓ cup fat-free, lower-sodium chicken broth
3 tablespoons lower-sodium soy sauce
1½ teaspoons cornstarch
⅓ cup thinly sliced green onions
¼ cup matchstick-cut carrot

1. Cook rice according to package directions.
2. Bring vinegars to a boil in a large saucepan. Add beans; cook 2 minutes. Drain beans (do not rinse).
3. Heat oil in a large nonstick skillet over medium-high heat. Add ginger, garlic, and pepper; sauté 30 seconds. Add pork to pan; cook 2 minutes or until browned, stirring to crumble. Add beans; cook 2 minutes, stirring occasionally. Combine broth, soy sauce, and cornstarch; stir with a whisk. Stir broth mixture into pork mixture, and cook 1 minute or until thickened. Divide rice among 4 plates; top evenly with pork mixture. Sprinkle evenly with green onions and carrot. Yield: 4 servings.

CALORIES 290; **FAT** 9.8g (sat 2.8g, mono 3.6g, poly 1.6g); **PROTEIN** 16.6g; **CARB** 34.4g; **FIBER** 5.5g; **CHOL** 43mg; **IRON** 2.6mg; **SODIUM** 483mg; **CALC** 66mg

Lemongrass Pork *(Pictured on page 8)*

A Southeast Asian–accented broth adds zest to pork and vegetables in this flavorful dish.

**4 (4-ounce) boneless center-cut loin pork
   chops (about ½ inch thick)**
¼ teaspoon freshly ground black pepper
⅛ teaspoon salt
2 tablespoons chopped green onions
**1 tablespoon finely chopped peeled fresh
   lemongrass**
**1 tablespoon finely chopped peeled
   fresh ginger**

1 tablespoon lower-sodium soy sauce
**8 ounces carrot, halved lengthwise and cut
   into 3-inch pieces**
**1 (14-ounce) can fat-free, lower-sodium
   chicken broth**
1 garlic clove, sliced
4 baby bok choy, halved
1 tablespoon chopped fresh cilantro
1 tablespoon fresh lime juice

1. Heat a large nonstick skillet over medium-high heat. Sprinkle pork with pepper and salt. Add pork to pan; cook 3½ minutes on each side or until pork is done. Remove from pan; keep warm.

2. Add onions and next 6 ingredients (through garlic) to pan. Bring to a simmer. Cook 6 minutes. Arrange bok choy in a single layer over carrot mixture. Cover, reduce heat to medium, and cook 4 minutes or until bok choy is tender. Stir in cilantro and juice. Cut each pork chop into ½-inch-thick slices. Spoon ½ cup vegetable mixture into each of 4 shallow bowls; top each serving with 3 ounces pork. Yield: 4 servings.

CALORIES 210; **FAT** 7.4g (sat 2.6g, mono 3.2g, poly 0.8g); **PROTEIN** 27.1g; **CARB** 8.9g; **FIBER** 2.2g; **CHOL** 67mg; **IRON** 1.9mg; **SODIUM** 357mg; **CALC** 104mg

Hoisin Pork and Snow Pea Stir-Fry

Slightly sweet, soy-based hoisin sauce is to Chinese food what ketchup is to American food.

4 ounces uncooked rice noodles or rice
2 tablespoons lower-sodium soy sauce, divided
1 (1-pound) pork tenderloin, thinly sliced
3/4 cup fat-free, lower-sodium chicken broth
1/4 cup hoisin sauce
1 tablespoon cornstarch

1 tablespoon honey
4 teaspoons dark sesame oil, divided
3 cups snow peas, trimmed (about 1/2 pound)
1/2 cup sliced red bell pepper
1 tablespoon bottled ground fresh ginger
1 teaspoon minced garlic
1/2 cup chopped green onions

1. Prepare rice noodles according to package directions, omitting salt and fat. Drain and keep warm.

2. Combine 1 tablespoon soy sauce and pork, tossing to coat. Set aside.

3. Combine remaining 1 tablespoon soy sauce, broth, hoisin, cornstarch, and honey in a medium bowl, stirring with a whisk until smooth.

4. Heat 1 tablespoon sesame oil in a large nonstick skillet over medium-high heat. Add pork mixture to pan; sauté 3 minutes or until browned. Remove pork from pan. Add remaining 1 teaspoon sesame oil to pan. Stir in snow peas, bell pepper, ginger, and garlic; sauté 30 seconds. Return pork mixture to pan; stir in broth mixture. Simmer 2 minutes or until thick, stirring occasionally. Remove from heat, and stir in green onions. Serve over rice noodles. Yield: 4 servings (serving size: 3/4 cup noodles and about 1 cup pork mixture).

CALORIES 395; **FAT** 9.6g (sat 2.1g, mono 3.7g, poly 2.5g); **PROTEIN** 28.1g; **CARB** 43.7g; **FIBER** 2.4g; **CHOL** 74mg; **IRON** 2.5mg; **SODIUM** 690mg; **CALC** 53mg

Ham and Cheese Hash Browns

A great use for leftover ham, this recipe resembles a skillet potato hash, but it's more easily prepared in the microwave. No need to thaw the hash brown potatoes; they go straight from the freezer to the microwave.

3 cups frozen hash brown potatoes with onions and peppers
⅓ cup fat-free, lower-sodium chicken broth
½ cup drained canned quartered artichoke hearts, chopped
¼ cup chopped green onions
⅛ teaspoon freshly ground black pepper
3 ounces smoked ham, cut into bite-sized pieces
½ cup (about 2 ounces) shredded Monterey Jack cheese

1. Combine potatoes and chicken broth in a 1-quart microwave-safe casserole. Cover with lid, and microwave at HIGH 12 minutes, stirring after 6 minutes.
2. Uncover dish. Stir in artichoke hearts, green onions, black pepper, and ham. Sprinkle with cheese. Microwave, uncovered, at HIGH 1 minute. Yield: 2 servings (serving size: 1¾ cups).

CALORIES 378; **FAT** 12.5g (sat 6.2g, mono 2.7g, poly 1.4g); **PROTEIN** 20g; **CARB** 41.8g; **FIBER** 6.1g; **CHOL** 55mg; **IRON** 1.3mg; **SODIUM** 817mg; **CALC** 204mg

Pork Tenderloin with Red and Yellow Peppers

Anchovies melt into the pepper mixture, adding a savory, salty quality. If you're not a fan of anchovies, omit them and add 3 tablespoons minced olives. Serve with mashed potatoes.

1 tablespoon extra-virgin olive oil
1 (1-pound) pork tenderloin, trimmed and
   cut crosswise into 1-inch-thick medallions
1/2 teaspoon kosher salt
1/2 teaspoon freshly ground black pepper
1 1/2 teaspoons chopped fresh rosemary, divided

4 canned anchovy fillets, drained and mashed
3 garlic cloves, thinly sliced
1 red bell pepper, cut into 1 1/2-inch strips
1 yellow bell pepper, cut into 1 1/2-inch strips
2 teaspoons balsamic vinegar

1. Heat oil in a large skillet over medium-high heat. Sprinkle pork with salt and pepper. Add pork to pan; cook 5 minutes. Reduce heat to medium; turn pork over. Add 1 teaspoon rosemary, anchovies, garlic, and bell peppers; cook 7 minutes or until peppers are tender and pork is done. Drizzle with vinegar. Top with remaining 1/2 teaspoon rosemary. Yield: 4 servings (serving size: 3 ounces pork and about 1/2 cup bell pepper mixture).

CALORIES 215; FAT 10.1g (sat 2.7g, mono 5.4g, poly 1.2g); PROTEIN 25.2g; CARB 5g; FIBER 1.4g; CHOL 78mg; IRON 2mg; SODIUM 441mg; CALC 26mg

Parmesan Polenta and Spicy Sausage Sauce

Use any variety of chicken sausage in the sauce.

1 tablespoon olive oil
3 ounces (2 links) sun-dried tomato chicken
   sausage, sliced
1 cup chopped onion
3 garlic cloves, minced
1 tablespoon chopped fresh oregano
1/2 teaspoon crushed red pepper
2 (14.5-ounce) cans no-salt-added diced
   tomatoes, undrained

1/2 cup chopped fresh basil, divided
2 cups fat-free, lower-sodium chicken broth
1 cup water
3/4 cup quick-cooking polenta
1/2 cup (2 ounces) grated Parmesan cheese,
   divided

1. Heat oil in a medium saucepan over medium-high heat. Add sausage; sauté 3 minutes or until browned. Add onion; sauté 5 minutes or until tender. Add garlic; sauté 30 seconds. Add oregano, pepper, and tomatoes; bring to a boil. Reduce heat, and simmer 15 minutes, stirring occasionally. Add ¼ cup basil to pan, and cook 5 minutes or until sauce thickens.
2. Combine broth and water in a large saucepan; bring to a boil. Add polenta; reduce heat, and simmer 5 minutes or until thick, stirring frequently with a whisk. Stir in ¼ cup cheese. Place ⅔ cup polenta in each of 4 bowls; top with about ¾ cup sauce. Top each serving with 1 tablespoon basil and 1 tablespoon cheese. Yield: 4 servings.

CALORIES 279; FAT 8.3g (sat 2.7g, mono 4.1g, poly 1g); PROTEIN 12.6g; CARB 31g; FIBER 5.3g; CHOL 25mg; IRON 1.7mg; SODIUM 524mg; CALC 170mg

FLAVOR HIT: Fresh basil and oregano make the difference in a sauce that relies on canned convenience products.

Chicken and Strawberry Salad

Pair this simple main-dish salad with toasted buttery baguette slices: Broil 8 (1/2-inch) slices French bread baguette for 1 1/2 minutes. Turn slices over; brush evenly with 2 tablespoons melted butter. Broil 1 1/2 minutes or until lightly browned.

Dressing:
1 tablespoon sugar
2 tablespoons red wine vinegar
1 tablespoon water
1/8 teaspoon salt
1/8 teaspoon freshly ground black pepper
2 tablespoons extra-virgin olive oil

Salad:
4 cups torn romaine lettuce
4 cups arugula
2 cups quartered strawberries
1/3 cup vertically sliced red onion
12 ounces skinless, boneless rotisserie chicken breast, sliced
2 tablespoons unsalted cashews, halved
1/2 cup (2 ounces) crumbled blue cheese

1. To prepare dressing, combine first 5 ingredients in a small bowl. Gradually drizzle in oil, stirring constantly with a whisk.

2. To prepare salad, combine romaine and next 4 ingredients (through sliced chicken breast) in a bowl; toss gently. Place about 2 cups chicken mixture on each of 4 plates. Top each serving with 1 1/2 teaspoons cashews and 2 tablespoons crumbled blue cheese. Drizzle about 4 teaspoons dressing over each serving. Yield: 4 servings.

CALORIES 333; **FAT** 16.4g (sat 4.9g, mono 8.3g, poly 2.1g); **PROTEIN** 32g; **CARB** 14.8g; **FIBER** 3.5g; **CHOL** 83mg; **IRON** 2.5mg; **SODIUM** 347mg; **CALC** 156mg

Spicy Asian Noodles with Chicken

Add a snow pea sauté to complete the meal: Heat 2 teaspoons canola oil in a large nonstick skillet over medium-high heat. Add 2 minced garlic cloves; sauté 15 seconds. Add 2 cups trimmed fresh snow peas and 1 cup drained sliced canned water chestnuts; sauté 3 minutes or until crisp-tender. Remove from heat; stir in 1 tablespoon lower-sodium soy sauce.

1 tablespoon dark sesame oil, divided
1 tablespoon grated peeled fresh ginger
2 garlic cloves, minced
2 cups chopped roasted chicken breast
1/2 cup chopped green onions
1/4 cup chopped fresh cilantro
3 tablespoons lower-sodium soy sauce

2 tablespoons rice vinegar
2 tablespoons hoisin sauce
2 teaspoons sambal oelek (ground fresh chile paste)
1 (6.75-ounce) package thin rice sticks (rice-flour noodles)
2 tablespoons chopped dry-roasted peanuts

1. Heat 2 teaspoons oil in a small skillet over medium-high heat. Add ginger and garlic to pan; cook 45 seconds, stirring constantly. Place in a large bowl. Stir in remaining 1 teaspoon oil, chicken, and next 6 ingredients (through sambal oelek).
2. Cook noodles according to package directions. Drain and rinse under cold water; drain. Cut noodles into smaller pieces. Add noodles to bowl; toss well to coat. Sprinkle with peanuts. Yield: 4 servings (serving size: 1¾ cups).

CALORIES 381; **FAT** 8.1g (sat 1.5g, mono 3.2g, poly 2.7g); **PROTEIN** 27.5g; **CARB** 47.1g; **FIBER** 2.3g; **CHOL** 60mg; **IRON** 3.1mg; **SODIUM** 614mg; **CALC** 55mg

Soba Noodles with Chicken and Vegetables

Substitute 1 teaspoon sugar and 1 tablespoon wine for mirin, if you prefer.

½ cup fat-free, lower-sodium chicken broth
3 tablespoons lower-sodium soy sauce
2 tablespoons oyster sauce
2 tablespoons mirin (sweet rice wine)
1 teaspoon Sriracha (hot chile sauce)
1 (12-ounce) package soba (buckwheat noodles)
1 tablespoon canola oil

1 teaspoon minced garlic
1 teaspoon grated peeled fresh ginger
1 pound chicken breast tenders, cut into bite-sized pieces
2 large zucchini, cut into julienne strips (about 2 cups)
1 large carrot, cut into julienne strips
1 tablespoon sesame seeds, toasted

1. Combine first 5 ingredients in a small bowl.

2. Prepare soba according to package directions, omitting salt and fat. Drain and rinse with cold water; drain.

3. Heat oil in a large nonstick skillet over medium-high heat. Add garlic, ginger, and chicken to pan; sauté 3 minutes. Add broth mixture, zucchini, and carrot to pan; cook 3 minutes, stirring constantly. Add noodles; cook 2 minutes or until thoroughly heated, tossing well. Sprinkle with sesame seeds. Yield: 6 servings (serving size: 1⅓ cups noodle mixture and ½ teaspoon sesame seeds).

CALORIES 353; **FAT** 5.2g (sat 0.8g, mono 2.2g, poly 1.6g); **PROTEIN** 25.7g; **CARB** 47.4g; **FIBER** 2.4g; **CHOL** 44mg; **IRON** 4mg; **SODIUM** 754mg; **CALC** 29mg

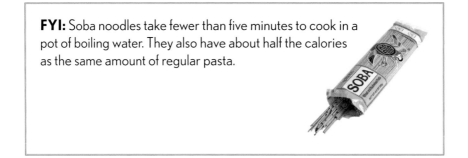

FYI: Soba noodles take fewer than five minutes to cook in a pot of boiling water. They also have about half the calories as the same amount of regular pasta.

Chicken, Cashew, and Bell Pepper Stir-Fry

This dish balances salty, sweet, tangy, and spicy ingredients. Spoon it alongside a quick rice pilaf: Cook 1 (10-ounce) package frozen white rice according to package directions. Combine cooked rice, 2 tablespoons drained chopped water chestnuts, 1/2 teaspoon crushed red pepper, 1/4 teaspoon salt, and 1/4 teaspoon freshly ground black pepper.

3³/₄ teaspoons cornstarch, divided
2 tablespoons lower-sodium soy sauce, divided
2 teaspoons dry sherry
1 teaspoon rice wine vinegar
³/₄ teaspoon sugar
1/2 teaspoon hot pepper sauce
1 pound chicken breast tenders, cut lengthwise
 into thin strips

1/2 cup unsalted cashews
2 tablespoons canola oil
2 cups julienne-cut red, green, or yellow bell
 pepper (about 1 large)
1 teaspoon minced garlic
1/2 teaspoon minced peeled fresh ginger
3 tablespoons thinly sliced green onions

1. Combine 1 teaspoon cornstarch, 1 tablespoon soy sauce, and next 4 ingredients (through hot pepper sauce) in a small bowl; stir with a whisk.

2. Combine remaining 2¾ teaspoons cornstarch, remaining 1 tablespoon soy sauce, and chicken in a medium bowl; toss well to coat.

3. Heat a large nonstick skillet over medium-high heat. Add cashews to pan; cook 3 minutes or until lightly toasted, stirring frequently. Remove from pan.

4. Add oil to pan, swirling to coat. Add chicken mixture to pan; sauté 2 minutes or until lightly browned. Remove chicken from pan; place in a bowl. Add bell pepper to pan; sauté 2 minutes, stirring occasionally. Add garlic and ginger; cook 30 seconds. Add chicken and cornstarch mixture to pan; cook 1 minute or until sauce is slightly thick. Sprinkle with cashews and green onions. Yield: 4 servings (serving size: 1 cup).

CALORIES 324; **FAT** 16.6g (sat 2.5g, mono 9.2g, poly 3.8g); **PROTEIN** 30g; **CARB** 13.5g; **FIBER** 2g; **CHOL** 66mg; **IRON** 2.4mg; **SODIUM** 350mg; **CALC** 33mg

Country Captain Chicken

Both South Carolina and Georgia lay claim to this Southern classic. Rice is a traditional side dish. To make it fast, cook 1 (3½-ounce) bag boil-in-bag rice, omitting salt and fat. Stir in ¼ teaspoon salt and ¼ teaspoon black pepper. Top each serving with 1 tablespoon bottled mango chutney.

1 tablespoon curry powder
¼ teaspoon salt
¼ teaspoon freshly ground black pepper
1 pound skinless, boneless chicken breast, cut into ¾-inch pieces
1½ tablespoons olive oil
2½ cups vertically sliced onion (about 2 medium)
¾ cup thinly sliced green bell pepper (about 1 medium)

2 garlic cloves, minced
⅔ cup fat-free, lower-sodium chicken broth
¼ cup dried currants
2 tablespoons chopped fresh thyme, divided
1 (14.5-ounce) can diced tomatoes with jalapeño peppers, undrained
½ cup sliced almonds, toasted

1. Combine curry powder, salt, and black pepper. Sprinkle chicken with curry powder mixture.

2. Heat oil in a large nonstick skillet over medium-high heat. Add chicken mixture to pan; sauté 5 minutes. Add onion, bell pepper, and garlic; sauté 3 minutes. Add broth, currants, 1 tablespoon thyme, and tomatoes; bring to a boil. Reduce heat, and simmer 5 minutes. Stir in remaining 1 tablespoon thyme; cook 1 minute. Sprinkle with almonds. Yield: 4 servings (serving size: 1½ cups chicken mixture and 2 tablespoons almonds).

CALORIES 314; **FAT** 11.2g (sat 1.4g, mono 7g, poly 1.9g); **PROTEIN** 30.5g; **CARB** 23.2g; **FIBER** 4.6g; **CHOL** 66mg; **IRON** 2.6mg; **SODIUM** 683mg; **CALC** 86mg

Chicken Biryani

Tender morsels of chicken are simmered in this spicy rice-based Indian dish. Serve with a simple salad of thinly sliced cucumber and plum tomato wedges topped with a yogurt dressing: Combine 1/3 cup plain low-fat yogurt, 1 tablespoon chopped green onions, 1 teaspoon fresh lemon juice, 1/4 teaspoon ground cumin, 1/8 teaspoon salt, and a dash of ground red pepper.

2 teaspoons canola oil

1 pound skinless, boneless chicken breast, cut into 1-inch pieces

1 cup chopped onion (about 1 medium)

1 jalapeño pepper, seeded and minced

1 teaspoon minced peeled fresh ginger

1 1/2 teaspoons garam masala

3/4 teaspoon ground cumin

1/2 teaspoon salt

2 garlic cloves, minced

2 cups chopped plum tomato (about 2 tomatoes)

1 cup uncooked basmati rice

1/3 cup golden raisins

1 (14-ounce) can fat-free, lower-sodium chicken broth

1/4 cup chopped fresh cilantro

1/4 cup sliced almonds

4 lime wedges

1. Heat oil in a large nonstick skillet over medium-high heat. Add chicken to pan; sauté 3 minutes. Add onion and jalapeño; sauté 3 minutes. Add ginger, garam masala, cumin, salt, and garlic; sauté 30 seconds. Add tomato, rice, raisins, and broth; bring to a boil. Cover, reduce heat, and simmer 15 minutes or until rice is tender. Stir in cilantro. Sprinkle with almonds; serve with lime wedges. Yield: 4 servings (serving size: 1½ cups rice mixture, 1 tablespoon almonds, and 1 lime wedge).

CALORIES 437; FAT 9.1g (sat 1.4g, mono 4.6g, poly 2.3g); PROTEIN 29.8g; CARB 63.2g; FIBER 4.5g; CHOL 66mg; IRON 3.4mg; SODIUM 555mg; CALC 58mg

Sherry-Soy Glazed Chicken

Pair this entrée with a simple rice pilaf: Heat 1 tablespoon canola oil in a large saucepan over medium-high heat. Add ½ cup chopped onion and 2 teaspoons grated peeled fresh ginger to pan; sauté 2 minutes. Stir in 1 cup water, ½ cup uncooked long-grain rice, and ¼ teaspoon salt; bring to a boil. Cover, reduce heat, and simmer 12 minutes or until liquid is absorbed. Remove from heat; stir in 2 tablespoons chopped fresh cilantro.

3 tablespoons lower-sodium soy sauce, divided
2 tablespoons dry sherry
4 teaspoons cornstarch, divided
1 pound skinless, boneless chicken breast, cut into bite-sized pieces
½ cup fat-free, lower-sodium chicken broth
2 tablespoons oyster sauce
1 tablespoon honey
2 teaspoons sesame oil, divided

¾ cup chopped onion
½ cup chopped celery
½ cup chopped red bell pepper
1 tablespoon grated peeled fresh ginger
2 garlic cloves, minced
½ cup thinly sliced green onions (about 3 green onions)
¼ cup chopped unsalted dry-roasted cashews

1. Combine 1 tablespoon soy sauce, sherry, 2 teaspoons cornstarch, and chicken in a large bowl; toss well to coat. Combine remaining 2 tablespoons soy sauce, remaining 2 teaspoons cornstarch, broth, oyster sauce, and honey in a small bowl.

2. Heat 1 teaspoon oil in a large nonstick skillet over medium-high heat. Add chicken mixture to pan; sauté 3 minutes. Remove from pan. Heat remaining 1 teaspoon oil in pan. Add onion, celery, and bell pepper to pan; sauté 2 minutes. Add ginger and garlic; sauté 1 minute. Return chicken mixture to pan; sauté 1 minute. Stir in broth mixture. Bring to a boil; cook 1 minute, stirring constantly. Remove from heat. Sprinkle with green onions and cashews. Yield: 4 servings (serving size: about ¾ cup).

CALORIES 257; **FAT** 9g (sat 1.9g, mono 4.2g, poly 2.3g); **PROTEIN** 26g; **CARB** 17g; **FIBER** 1.9g; **CHOL** 63mg; **IRON** 2mg; **SODIUM** 584mg; **CALC** 45mg

Curried Chicken and Cashews

Madras curry powder delivers more intensity than regular curry powder. For less heat, leave the chiles whole when you add them to the wok with the curry powder.

Sauce:
1/3 cup fat-free, lower-sodium chicken broth
3 tablespoons water
1 1/2 tablespoons fish sauce
1 teaspoon sugar
1 teaspoon rice vinegar
Remaining ingredients:
3/4 pound skinless, boneless chicken breast
2 tablespoons canola oil, divided

1 1/2 cups vertically sliced onion
1 tablespoon minced peeled fresh ginger
1 tablespoon minced garlic
1 teaspoon Madras curry powder
3 small dried hot red chiles, broken in half
1/3 cup chopped fresh cilantro
1/4 cup salted dry-roasted cashews, chopped
3 cups hot cooked short-grain rice

1. To prepare sauce, combine first 5 ingredients.
2. Cut chicken across grain into 1/4-inch slices; cut slices into 1/2-inch-wide strips. Cut chicken strips into 3-inch-long pieces.
3. Heat 1 tablespoon oil in a 14-inch wok over high heat. Add half of chicken strips to wok; stir-fry 2 minutes. Spoon cooked chicken into a bowl. Repeat procedure with 2 teaspoons canola oil and remaining chicken strips.
4. Add remaining 1 teaspoon oil to wok, swirling to coat. Add onion, ginger, and garlic to wok; stir-fry 1 minute or until lightly browned. Add curry powder and chiles; stir-fry 30 seconds. Add sauce and chicken to wok; stir-fry 1 minute. Spoon into a serving dish. Sprinkle with chopped cilantro and cashews. Serve over rice. Yield: 4 servings (serving size: 3/4 cup rice and 1 cup chicken mixture).

CALORIES 439; **FAT** 13g (sat 1.7g, mono 6.9g, poly 3.2g); **PROTEIN** 26g; **CARB** 52.6g; **FIBER** 3.2g; **CHOL** 49mg; **IRON** 3.9mg; **SODIUM** 669mg; **CALC** 37mg

Curried Chicken Sauté

This simple dish delivers bold, complex flavors and requires picking up just five ingredients at the super-market (excluding salt and pepper).

1½ teaspoons curry powder, divided
¾ teaspoon salt, divided
½ teaspoon freshly ground black pepper
1 pound skinless, boneless chicken breast
1 (8-ounce) package presliced mixed bell
peppers

1 cup light coconut milk
1 tablespoon fresh lime juice
4 lime wedges

1. Heat a nonstick skillet over medium-high heat. Sprinkle 1 teaspoon curry powder, ½ teaspoon salt, and black pepper over chicken. Add chicken to pan; cook 5 minutes on each side or until done. Remove chicken from pan; keep warm.

2. Add bell peppers and remaining ½ teaspoon curry powder to pan; sauté 1 minute. Add coconut milk, and bring to a boil; reduce heat, and simmer 4 minutes or until mixture is slightly thickened. Stir juice and remaining ¼ teaspoon salt into bell pepper mixture. Cut chicken across grain into thin slices. Serve chicken with bell pepper mixture and lime wedges. Yield: 4 servings (serving size: 3 ounces chicken, ½ cup pepper mixture, and 1 lime wedge).

CALORIES 175; **FAT** 5.9g (sat 3.6g, mono 1g, poly 0.7g); **PROTEIN** 24.4g; **CARB** 7.1g; **FIBER** 1.7g; **CHOL** 63mg; **IRON** 1.6mg; **SODIUM** 515mg; **CALC** 20mg

SIMPLE SIDE: Serve with steamed long-grain rice to round out the meal.

Weeknight Coq au Vin

Serve this robust French classic over egg noodles.

2 bacon slices, chopped
4 (4-ounce) bone-in chicken thighs, skinned
4 (4-ounce) chicken drumsticks, skinned
½ teaspoon salt
½ teaspoon freshly ground black pepper
¼ cup finely chopped fresh flat-leaf parsley, divided
1½ cups sliced cremini mushrooms

1½ cups dry red wine
1 cup chopped carrot
½ cup chopped shallots
½ cup fat-free, lower-sodium chicken broth
1 tablespoon brandy
1 teaspoon minced fresh thyme
2 teaspoons tomato paste
1 garlic clove, minced

1. Cook bacon in a large Dutch oven over medium-high heat 2 minutes. Sprinkle chicken with salt and pepper. Add chicken to pan; cook 2 minutes. Stir in 3 tablespoons parsley, mushrooms, and remaining ingredients; bring to a boil. Cover, reduce heat, and simmer 25 minutes or until chicken is done.

2. Remove chicken with a slotted spoon; keep warm. Bring cooking liquid to a boil; cook until reduced to 3 cups (about 6 minutes). Return chicken to pan; cook 1 minute or until thoroughly heated. Sprinkle with remaining 1 tablespoon parsley. Yield: 4 servings (serving size: 1 thigh, 1 drumstick, and ¾ cup sauce).

CALORIES 345; **FAT** 12.7g (sat 3.7g, mono 4.7g, poly 2.7g); **PROTEIN** 43.7g; **CARB** 11g; **FIBER** 1.6g; **CHOL** 150mg; **IRON** 3.3mg; **SODIUM** 595mg; **CALC** 60mg

Roasted Butternut Squash and Bacon Pasta, page 100

casseroles

Roasted Garlic and Butternut Squash Cassoulet

To get a head start, roast the garlic, caramelize the onions, and even assemble this robust casserole the day before you plan to serve it. Use leftover roasted garlic to flavor soups, or combine with olive oil as a spread for toasted baguette slices. Pancetta is an Italian unsmoked bacon. You can substitute regular smoked bacon, but you'll need less, as the flavor is more assertive.

1 whole garlic head
4 ounces pancetta, chopped
2 cups vertically sliced onion
1 tablespoon olive oil
1 tablespoon white wine vinegar
4½ cups (½-inch) cubed peeled butternut squash (about 2 pounds)
½ cup organic vegetable broth
½ teaspoon dried thyme
¼ teaspoon salt
⅛ teaspoon freshly ground black pepper
4 (16-ounce) cans cannellini or other white beans, rinsed and drained
1 bay leaf
2 (1-ounce) slices white bread
2 tablespoons grated fresh Parmesan cheese
½ teaspoon olive oil
1 tablespoon chopped fresh parsley

1. Preheat oven to 350°.
2. Remove white papery skin from garlic head (do not peel or separate cloves). Wrap garlic head in foil. Bake at 350° for 1 hour; cool 10 minutes. Separate cloves; squeeze to extract garlic pulp. Set half of garlic pulp aside; reserve remaining garlic pulp for another use. Discard skins.
3. Heat a large Dutch oven over medium-high heat. Add pancetta; sauté 5 minutes or until crisp. Remove pancetta from pan, reserving drippings in pan. Add onion and 1 tablespoon oil to drippings in pan; sauté 5 minutes. Reduce heat to medium-low; cook 25 minutes or until onion is very tender and browned, stirring frequently. Stir in vinegar.
4. Preheat oven to 375°.
5. Add garlic pulp, pancetta, squash, and next 6 ingredients (through bay leaf) to onion mixture, stirring well. Place bread in a food processor, and pulse 10 times or until coarse crumbs measure about 1 cup. Combine breadcrumbs, Parmesan cheese, and ½ teaspoon oil; sprinkle evenly over squash mixture. Cover and bake at 375° for 50 minutes or until squash is tender. Uncover and bake an additional 15 minutes or until topping is browned. Discard bay leaf. Sprinkle with parsley. Yield: 8 servings (serving size: 1¾ cups).

CALORIES 259; **FAT** 7.7g (sat 2.6g, mono 3.6g, poly 1.4g); **PROTEIN** 9.5g; **CARB** 38.8g; **FIBER** 8g; **CHOL** 11mg; **IRON** 3mg; **SODIUM** 679mg; **CALC** 131mg

Parmesan and Root Vegetable Lasagna

Wash the pan well before using it again to cook the strained milk mixture—this helps ensure a silken sauce.

6 cups ($\frac{1}{2}$-inch) cubed peeled butternut squash (about $2\frac{1}{2}$ pounds)
$2\frac{1}{4}$ cups ($\frac{1}{2}$-inch) cubed peeled sweet potato (about 1 pound)
2 cups coarsely chopped onion, divided
1 tablespoon olive oil
Cooking spray
4 cups 1% low-fat milk
$\frac{1}{8}$ teaspoon ground nutmeg
$\frac{1}{8}$ teaspoon ground cinnamon

1 bay leaf
1.5 ounces all-purpose flour (about $\frac{1}{3}$ cup)
$\frac{1}{2}$ teaspoon salt
$\frac{1}{4}$ teaspoon freshly ground black pepper
$1\frac{1}{4}$ cups (5 ounces) grated Parmigiano-Reggiano cheese
9 packaged no-boil lasagna noodles
$1\frac{1}{2}$ cups (6 ounces) shredded part-skim mozzarella cheese

1. Preheat oven to 450°.

2. Combine squash, sweet potato, 1 cup chopped onion, and oil in a roasting pan coated with cooking spray, tossing to coat vegetables. Bake at 450° for 30 minutes or until vegetables are tender, stirring once.

3. Combine remaining 1 cup onion, milk, nutmeg, cinnamon, and bay leaf in a medium saucepan over medium-high heat; bring to a simmer. Remove from heat; let stand 15 minutes. Strain milk mixture through a fine sieve over a bowl; discard solids. Return milk mixture to pan. Weigh or lightly spoon flour into a dry measuring cup; level with a knife. Add flour, salt, and pepper to milk mixture, stirring with a whisk. Cook over medium heat 10 minutes or until thick, stirring frequently with a whisk. Remove from heat; stir in Parmigiano-Reggiano cheese.

4. Preheat oven to 375°.

5. Spread ½ cup milk mixture in bottom of a 13 x 9–inch glass or ceramic baking dish coated with cooking spray. Arrange 3 noodles over milk mixture; top with half of squash mixture, ½ cup mozzarella, and 1 cup milk mixture. Repeat layers with noodles, squash mixture, mozzarella, and milk mixture. Top with remaining 3 noodles. Spread remaining milk mixture over noodles, and sprinkle with remaining ½ cup mozzarella. Cover with foil coated with cooking spray. Bake at 375° for 30 minutes. Uncover and bake an additional 20 minutes. Let stand 10 minutes. Yield: 10 servings.

CALORIES 322; FAT 8.4g (sat 3.9g, mono 2.2g, poly 0.5g); PROTEIN 16.6g; CARB 45.8g; FIBER 4.6g; CHOL 19mg; IRON 2.1mg; SODIUM 471mg; CALC 422mg

Mushroom and Root Vegetable Potpies

2 cups (¹/₂-inch-thick) slices carrot
2 cups (¹/₂-inch-thick) slices rutabaga
2 cups (¹/₂-inch-thick) slices parsnip
3 cups organic vegetable broth
2 cups fat-free milk
1 bay leaf
1 tablespoon butter, divided
1 tablespoon chopped fresh thyme, divided
3 (4-ounce) packages presliced exotic
  mushroom blend
²/₃ cup finely chopped shallots
2 garlic cloves, minced

1.5 ounces all-purpose flour (about ¹/₃ cup)
2 tablespoons heavy whipping cream
1 tablespoon dry sherry
Cooking spray
3.2 ounces whole-wheat flour (about ²/₃ cup)
3 ounces all-purpose flour (about ²/₃ cup)
1¹/₂ teaspoons baking powder
2 teaspoons minced fresh parsley
3 tablespoons chilled butter, cut into
  small pieces
²/₃ cup plus 2 tablespoons fat-free
  buttermilk, divided

1. Place first 6 ingredients in a large saucepan; bring to a boil. Reduce heat; simmer 5 minutes or until vegetables are tender. Remove carrot mixture from pan with a slotted spoon, and set aside. Reserve cooking liquid, and set aside. Discard bay leaf.

2. Heat 1½ teaspoons butter in a large nonstick skillet over medium heat. Add 1½ teaspoons thyme and mushrooms; cook 12 minutes or until mushrooms are tender, stirring occasionally. Remove from heat.

3. Melt remaining 1½ teaspoons butter in a medium, heavy saucepan over medium heat. Add shallots and garlic; cook 3 minutes or until tender, stirring frequently. Pour ½ cup reserved cooking liquid into a bowl. Weigh or lightly spoon 1.5 ounces (about ⅓ cup) all-purpose flour into a dry measuring cup; level with a knife. Add 1.5 ounces all-purpose flour to ½ cup reserved cooking liquid in bowl; stir with a whisk.

4. Add remaining reserved cooking liquid, remaining thyme, whipping cream, and sherry to shallots in pan; bring to a boil. Add flour mixture; stir with whisk. Bring to a boil; reduce heat. Simmer until mixture thickens and is reduced to 3 cups (about 10 minutes); stir frequently.

5. Combine reserved carrot mixture, mushroom mixture, and shallot mixture in a bowl. Spoon 1⅓ cups mixture into each of 6 (10-ounce) ramekins coated with cooking spray.

6. Preheat oven to 400°.

7. Weigh or lightly spoon whole-wheat flour and 3 ounces (about ⅔ cup) all-purpose flour into dry measuring cups; level with a knife. Combine flours, baking powder, and parsley in a bowl; stir with a whisk. Cut in 3 tablespoons chilled butter with pastry blender or 2 knives until mixture resembles coarse meal. Add ⅔ cup buttermilk to whole-wheat flour mixture; stir until moist. Drop dough by tablespoonfuls onto vegetable mixture, dividing evenly among ramekins. Brush remaining buttermilk over topping. Bake at 400° for 45 minutes or until crust is golden brown. Yield: 6 servings (serving size: 1 pie).

CALORIES 351; FAT 10.5g (sat 6.2g, mono 2.6g, poly 0.8g); PROTEIN 12.2g; CARB 53.7g; FIBER 6.9g; CHOL 29mg; IRON 2.7mg; SODIUM 561mg; CALC 253mg

Chiles Rellenos Gratin

8 poblano chiles
1 cup finely chopped red bell pepper
1½ cups fresh corn kernels
½ cup chopped green onions
2 tablespoons pine nuts, toasted
2 garlic cloves, minced
¾ cup (3 ounces) crumbled queso
  fresco, divided
2 tablespoons chopped fresh cilantro
1 teaspoon salt, divided
¼ teaspoon ground red pepper, divided

1 (15-ounce) can black beans, rinsed,
  drained, and divided
Cooking spray
2 tablespoons butter
½ teaspoon ground cumin
⅛ teaspoon ground nutmeg
2 tablespoons all-purpose flour
2 cups 2% reduced-fat milk
1 tablespoon fresh lime juice
½ cup dry breadcrumbs

1. Preheat broiler.
2. Place chiles on a foil-lined baking sheet; broil 3 inches from heat 8 minutes or until blackened, turning after 4 minutes. Place in paper bag; fold to close tightly. Let stand 15 minutes. Peel and discard skins. Cut a lengthwise slit in each chile; discard seeds, leaving stems intact.
3. Preheat oven to 350°.
4. Heat a large nonstick skillet over medium heat. Add bell pepper; cook 4 minutes, stirring frequently. Add corn, onions, nuts, and garlic; cook 2 minutes, stirring frequently. Remove from heat; stir in ½ cup cheese, cilantro, ½ teaspoon salt, and ⅛ teaspoon ground red pepper.
5. Place half of black beans in a bowl; mash with a fork. Add mashed beans and whole beans to corn mixture. Spoon about ⅓ cup bean mixture into each chile; fold sides of chile over filling. Arrange stuffed chiles in an 8-inch square glass or ceramic baking dish coated with cooking spray.
6. Melt butter in a medium saucepan over medium-low heat; add remaining ⅛ teaspoon ground red pepper, cumin, and nutmeg; stir with a whisk. Cook 30 seconds, stirring constantly. Gradually add flour, and stir with a whisk; cook 5 minutes, stirring constantly. Gradually add milk. Stir with a whisk until blended.
7. Increase heat to medium. Cook milk mixture 8 minutes or until thick. Remove from heat; stir in remaining ½ teaspoon salt and lime juice. Pour milk mixture over stuffed chiles.
8. Combine remaining ¼ cup queso fresco and breadcrumbs; sprinkle over milk mixture. Bake at 350° for 20 minutes or until sauce is bubbly.
9. Preheat broiler.
10. Broil 1 minute or until top is golden brown. Yield: 8 servings (serving size: 1 stuffed chile).

CALORIES 216; **FAT** 7.1g (sat 3.3g, mono 1.9g, poly 0.8g); **PROTEIN** 9.1g; **CARB** 33.1g; **FIBER** 5.9g; **CHOL** 16mg; **IRON** 2.3mg; **SODIUM** 574mg; **CALC** 148mg

Mushroom Pasta Bake

8 ounces uncooked gigli or radiatore pasta
2 teaspoons butter
¼ cup sliced shallots
8 ounces sliced shiitake mushroom caps
4 ounces sliced cremini mushrooms
1 tablespoon chopped fresh thyme
½ teaspoon salt
¼ teaspoon freshly ground black pepper

3 garlic cloves, minced
1 tablespoon dry sherry
1.1 ounces all-purpose flour (about ¼ cup)
2 cups 2% reduced-fat milk
1 cup (4 ounces) grated Asiago cheese, divided
Cooking spray
Thyme sprigs (optional)

1. Preheat oven to 375°.
2. Cook pasta according to package directions, omitting salt and fat. Drain well. Set aside.
3. Melt butter in a large nonstick skillet over medium-high heat. Add sliced shallots; sauté 3 minutes. Add mushrooms, 1 tablespoon thyme, salt, pepper, and garlic; sauté 8 minutes or until mushrooms are tender. Add sherry; cook 1 minute, stirring frequently. Remove from heat.
4. Place flour in a Dutch oven over medium-high heat; gradually add milk, stirring constantly with a whisk. Bring mixture to a boil, and cook 1 minute or until slightly thick, stirring constantly with a whisk. Remove from heat; add ½ cup Asiago cheese, stirring until melted. Add pasta and mushroom mixture to cheese mixture, tossing well to combine. Spoon pasta mixture into an 8-inch square glass or ceramic baking dish lightly coated with cooking spray; sprinkle evenly with remaining ½ cup Asiago cheese. Bake at 375° for 30 minutes or until cheese melts and begins to brown. Garnish with thyme sprigs, if desired. Yield: 4 servings.

CALORIES 474; **FAT** 16g (sat 8g, mono 4.6g, poly 2.2g); **PROTEIN** 21.8g; **CARB** 61.4g; **FIBER** 3.3g; **CHOL** 40mg; **IRON** 3.9mg; **SODIUM** 745mg; **CALC** 386mg

Tex-Mex Lasagna

Try different salsas to vary the flavor of this lasagna. Make it smoky with chipotle salsa, or spice it up with the hot stuff.

¾ cup bottled low-sodium salsa
1½ teaspoons ground cumin
1 (14.5-ounce) can no-salt-added
  diced tomatoes
1 (8-ounce) can no-salt-added tomato sauce
Cooking spray
6 no-boil lasagna noodles

1 cup frozen whole-kernel corn, thawed
1 (15-ounce) can 50%-less-sodium black
  beans, rinsed and drained
1½ cups (6 ounces) preshredded reduced-fat
  4-cheese Mexican blend cheese
¼ cup chopped green onions

1. Preheat oven to 450°.
2. Combine first 4 ingredients; spread ⅔ cup sauce in bottom of an 8-inch square glass or ceramic baking dish coated with cooking spray. Arrange 2 noodles over sauce; top with ½ cup corn and half of beans. Sprinkle with ½ cup cheese; top with ⅔ cup sauce. Repeat layers once; top with remaining 2 noodles. Spread remaining sauce over noodles. Sprinkle with remaining ½ cup cheese. Cover and bake at 450° for 30 minutes or until noodles are tender. Let stand 15 minutes. Sprinkle with green onions. Yield: 4 servings (serving size: 1 piece).

CALORIES 376; FAT 10.3g (sat 4.6g, mono 2.4g, poly 0.4g); PROTEIN 23.4g; CARB 56g; FIBER 9.9g; CHOL 31mg; IRON 3.6mg; SODIUM 871mg; CALC 455mg

Chipotle Macaroni and Cheese

This mac and cheese is incredibly tasty and easy to prepare. Here's more good news: You don't even have to make a white sauce.

1 (7-ounce) can chipotle chiles in adobo sauce
1 tablespoon butter
½ cup finely chopped onion
½ cup finely chopped green bell pepper
1 garlic clove, minced
2 tablespoons all-purpose flour
1 (14.5-ounce) can diced tomatoes and green chiles, undrained
4 cups hot cooked elbow macaroni (2 cups uncooked)

2 cups (8 ounces) shredded reduced-fat sharp cheddar cheese
1 cup 1% low-fat cottage cheese
1 cup 2% reduced-fat milk
¼ cup (1 ounce) grated fresh Parmesan cheese
1 large egg, lightly beaten
Cooking spray
3 tablespoons dry breadcrumbs

1. Preheat oven to 350°.

2. Remove 1 teaspoon adobo sauce from can; set aside. Remove 2 chipotle chiles from can; finely chop to measure 1 tablespoon. Reserve remaining chipotle chiles and adobo sauce for another use.

3. Melt butter in a Dutch oven over medium-high heat. Add chopped chiles, onion, bell pepper, and garlic; cook 4 minutes or until onion is tender, stirring frequently. Sprinkle with flour; cook 30 seconds, stirring constantly. Reduce heat to medium; add tomatoes. Cook 3 minutes or until thickened. Add reserved 1 teaspoon adobo sauce, pasta, cheddar cheese, cottage cheese, milk, Parmesan, and egg; stir to combine. Spoon pasta mixture into a 2-quart baking dish coated with cooking spray; top with breadcrumbs. Bake at 350° for 30 minutes or until bubbly. Yield: 6 servings (serving size: about 1 cup).

CALORIES 324; **FAT** 8.5g (sat 4.6g, mono 2.4g, poly 0.6g); **PROTEIN** 34.2g; **CARB** 39.6g; **FIBER** 2g; **CHOL** 56mg; **IRON** 2.4mg; **SODIUM** 756mg; **CALC** 307mg

Artichoke and Goat Cheese Strata

To make ahead, prepare through step 2, cover, and chill. Before baking, let the bread mixture stand at room temperature 10 minutes while the oven preheats. Then assemble and bake. The cook time will increase by about 10 minutes. Garnish with fresh flat-leaf parsley.

1 teaspoon olive oil
1/2 cup finely chopped shallots
1 (10-ounce) package frozen artichoke
  hearts, thawed
2 garlic cloves, minced
1/2 teaspoon dried herbes de Provence
1 3/4 cups 1% low-fat milk
1/2 teaspoon freshly ground black pepper
1/4 teaspoon salt

4 large eggs
1/3 cup (about 1 1/2 ounces) grated
  Parmigiano-Reggiano cheese
1/2 (1-pound) loaf country-style white bread,
  cut into 1-inch cubes (about 5 cups)
Cooking spray
3/4 cup (3 ounces) crumbled goat cheese,
  divided

1. Heat oil in a large nonstick skillet over medium heat. Add shallots; cook 2 minutes, stirring frequently. Stir in artichokes and garlic; cook 8 minutes or until artichoke hearts begin to brown, stirring occasionally. Remove from heat; stir in herbes de Provence. Cool 10 minutes.

2. Combine milk, black pepper, salt, and eggs in a large bowl, stirring with a whisk. Add Parmigiano-Reggiano cheese and bread; toss gently to combine. Stir in artichoke mixture, and let stand 20 minutes.

3. Preheat oven to 375°.

4. Spoon half of bread mixture into a 2-quart glass or ceramic baking dish coated with cooking spray. Sprinkle with half of goat cheese; top with remaining bread mixture. Sprinkle remaining half of goat cheese over top. Bake at 375° for 50 minutes or until browned and bubbly. Yield: 6 servings (serving size: about 1 cup).

CALORIES 286; **FAT** 10.7g (sat 5.1g, mono 3.4g, poly 0.9g); **PROTEIN** 16.8g; **CARB** 31.1g; **FIBER** 2.7g; **CHOL** 139mg; **IRON** 2.5mg; **SODIUM** 561mg; **CALC** 272mg

Spinach Pie with Goat Cheese, Raisins, and Pine Nuts

⅓ cup olive oil, divided
2 cups minced onion (about 1 large)
5 (9-ounce) packages fresh spinach
½ cup golden raisins
2 cups (8 ounces) crumbled goat cheese

⅓ cup pine nuts, toasted
½ teaspoon kosher salt
¼ teaspoon freshly ground black pepper
12 sheets frozen phyllo dough, thawed
Cooking spray

1. Preheat oven to 400°.
2. Heat 3 tablespoons oil in a large Dutch oven over medium heat. Add onion to pan; cook 5 minutes or until browned, stirring occasionally. Add spinach, 1 bag at a time; cook 3 minutes or until spinach wilts, stirring frequently. Simmer spinach mixture 40 minutes or until liquid evaporates. Stir in raisins. Cool completely. Stir in cheese, nuts, salt, and pepper.
3. Press 1 phyllo sheet into bottom and up sides of a 13 x 9–inch glass or ceramic baking dish coated with cooking spray (cover remaining dough to keep from drying); lightly coat phyllo with cooking spray. Repeat procedure with 7 phyllo sheets. Spread spinach mixture in an even layer onto phyllo. Place 1 phyllo sheet on a large cutting board or work surface (cover remaining dough to keep from drying); lightly brush with 1½ teaspoons oil. Repeat procedure with remaining 3 phyllo sheets and remaining 1½ tablespoons oil. Place phyllo layer over spinach mixture; tuck in sides to enclose spinach fully. Bake at 400° for 30 minutes. Remove from oven; let stand 15 minutes. Yield: 8 servings (serving size: 1 piece).

CALORIES 363; FAT 21.8g (sat 6.6g, mono 9.9g, poly 3.6g); PROTEIN 14.9g; CARB 31.9g; FIBER 6.4g; CHOL 13mg; IRON 5.3mg; SODIUM 480mg; CALC 300mg

FYI: Pungent imported fresh Parmigiano-Reggiano cheese in the ricotta tart (at right) and a high-quality goat cheese in the spinach pie are worth the splurge. They contribute wonderful flavors to these meatless dishes.

Herbed Ricotta Tart

1 (11-ounce) can refrigerated pizza
  crust dough
Cooking spray
2 cups thinly sliced green onions
1⅓ cups part-skim ricotta cheese
½ cup thinly sliced fresh chives
2 tablespoons minced fresh dill

½ teaspoon salt
½ teaspoon freshly ground black pepper
2 large eggs, lightly beaten
1 large egg white, lightly beaten
2 tablespoons finely grated fresh
  Parmigiano-Reggiano cheese

1. Preheat oven to 375°.
2. Unroll dough, and press into the bottom and up sides of a 9-inch round removable-bottom tart pan coated with cooking spray.
3. Heat a medium nonstick skillet over medium heat. Add onions to pan, and cook 5 minutes, stirring occasionally. Combine cooked onions, ricotta cheese, chives, dill, salt, pepper, eggs, and egg white, stirring well with a whisk. Pour onion mixture into prepared crust; sprinkle mixture with Parmigiano-Reggiano. Bake at 375° for 35 minutes or until center is set. Let stand 5 minutes. Cut into 6 wedges. Yield: 6 servings (serving size: 1 wedge).

CALORIES 259; FAT 8.4g (sat 3.5g, mono 2.1g, poly 0.4g); PROTEIN 14.9g; CARB 30.4g; FIBER 1.7g; CHOL 89mg; IRON 2.5mg; SODIUM 673mg; CALC 206mg

Baked Ziti and Summer Veggies

4 ounces uncooked ziti
1 tablespoon olive oil
2 cups chopped yellow squash
1 cup chopped zucchini
½ cup chopped onion
2 cups chopped tomato
2 garlic cloves, minced
1 cup shredded part-skim mozzarella
  cheese, divided

2 tablespoons chopped fresh basil
2 teaspoons chopped fresh oregano
¾ teaspoon salt, divided
⅛ teaspoon crushed red pepper
¼ cup part-skim ricotta cheese
1 large egg, lightly beaten
Cooking spray

1. Cook pasta according to package directions, omitting salt and fat; drain.

2. Preheat oven to 400°.

3. Heat oil in a large skillet over medium-high heat. Add squash, zucchini, and onion; sauté 5 minutes. Add tomato and garlic; sauté 3 minutes. Remove from heat; stir in pasta, ½ cup mozzarella, herbs, ½ teaspoon salt, and red pepper.

4. Combine ricotta, remaining ¼ teaspoon salt, and egg. Stir into pasta mixture. Spoon into an 8-inch square glass or ceramic baking dish coated with cooking spray; top with remaining ½ cup mozzarella. Bake at 400° for 15 minutes. Yield: 4 servings (serving size: 1½ cups).

CALORIES 301; **FAT** 12.1g (sat 5.3g, mono 5g, poly 0.9g); **PROTEIN** 16.5g; **CARB** 32.8g; **FIBER** 4.1g; **CHOL** 65mg; **IRON** 1.9mg; **SODIUM** 640mg; **CALC** 291mg

Gnocchi Gratin

Gnocchi are Italian dumplings cooked and sauced like pasta. Here, they're turned into a creamy casserole that's quick to prepare on busy days. Look for vacuum-packed gnocchi on the pasta aisle.

1 (22-ounce) package vacuum-packed gnocchi
1 tablespoon butter
1.5 ounces all-purpose flour (about ⅓ cup)
¼ teaspoon salt
¼ teaspoon freshly ground black pepper
2 cups fat-free milk
½ cup fat-free, lower-sodium chicken broth
¾ cup (3 ounces) shredded Gruyère cheese
⅓ cup chopped fresh chives
2 bacon slices, cooked and crumbled
Cooking spray
¼ cup (1 ounce) grated fresh Parmesan cheese

1. Preheat oven to 400°.

2. Cook gnocchi according to package directions, omitting salt and fat. Drain.

3. Melt butter in a large saucepan over medium heat. Lightly spoon flour into a dry measuring cup; level with a knife. Add flour, salt, and pepper to pan; cook 1 minute, stirring constantly. Gradually add milk and broth, stirring with a whisk until blended. Bring to a boil; cook until thick, stirring constantly. Remove from heat. Add Gruyère, chives, and bacon; stir until smooth. Add gnocchi; toss well.

4. Spoon mixture into an 11 x 7–inch glass or ceramic baking dish coated with cooking spray; sprinkle with Parmesan. Bake at 400° for 20 minutes or until lightly browned. Serve immediately. Yield: 6 servings (serving size: about ¾ cup).

CALORIES 328; **FAT** 9.2g (sat 5.1g, mono 2.7g, poly 0.5g); **PROTEIN** 14.1g; **CARB** 47.7g; **FIBER** 1.7g; **CHOL** 29mg; **IRON** 1.3mg; **SODIUM** 726mg; **CALC** 304mg

Vegetarian Moussaka

Eggplant and bulgur boost the fiber in this Greek dish. Garnish with fresh flat-leaf parsley.

3 peeled eggplants, cut into ½-inch-thick
   slices (about 2½ pounds)
2 tablespoons extra-virgin olive oil, divided
Cooking spray
2 cups chopped onion
4 garlic cloves, minced
½ cup uncooked bulgur
¼ teaspoon ground allspice
¼ teaspoon ground cinnamon
⅛ teaspoon ground cloves
2 cups organic vegetable broth

2 teaspoons chopped fresh oregano
1 (14.5-ounce) can no-salt-added diced
   tomatoes, undrained
1 tablespoon butter
2 tablespoons all-purpose flour
1 cup 1% low-fat milk
2 tablespoons finely grated fresh
   Romano cheese
¼ teaspoon salt
1 large egg, lightly beaten

1. Preheat broiler.

2. Brush eggplant slices with 1 tablespoon oil. Place half of eggplant on a foil-lined baking sheet coated with cooking spray; broil 5 inches from heat 5 minutes on each side or until browned. Repeat procedure with remaining eggplant. Set eggplant aside.

3. Heat remaining 1 tablespoon oil in a large skillet over medium-high heat. Add chopped onion to pan; sauté 8 minutes. Add garlic; sauté 1 minute. Add bulgur; cook 3 minutes or until bulgur is lightly toasted, stirring frequently. Add ground allspice, cinnamon, and cloves; cook 1 minute, stirring constantly. Stir in broth, oregano, and tomatoes. Bring to a boil; reduce heat, and simmer 20 minutes or until thickened, stirring occasionally.

4. Melt butter in a saucepan over medium heat. Add flour; cook 1 minute, stirring constantly with a whisk until well blended. Gradually add milk, stirring constantly with a whisk. Bring to a boil; reduce heat to medium-low, and simmer 5 minutes or until thickened, stirring frequently. Stir in cheese and salt. Remove from heat, and cool slightly. Add egg, stirring well with a whisk.

5. Preheat oven to 350°.

6. Arrange half of eggplant in an 11 x 7–inch glass or ceramic baking dish coated with cooking spray. Spread bulgur mixture evenly over eggplant; arrange remaining eggplant over bulgur mixture. Top with milk mixture. Bake at 350° for 40 minutes; remove from oven. Increase oven temperature to 475°. Return dish to oven for 4 minutes or until top is browned. Let stand 10 minutes before serving. Yield: 4 servings.

CALORIES 343; **FAT** 13.1g (sat 4.2g, mono 6.4g, poly 1.3g); **PROTEIN** 11.4g; **CARB** 47.8g; **FIBER** 13.4g; **CHOL** 57mg; **IRON** 2.3mg; **SODIUM** 583mg; **CALC** 203mg

> **SIMPLE SUB:** Bulgur wheat stands in for ground meat in this well-spiced tomato-eggplant dish.

Green Chile Tamale Pie

1 cup masa harina
1 teaspoon kosher salt, divided
¼ teaspoon ground red pepper
1 cup boiling water
1 tablespoon olive oil
8 ounces ground sirloin
1½ cups chopped onion
3 garlic cloves, minced
1 poblano chile, seeded and chopped

¼ teaspoon freshly ground black pepper
8 small tomatillos, chopped
1 cup frozen baby lima beans
2 tablespoons butter, melted
½ teaspoon baking powder
¼ cup crumbled queso fresco
2 tablespoons chopped fresh cilantro
4 lime wedges

1. Preheat oven to 400°.

2. Combine masa harina, ¼ teaspoon salt, and ground red pepper, stirring well with a whisk. Add 1 cup boiling water to masa mixture, and stir until a soft dough forms. Cover until ready to use.

3. Heat oil in a 9-inch cast-iron skillet over medium-high heat. Add beef; cook 5 minutes or until browned, stirring to crumble. Add onion, garlic, poblano chile, remaining ¾ teaspoon salt, and black pepper; sauté 5 minutes or until onion is tender, stirring frequently. Add tomatillos and lima beans; cook 2 minutes. Remove from heat.

4. Add butter and baking powder to masa mixture, stirring until smooth. Dollop batter over filling, and spread into an even layer. Cover pan with foil; bake at 400° for 30 minutes. Uncover and bake an additional 10 minutes or until crust is lightly browned around edges. Remove from oven; let stand 3 minutes. Sprinkle with crumbled queso fresco and cilantro; serve with lime wedges. Yield: 4 servings (serving size: 1½ cups pie, 1 tablespoon queso fresco, and 1 lime wedge).

CALORIES 378; FAT 15.2g (sat 6.2g, mono 5.7g, poly 1.9g); PROTEIN 20.5g; CARB 43.4g; FIBER 8.6g; CHOL 50mg; IRON 5mg; SODIUM 643mg; CALC 154mg

> **FYI:** Masa harina has a distinctive tortilla-like, hint-of-lime taste. The flour used to make tamales, it stands in for cornmeal in this lightened retro version of the Mexican classic.

Eggplant Parmesan

Whole-wheat panko is best in this recipe; the regular type became soggy when we tested it. To save time, prepare the filling while the eggplant bakes.

Eggplant:
2 large eggs, lightly beaten
1 tablespoon water
2 cups whole-wheat panko
  (Japanese breadcrumbs)
$1/4$ cup (1 ounce) grated fresh
  Parmigiano-Reggiano cheese
2 (1-pound) eggplants, peeled and cut
  crosswise into $1/2$-inch-thick slices
Cooking spray
Filling:
$1/2$ cup torn fresh basil
$1/4$ cup (1 ounce) grated fresh
  Parmigiano-Reggiano cheese

$1/2$ teaspoon crushed red pepper
$1 1/2$ teaspoons minced garlic
$1/4$ teaspoon salt
1 (16-ounce) container part-skim
  ricotta cheese
1 large egg, lightly beaten
Remaining ingredients:
1 (24-ounce) jar premium pasta sauce
$1/4$ teaspoon salt, divided
8 ounces thinly sliced mozzarella cheese
$3/4$ cup (3 ounces) finely grated fontina
  cheese
Chopped fresh basil (optional)

1. Preheat oven to 375°.
2. To prepare eggplant, combine 2 eggs and 1 tablespoon water in a shallow dish. Combine panko and ¼ cup Parmigiano-Reggiano in a second shallow dish. Dip eggplant in egg mixture; dredge in panko mixture, pressing gently to adhere and shaking off excess. Place eggplant slices 1 inch apart on baking sheets coated with cooking spray. Bake at 375° for 30 minutes or until golden, turning once and rotating baking sheets after 15 minutes.
3. To prepare filling, combine basil and next 6 ingredients (through egg).
4. To assemble, spoon ½ cup pasta sauce in bottom of a 13 x 9–inch glass or ceramic baking dish coated with cooking spray. Layer half of eggplant slices over pasta sauce. Sprinkle eggplant with ⅛ teaspoon salt. Top with about ¾ cup pasta sauce; spread half of ricotta mixture over sauce, and top with a third of mozzarella and ¼ cup fontina. Repeat layers once, ending with about 1 cup pasta sauce. Cover tightly with aluminum foil coated with cooking spray. Bake at 375° for 35 minutes. Remove foil; top with remaining third of mozzarella and ¼ cup fontina. Bake at 375° for 10 minutes or until sauce is bubbly and cheese melts; cool 10 minutes. Garnish with basil, if desired. Yield: 10 servings (serving size: 1 slice).

CALORIES 318; **FAT** 15.1g (sat 8.2g, mono 2.7g, poly 0.6g); **PROTEIN** 19.3g; **CARB** 26.8g; **FIBER** 4.8g; **CHOL** 99mg; **IRON** 1.6mg; **SODIUM** 655mg; **CALC** 365mg

Paella with Poblanos, Corn, and Clams

The crust won't form until all the liquid from the clams and the tomatoes has boiled off, so be patient with that last step; it's worth it.

2 tablespoons olive oil
2 cups chopped yellow onion
3 garlic cloves, minced
2 poblano chiles, seeded and chopped
1¼ teaspoons kosher salt, divided
½ teaspoon freshly ground black pepper, divided
¾ cup uncooked short-grain brown rice

¼ teaspoon saffron threads, crushed
2 cups water
⅛ teaspoon ground red pepper
1½ cups fresh corn kernels (about 2 ears)
1 cup halved cherry tomatoes
2 pounds littleneck clams
2 tablespoons chopped fresh flat-leaf parsley
8 lemon wedges

1. Preheat oven to 450°.

2. Heat oil in a 12-inch ovenproof skillet over medium-high heat. Add onion, garlic, poblanos, ½ teaspoon salt, and ¼ teaspoon black pepper; sauté 3 minutes. Add rice and saffron. Cook 2 minutes, stirring constantly. Add 2 cups water, remaining ¾ teaspoon salt, remaining ¼ teaspoon black pepper, and red pepper; bring to a boil.

3. Bake at 450° for 50 minutes or until rice is done. Stir in corn and tomatoes. Nestle clams into rice mixture. Bake at 450° for 12 minutes or until shells open; discard unopened shells.

4. Return pan to medium-high heat; cook, without stirring, 10 minutes or until liquid evaporates and rice browns. (It should smell toasty but not burned.) Top with parsley; serve with lemon wedges. Yield: 4 servings (serving size: 1¼ cups rice mixture, about 7 clams, and 2 lemon wedges).

CALORIES 340; **FAT** 9.1g (sat 1.1g, mono 5.2g, poly 1.3g); **PROTEIN** 14.8g; **CARB** 52.7g; **FIBER** 5.6g; **CHOL** 21mg; **IRON** 10mg; **SODIUM** 651mg; **CALC** 68mg

Lobster Thermidor

To save time, buy fresh lobster tails and have them steamed at the store. If using whole lobster, reserve the shells to cook the meat in, and use the body and claw shells to simmer in the milk. This entrée makes an impressive offering for a small, elegant dinner party.

3 cups water
4 large lobster tails (about 28 ounces)
2 cups fat-free milk
1 teaspoon olive oil
3 tablespoons chopped shallots (about 1 large)
2 (8-ounce) packages presliced mushrooms
3 tablespoons dry sherry
1 1/2 tablespoons all-purpose flour
1/4 teaspoon freshly ground black pepper
Dash of white pepper

1 tablespoon chopped fresh basil
2 teaspoons chopped fresh tarragon
3 tablespoons whipping cream
1/4 teaspoon kosher salt
Cooking spray
3/4 cup (3 ounces) shredded reduced-fat, reduced-sodium Swiss cheese
2/3 cup panko (Japanese breadcrumbs)
2 teaspoons unsalted butter, melted

1. Bring 3 cups water to a boil in a stockpot. Place a vegetable steamer or rack in bottom of pan. Add lobster tails. Cover and steam 8 minutes or until done. Cool to room temperature. Remove meat from cooked lobster tails; set shells aside. Chop meat into bite-sized pieces. (You should have about 1¾ cups chopped meat.) Cover and chill.
2. Place lobster shells in a large zip-top plastic bag. Coarsely crush shells using a meat mallet or rolling pin. Combine shells and milk in a small saucepan over medium heat. Bring to a simmer; cook 5 minutes (do not boil). Remove from heat; cover and let stand 30 minutes. Strain mixture through a fine mesh sieve into a bowl; discard solids. Set aside.
3. Preheat oven to 450°.
4. Heat oil in a large nonstick skillet over medium-high heat. Add shallots; sauté 2 minutes or until soft. Add mushrooms; sauté 4 minutes or until liquid begins to evaporate. Stir in sherry, and cook 1 minute.
5. Combine reserved milk mixture, flour, black pepper, and white pepper in a small bowl; stir with a whisk until smooth. Add milk mixture to pan; bring to a boil. Cook 1 minute or until thickened, stirring constantly. Stir in basil and tarragon; cook 1 minute, stirring occasionally. Add reserved lobster meat, cream, and salt; stir well. Divide mixture evenly among 4 (1½-cup) gratin dishes coated with cooking spray.
6. Combine cheese, panko, and melted butter in a small bowl; toss well. Sprinkle about ⅓ cup panko mixture over each gratin. Bake at 450° for 12 minutes or until topping is browned. Yield: 4 servings (serving size: 1 gratin).

CALORIES 419; **FAT** 13.5g (sat 7.1g, mono 4.1g, poly 0.7g); **PROTEIN** 50.2g; **CARB** 23.3g; **FIBER** 1.7g; **CHOL** 159mg; **IRON** 1.7mg; **SODIUM** 883mg; **CALC** 480mg

Provençal Cod Fillets with Wilted Lettuce and Tomato

The fish is surrounded by layers of onion, tomato, and lettuce, and then topped with lettuce leaves instead of a lid. Any firm fish can stand in for the cod.

6 (6-ounce) cod fillets
3 tablespoons red wine vinegar
3 tablespoons water
1 lemon
1 (12-ounce) head romaine lettuce, trimmed
2 pounds tomato, peeled, seeded, and chopped
2 cups coarsely chopped onion
3 garlic cloves, minced
Cooking spray
1 teaspoon salt, divided
½ teaspoon freshly ground black pepper, divided
¼ cup extra-virgin olive oil

1. Place fillets in a shallow dish. Combine vinegar and 3 tablespoons water; drizzle over fillets. Cover and refrigerate 30 minutes.

2. Carefully cut rind and white pithy part from lemon using a small knife. Cut lemon cross-wise into thin slices; discard seeds. Reserve 6 whole lettuce leaves; coarsely shred remaining lettuce.

3. Preheat oven to 325°.

4. Layer about 2 cups shredded lettuce, 1½ cups tomato, 1 cup onion, 1½ teaspoons garlic, and half the lemon slices in a 13 x 9–inch glass or ceramic baking dish coated with cooking spray. Sprinkle vegetable mixture with ¼ teaspoon salt and ⅛ teaspoon pepper. Place fillets on top of vegetable mixture. Sprinkle fish evenly with ½ teaspoon salt and ¼ teaspoon pepper. Repeat layers with remaining chopped lettuce, tomato, onion, garlic, and lemon slices. Sprinkle with remaining ¼ teaspoon salt and ⅛ teaspoon pepper. Top with reserved whole lettuce leaves; drizzle with oil.

5. Bake at 325° for 20 minutes or until fish flakes easily when tested with a fork or until desired degree of doneness. Remove whole lettuce leaves and fillets from pan; keep warm. Return vegetables to oven. Bake an additional 20 minutes or until vegetables are tender. Place 1 whole lettuce leaf on each of 6 plates; top each serving with 1 fillet. Spoon about 1 cup vegetable mixture over each fillet. Yield: 6 servings.

CALORIES 269; FAT 10.4g (sat 1.5g, mono 6.8g, poly 1.4g); PROTEIN 29.6g; CARB 14.5g; FIBER 3.8g; CHOL 65mg; IRON 1.8mg; SODIUM 502mg; CALC 77mg

Roasted Butternut Squash and Bacon
Pasta *(Pictured on page 70)*

Mini penne pasta works well in this dish because it's about the same size as the squash.

¾ teaspoon salt, divided
½ teaspoon dried rosemary
¼ teaspoon freshly ground black pepper
3 cups (1-inch) cubed peeled butternut squash
Cooking spray
6 sweet hickory-smoked bacon slices
1 cup thinly sliced shallots
8 ounces uncooked mini penne
   (tube-shaped pasta)

1.1 ounces all-purpose flour (about ¼ cup)
2 cups 2% reduced-fat milk
¾ cup (3 ounces) shredded sharp
   provolone cheese
⅓ cup (1½ ounces) grated fresh
   Parmesan cheese

1. Preheat oven to 425°.
2. Combine ¼ teaspoon salt, rosemary, and pepper. Place squash on a foil-lined baking sheet coated with cooking spray; sprinkle with salt mixture. Bake at 425° for 45 minutes or until tender and lightly browned. Increase oven temperature to 450°.
3. Cook bacon in a large nonstick skillet over medium heat until crisp. Remove bacon from pan, reserving 1½ teaspoons drippings in pan; crumble bacon. Increase heat to medium-high. Add shallots to pan; sauté 8 minutes or until tender. Combine squash mixture, bacon, and shallots; set aside.
4. Cook pasta according to package directions, omitting salt and fat. Drain well.
5. Combine flour and remaining ½ teaspoon salt in a Dutch oven over medium-high heat. Gradually add milk, stirring constantly with a whisk; bring to a boil. Cook 1 minute or until slightly thick, stirring constantly. Remove from heat. Add provolone, stirring until cheese melts. Add pasta to cheese mixture, tossing well to combine. Spoon pasta mixture into an 11 x 7–inch glass or ceramic baking dish lightly coated with cooking spray; top with squash mixture. Sprinkle evenly with Parmesan cheese. Bake at 450° for 10 minutes or until cheese melts and begins to brown. Yield: 5 servings.

CALORIES 469; **FAT** 14.4g (sat 7.3g, mono 4.4g, poly 0.9g); **PROTEIN** 22.1g; **CARB** 66.6g; **FIBER** 6.8g; **CHOL** 40mg; **IRON** 3.5mg; **SODIUM** 849mg; **CALC** 443mg

Beef, Cheese, and Noodle Bake

1 (8-ounce) package small elbow macaroni
Cooking spray
1 cup chopped onion
1 cup shredded carrot
2 teaspoons minced garlic
1 pound lean ground sirloin
1 cup tomato sauce

1 teaspoon kosher salt, divided
1/2 teaspoon freshly ground black pepper
1 cup fat-free milk
2 tablespoons all-purpose flour
1/8 teaspoon ground nutmeg
1 1/2 cups (6 ounces) shredded reduced-fat
 sharp cheddar cheese, divided

1. Preheat oven to 350°.
2. Cook pasta according to package directions, omitting salt and fat; drain well. Lightly coat pasta with cooking spray.
3. Heat a Dutch oven over medium-high heat. Coat pan with cooking spray. Add onion and carrot; sauté 4 minutes. Add garlic; sauté 1 minute. Add beef; cook 5 minutes or until browned, stirring to crumble. Add tomato sauce, 1/2 teaspoon salt, and pepper. Cook 2 minutes or until most of liquid evaporates.
4. Add pasta to beef mixture in pan, stirring to combine. Spoon pasta mixture into an 11 x 7–inch glass or ceramic baking dish coated with cooking spray.
5. Place milk, flour, nutmeg, and remaining 1/2 teaspoon salt in a medium saucepan; stir with a whisk until blended. Cook over medium heat 2 minutes or until thickened, stirring constantly with a whisk. Add 1 cup cheese, stirring until smooth. Pour cheese mixture over pasta mixture; stir well. Top evenly with remaining 1/2 cup cheese. Bake at 350° for 20 minutes or until lightly browned. Let stand 5 minutes before serving. Yield: 8 servings (serving size: about 1 cup).

CALORIES 283; FAT 7.7g (sat 4.2g, mono 2.4g, poly 0.7g); PROTEIN 22.3g; CARB 30.1g; FIBER 2.1g; CHOL 46mg; IRON 3.1mg; SODIUM 622mg; CALC 209mg

Chili and Cheddar Bow Tie Casserole

If you don't have farfalle, substitute ziti, rigatoni, or macaroni.

1 (7-ounce) can chipotle chiles in adobo sauce
1 tablespoon butter
1 cup chopped red bell pepper
1/2 cup diced Canadian bacon (about 2 ounces)
1 cup thinly sliced green onions
2 tablespoons all-purpose flour
1 teaspoon chili powder
1/2 teaspoon salt

1/2 teaspoon ground cumin
2 1/4 cups 2% reduced-fat milk
2 cups (8 ounces) shredded reduced-fat sharp cheddar cheese, divided
2 tablespoons chopped fresh cilantro
8 cups hot cooked farfalle (bow tie pasta)
Cooking spray

1. Preheat oven to 400°.

2. Remove 1 teaspoon adobo sauce and 1 chile from canned chiles; mince chile. Place remaining sauce and chiles in a zip-top plastic bag; freeze for another use.

3. Melt butter in a large Dutch oven over medium-high heat. Add bell pepper and bacon; sauté 4 minutes. Add onions; sauté 1 minute. Stir in adobo sauce, minced chile, flour, chili powder, salt, and cumin; cook 1 minute. Gradually add milk; cook until thick and bubbly (about 4 minutes), stirring constantly with a whisk. Remove from heat. Gradually add 1½ cups cheese and cilantro, stirring until cheese melts. Add pasta to pan; toss well.

4. Spoon pasta mixture into an 11 x 7–inch glass or ceramic baking dish coated with cooking spray. Sprinkle remaining ½ cup cheese over pasta mixture. Bake at 400° for 15 minutes or until browned. Yield: 6 servings (serving size: 1⅓ cups).

CALORIES 369; FAT 12.4g (sat 7.4g, mono 1.6g, poly 1g); PROTEIN 23.2g; CARB 43g; FIBER 3.1g; CHOL 44mg; IRON 1.6mg; SODIUM 758mg; CALC 472mg

Potato and Lamb Moussaka

Add a simple Greek salad, a few wedges of warm pita bread, and a red wine to complete this Mediterranean menu.

Cooking spray
2 pounds peeled baking potato, cut into
  ¼-inch-thick slices
1 cup chopped onion (about 1 medium)
2 garlic cloves, chopped
1 pound ground lamb
½ cup chopped green bell pepper
½ cup chopped red bell pepper

1 cup no-salt-added tomato sauce
1 teaspoon salt
1 teaspoon ground cumin
½ teaspoon freshly ground black pepper
¼ teaspoon ground cinnamon
½ cup finely chopped fresh flat-leaf parsley
1 cup 1% low-fat milk
2 large eggs, lightly beaten

1. Heat a large skillet over medium heat. Coat pan with cooking spray. Add one-third of the potato slices to pan; cook 3 minutes on each side or until lightly browned. Transfer potato to a large bowl. Repeat procedure with cooking spray and remaining potato slices.
2. Preheat oven to 350°.
3. Recoat pan with cooking spray. Add onion, garlic, and lamb to pan; cook 3 minutes or until lamb begins to brown. Add bell peppers, tomato sauce, salt, cumin, black pepper, cinnamon, and parsley; cook 10 minutes.
4. Arrange half of the potato slices in a 13 x 9–inch glass or ceramic baking dish coated with cooking spray. Arrange lamb mixture over potato slices, and top with remaining potato slices. Combine milk and lightly beaten eggs in a small bowl; pour over potato mixture. Bake at 350° for 30 minutes or until top is golden and set. Remove from oven; let stand 10 minutes before serving. Yield: 6 servings (serving size: 1 piece).

CALORIES 369; FAT 13.7g (sat 5.5g, mono 5.5g, poly 1.2g); PROTEIN 21.4g; CARB 40.3g; FIBER 4.7g; CHOL 127mg; IRON 2.8mg; SODIUM 501mg; CALC 111mg

Moroccan Shepherd's Pie

1 tablespoon olive oil
1 pound bone-in lamb shoulder,
   trimmed and cut into 1/2-inch pieces
1 teaspoon ground cumin, divided
1/2 teaspoon kosher salt, divided
1 1/2 cups chopped onion
4 garlic cloves, minced
1 tablespoon tomato paste
1 1/2 cups fat-free, lower-sodium chicken broth
1/2 cup water
1/3 cup sliced pimiento-stuffed green olives
1/3 cup raisins
2 tablespoons honey
1/2 teaspoon ground red pepper
1/4 teaspoon ground turmeric
1/2 teaspoon cinnamon, divided
1 cup frozen green peas
4 cups chopped peeled sweet potato
1 large egg, lightly beaten
Cooking spray

1. Preheat oven to 350°.
2. Heat oil in a large skillet over medium-high heat. Sprinkle lamb evenly with 1/2 teaspoon ground cumin and 1/4 teaspoon salt. Add lamb to pan; sauté 4 minutes, turning to brown on all sides. Remove lamb from pan. Add onion to pan; sauté 3 minutes. Add garlic, and sauté 30 seconds, stirring constantly. Stir in tomato paste, and sauté 30 seconds.
3. Add broth and 1/2 cup water to pan; bring to a boil, scraping pan to loosen browned bits. Return lamb to pan. Stir in remaining 1/2 teaspoon ground cumin, olives, raisins, honey, red pepper, and turmeric. Stir in 1/8 teaspoon cinnamon. Reduce heat, and simmer 30 minutes, stirring occasionally. Remove from heat; stir in peas.
4. Cook potato in boiling water 10 minutes or until tender; drain. Cool 5 minutes. Place in a bowl. Sprinkle with remaining 1/4 teaspoon salt and remaining 3/8 teaspoon cinnamon. Beat potato with a mixer at high speed until smooth. Add egg; beat until combined. Spoon lamb mixture into 4 (10-ounce) ramekins coated with cooking spray; spread potato mixture evenly over lamb mixture. Place ramekins on a baking sheet; bake at 350° for 25 minutes or until bubbly. Yield: 4 servings (serving size: 1 pie).

CALORIES 515; **FAT** 22g (sat 7.9g, mono 10.6g, poly 2.1g); **PROTEIN** 22.1g; **CARB** 58.3g; **FIBER** 7.9g; **CHOL** 105mg; **IRON** 4mg; **SODIUM** 885mg; **CALC** 112mg

Cassoulet

Cassoulet serves a large gathering, and leftovers reheat well. Precooked spicy Italian sausage or Polish kielbasa is a close match to the lively garlic sausage from southwestern France that traditionally graces this dish. The recipe can be prepared two days ahead and refrigerated. Top with breadcrumbs and finish in the oven before serving.

1/4 cup salt
6 (8-ounce) duck leg quarters
1 1/2 tablespoons canola oil
4 thick-cut bacon slices, sliced crosswise into (1/2-inch-thick) strips
1 (3/4-pound) boneless leg of lamb, trimmed and cut into 1-inch cubes
1 1/2 cups chopped onion
1/4 teaspoon freshly ground black pepper

1/4 cup no-salt-added tomato puree
3 garlic cloves, minced
2 cups fat-free, lower-sodium chicken broth
2 cups water
4 (15-ounce) cans organic Great Northern beans, rinsed and drained
8 ounces cooked spicy Italian sausage, diagonally sliced
1/4 cup dry breadcrumbs

1. Rub salt evenly over duck; cover and refrigerate 30 minutes.
2. Heat oil in a large Dutch oven over medium heat. Add bacon to pan; cook 7 minutes or until crisp, stirring occasionally. Remove bacon from pan using a slotted spoon; set aside. Increase heat to medium-high. Add lamb to drippings in pan; cook 8 minutes, turning to brown on all sides. Remove lamb from pan, and set aside.
3. Preheat oven to 300°.
4. Rinse duck with cold water; pat dry with paper towels. Add half of duck, skin side down, to pan; cook over medium heat 15 minutes or until golden brown. Turn duck over, and cook 10 minutes or until browned and fat under skin is melted. Remove duck from pan. Repeat procedure with remaining duck, reserving 1 tablespoon duck fat in pan; set duck aside. Add onion and pepper to pan; cook 7 minutes or until lightly browned, stirring occasionally. Stir in tomato puree and garlic; cook 1 minute. Return lamb to pan. Nestle duck into lamb mixture; add broth and 2 cups water. Cover and bake at 300° for 2 1/2 hours or until lamb and duck are very tender. Remove pan from oven. Remove duck from pan to a cutting board; let stand until tepid. Remove skin from duck pieces; discard. Cut duck legs in half through the joint. Return duck to lamb mixture. Taste and adjust the seasoning, if desired.
5. Increase oven temperature to 375°.
6. Stir 2 cans of Great Northern beans into lamb mixture. Add bacon and Italian sausage; top mixture with remaining 2 cans of beans. Sprinkle breadcrumbs evenly over top. Cover and cook 1 hour and 10 minutes. Uncover and cook an additional 20 minutes or until browned and bubbly. Yield: 12 servings (serving size: 1 drumstick or thigh and about 3/4 cup bean mixture).

CALORIES 323; FAT 14.4g (sat 4.6g, mono 4.4g, poly 1.2g); PROTEIN 27.1g; CARB 20g; FIBER 7.1g; CHOL 79mg; IRON 2.9mg; SODIUM 821mg; CALC 88mg

Chicken Tamale Casserole

Homemade tamales are too time-consuming to prepare for weeknight meals; a corn muffin mix approximates the flavor.

1 cup (4 ounces) preshredded 4-cheese
  Mexican blend cheese, divided
$1/3$ cup fat-free milk
$1/4$ cup egg substitute
1 teaspoon ground cumin
$1/8$ teaspoon ground red pepper
1 ($14^3/4$-ounce) can cream-style corn

1 ($8^1/2$-ounce) package corn muffin mix
1 (4-ounce) can chopped green chiles,
  drained
Cooking spray
1 (10-ounce) can red enchilada sauce
2 cups shredded cooked chicken breast
$1/2$ cup fat-free sour cream

1. Preheat oven to 400°.

2. Combine ¼ cup cheese and next 7 ingredients (through chiles) in a large bowl, stirring just until moist. Pour mixture into a 13 x 9–inch glass or ceramic baking dish coated with cooking spray.

3. Bake at 400° for 15 minutes or until set. Pierce entire surface liberally with a fork; pour enchilada sauce over top. Top with chicken; sprinkle with remaining ¾ cup cheese. Bake at 400° for 15 minutes or until cheese melts. Remove from oven; let stand 5 minutes. Cut into 8 pieces; top each serving with 1 tablespoon sour cream. Yield: 8 servings.

CALORIES 354; **FAT** 14.1g (sat 7.1g, mono 3.3g, poly 1.2g); **PROTEIN** 18.9g; **CARB** 36.3g; **FIBER** 2.5g; **CHOL** 58mg; **IRON** 1.7mg; **SODIUM** 620mg; **CALC** 179mg

Black Bean and Chicken Chilaquiles

Refrigerate leftover chilaquiles in individual microwave-safe containers with tight-fitting lids. To reheat, drizzle with a tablespoon of water, and microwave just until thoroughly heated.

1 cup thinly sliced onion
5 garlic cloves, minced
2 cups shredded cooked chicken breast
1 (15-ounce) can black beans, rinsed
  and drained

1 cup fat-free, lower-sodium chicken broth
1 (7³/₄-ounce) can salsa de chile fresco
15 (6-inch) corn tortillas, cut into 1-inch strips
Cooking spray
1 cup (4 ounces) shredded queso blanco

1. Preheat oven to 450°.

2. Heat a large nonstick skillet over medium-high heat. Add onion; sauté 5 minutes or until lightly browned. Add garlic; sauté 1 minute. Add chicken; cook 30 seconds. Transfer mixture to a medium bowl; stir in beans. Add broth and salsa de chile fresco to pan; bring to a boil. Reduce heat, and simmer 5 minutes, stirring occasionally. Set aside.

3. Place half of tortilla strips in bottom of an 11 x 7–inch baking dish coated with cooking spray. Layer half of chicken mixture over tortillas, and top with remaining tortillas and chicken mixture. Pour broth mixture evenly over chicken mixture. Sprinkle with cheese. Bake at 450° for 10 minutes or until tortillas are lightly browned and cheese is melted. Yield: 6 servings (serving size: 1 [3½-inch] square).

CALORIES 293; **FAT** 4.9g (sat 1.7g, mono 1.5g, poly 1.2g); **PROTEIN** 22.9g; **CARB** 40g; **FIBER** 5.9g; **CHOL** 46mg; **IRON** 2.3mg; **SODIUM** 602mg; **CALC** 200mg

Chicken Chilaquiles

For even more heat, add ¼ teaspoon ground red pepper to the tomatillo mixture. Serve with coleslaw and fruit on the side.

2 cups shredded cooked chicken breast
½ cup chopped green onions
½ cup (2 ounces) shredded Monterey Jack cheese with jalapeño peppers, divided
2 tablespoons grated Parmesan cheese
1 teaspoon chili powder
¼ teaspoon salt
¼ teaspoon freshly ground black pepper

¾ cup 1% low-fat milk
¼ cup chopped fresh cilantro
1 (11-ounce) can tomatillos, drained
1 (4.5-ounce) can chopped green chiles, drained
12 (6-inch) corn tortillas
Cooking spray

1. Preheat oven to 375°.

2. Combine cooked chicken, onions, ¼ cup Monterey Jack cheese, Parmesan, chili powder, salt, and pepper in a medium bowl. Place milk and next 3 ingredients (through chiles) in a food processor or blender; process until smooth.

3. Heat corn tortillas according to package directions. Pour ⅓ cup tomatillo mixture into bottom of an 11 x 7–inch glass or ceramic baking dish coated with cooking spray. Arrange 4 corn tortillas in dish, and top with half of chicken mixture. Repeat layer with remaining tortillas and chicken mixture, ending with tortillas.

4. Pour remaining 1½ cups tomatillo mixture over tortillas; sprinkle with remaining ¼ cup Monterey Jack cheese. Bake at 375° for 20 minutes or until bubbly. Yield: 4 servings (serving size: 1½ cups).

CALORIES 347; **FAT** 10.9g (sat 4.5g, mono 2.9g, poly 1.9g); **PROTEIN** 30.9g; **CARB** 33.3g; **FIBER** 5.9g; **CHOL** 79mg; **IRON** 1.5mg; **SODIUM** 560mg; **CALC** 272mg

Mexican Chicken Casserole with Charred Tomato Salsa

Salsa:
8 plum tomatoes, halved and seeded
3 garlic cloves, peeled and crushed
1 small onion, peeled and chopped
1 seeded jalapeño pepper, quartered
Cooking spray
⅓ cup chopped fresh cilantro
3 tablespoons fresh lime juice
⅛ teaspoon freshly ground black pepper

Casserole:
1 cup chopped onion
1 cup fresh or frozen corn kernels

1 cup diced zucchini
1 cup chopped red bell pepper
3 cups shredded cooked chicken breast
1 tablespoon minced garlic
2 teaspoons chili powder
1 teaspoon ground cumin
1 (10-ounce) can green chile enchilada sauce
1 (4-ounce) can chopped green chiles
12 (6-inch) corn tortillas
1 cup (4 ounces) shredded Monterey Jack cheese
1 cup (4 ounces) crumbled feta cheese

1. Preheat broiler.

2. To prepare salsa, combine first 4 ingredients on a baking sheet coated with cooking spray. Broil 20 minutes or until charred, stirring once. Remove from oven; cool slightly. Place mixture in a food processor; add cilantro, lime juice, and black pepper. Process until smooth. Set aside.

3. Preheat oven to 350°.

4. To prepare casserole, heat a large nonstick skillet over medium-high heat. Add 1 cup onion, corn, zucchini, and bell pepper; sauté 6 minutes or until tender. Add chicken and next 5 ingredients (through green chiles); sauté 2 minutes or until thoroughly heated. Remove from heat.

5. Spread ½ cup salsa over bottom of a 13 x 9–inch glass or ceramic baking dish coated with cooking spray. Arrange half of tortillas over salsa. Spoon 2 cups chicken mixture evenly over tortillas. Top with ¾ cup salsa. Sprinkle with ½ cup of each cheese. Repeat layers, starting with remaining tortillas and ending with remaining cheeses. Bake at 350° for 25 minutes or until bubbly. Yield: 8 servings.

CALORIES 331; **FAT** 12.3g (sat 6.1g, mono 2.8g, poly 1.2g); **PROTEIN** 26.1g; **CARB** 30.8g; **FIBER** 4.2g; **CHOL** 74mg; **IRON** 1.6mg; **SODIUM** 535mg; **CALC** 242mg

Chicken Enchilada Casserole

Cooking spray
4 bone-in chicken thighs, skinned
1/3 cup chopped fresh cilantro, divided
1 cup frozen corn kernels, thawed
1/3 cup (3 ounces) 1/3-less-fat cream
  cheese, softened
1/2 teaspoon ground red pepper
1/2 teaspoon ground cumin
1/4 teaspoon kosher salt
1/4 teaspoon freshly ground black pepper

2 cups chopped onion, divided
6 garlic cloves, minced and divided
1 cup fat-free, lower-sodium chicken broth
2/3 cup salsa verde
1/4 cup water
2 tablespoons chopped pickled jalapeño
  pepper
9 (6-inch) corn tortillas
1/2 cup (2 ounces) shredded sharp
  cheddar cheese

1. Preheat oven to 425°.
2. Heat a large ovenproof skillet over medium-high heat. Coat pan with cooking spray. Add chicken to pan; sauté 4 minutes on each side. Place skillet in oven; bake at 425° for 10 minutes or until done. Remove chicken from pan; let stand 15 minutes. Remove meat from bones; shred. Discard bones. Place chicken in a medium bowl. Add 1½ tablespoons cilantro, corn, and next 5 ingredients (through black pepper) to chicken; toss to combine.
3. Return pan to medium-high heat. Add ½ cup onion; sauté 5 minutes, stirring occasionally. Add 3 garlic cloves; sauté 30 seconds, stirring constantly. Add onion mixture to chicken mixture; stir to combine.
4. Combine remaining 1½ cups onion, remaining 3 garlic cloves, broth, salsa, ¼ cup water, and jalapeño in a medium saucepan over medium-high heat; bring to a boil. Reduce heat, and simmer 15 minutes, stirring occasionally. Remove from heat; let stand 10 minutes. Carefully pour mixture into a blender; add 2 tablespoons cilantro. Process until smooth.
5. Heat a large skillet over medium-high heat. Add 2 tortillas; cook 1½ minutes on each side. Remove tortillas from pan; repeat procedure with remaining tortillas. Cut tortillas into quarters.
6. Spread ½ cup salsa mixture in bottom of a 2-quart glass or ceramic baking dish coated with cooking spray. Arrange 12 tortilla quarters over salsa mixture. Spoon half of chicken mixture over tortillas. Repeat layers, ending with tortillas. Pour remaining salsa mixture over tortillas; sprinkle evenly with cheddar cheese. Bake at 425° for 15 minutes or until bubbly and lightly browned. Top with remaining cilantro. Yield: 4 servings (serving size: about 1¾ cups).

CALORIES 399; FAT 14.7g (sat 6.5g, mono 3.6g, poly 1.8g); PROTEIN 24.9g; CARB 45.4g; FIBER 5.4g; CHOL 88mg; IRON 1.6mg; SODIUM 803mg; CALC 192mg

> **TIME-SAVER:** Rotisserie chicken is a convenient substitute, but it is higher in sodium than fresh chicken thighs.

Swiss Enchiladas

Add a dash of ground cumin or paprika to the onions, if you'd like. Purchase rotisserie chicken to cut down on the prep time.

1½ cups chopped onion
2 cups chopped roasted skinless, boneless
  chicken breast (about 2 breasts)
2 garlic cloves, minced
2 (4.5-ounce) cans diced green
  chiles, undrained
1 (14.5-ounce) can petite-cut diced
  tomatoes, undrained

2 cups 2% reduced-fat milk
2 tablespoons all-purpose flour
¼ teaspoon salt
6 (8-inch) fat-free flour tortillas
2 cups (8 ounces) shredded Swiss cheese,
  divided
Cooking spray

1. Preheat oven to 350°.

2. Heat a large nonstick skillet over medium-high heat. Add onion; cook 5 minutes or until tender, stirring occasionally. Stir in chicken, garlic, chiles, and tomatoes. Reduce heat, and simmer 7 minutes or until liquid evaporates. Remove from heat; set aside.

3. Combine milk and flour in a small saucepan over medium-high heat; cook 5 minutes or until mixture thickens, stirring constantly with a whisk. Stir in salt.

4. Warm tortillas according to package directions. Spoon about ½ cup chicken mixture and about 2½ tablespoons cheese down center of each tortilla; roll up. Arrange filled tortillas in bottom of a 13 x 9–inch glass or ceramic baking dish coated with cooking spray. Pour milk mixture over tortillas, and top evenly with remaining 1 cup cheese. Bake at 350° for 25 minutes or until cheese is bubbly. Remove from oven.

5. Preheat broiler.

6. Broil casserole 3 minutes or until cheese begins to brown. Yield: 6 servings (serving size: 1 enchilada and about ⅓ cup sauce).

CALORIES 419; **FAT** 13.2g (sat 7.9g, mono 3.7g, poly 0.8g); **PROTEIN** 33.2g; **CARB** 41.8g; **FIBER** 4.3g; **CHOL** 79mg; **IRON** 2.1mg; **SODIUM** 726mg; **CALC** 474mg

Chicken Spaghetti Casserole

Since this recipe makes two casseroles, you will have one for later. Prepare as directed; cover and freeze before baking. Bake a frozen casserole, covered, for 55 minutes at 350°; uncover and bake an additional 10 minutes or until hot and bubbly.

2 cups chopped cooked chicken breast
2 cups uncooked spaghetti, broken
   into 2-inch pieces (about 7 ounces)
1 cup (¼-inch-thick) slices celery
1 cup chopped onion
1 cup chopped red bell pepper
1 cup fat-free, lower-sodium chicken broth
½ teaspoon salt

¼ teaspoon freshly ground black pepper
2 (10.75-ounce) cans condensed 30%
   reduced-sodium 98% fat-free cream
   of mushroom soup, undiluted
Cooking spray
1 cup (4 ounces) shredded cheddar
   cheese, divided

1. Preheat oven to 350°.
2. Combine first 5 ingredients in a large bowl. Combine broth, salt, pepper, and soup in a medium bowl, stirring with a whisk. Add soup mixture to chicken mixture; toss. Divide mixture evenly between 2 (8-inch) square or (2-quart) glass or ceramic baking dishes coated with cooking spray. Sprinkle ½ cup cheese over each casserole. Cover with foil coated with cooking spray. Bake at 350° for 35 minutes. Uncover and bake an additional 10 minutes. Yield: 2 casseroles, 4 servings each (serving size: about 1 cup).

CALORIES 261; **FAT** 7.8g (sat 3.9g, mono 2.2g, poly 1.1g); **PROTEIN** 19g; **CARB** 28g; **FIBER** 2.1g; **CHOL** 47mg; **IRON** 1.8mg; **SODIUM** 652mg; **CALC** 134mg

Chicken and Root Vegetable Potpie

Instead of a baking dish, you can use 8 (10-ounce) ramekins. Garnish with fresh thyme sprigs.

3 cups fat-free, lower-sodium chicken broth
1½ cups frozen green peas, thawed
1 cup (½-inch) cubed peeled baking potato
1 cup (½-inch) cubed peeled sweet potato
1 cup (½-inch) cubed peeled celeriac
  (celery root)
1 cup (½-inch-thick) slices parsnip
1 (10-ounce) package frozen pearl onions
1 pound skinless, boneless chicken breast,
  cut into bite-sized pieces
3 ounces all-purpose flour (about ²/₃ cup),
  divided
1½ cups fat-free milk
¼ cup chopped fresh parsley
2 tablespoons chopped fresh thyme
1½ teaspoons salt
1 teaspoon freshly ground black pepper
Cooking spray
1 sheet frozen puff pastry dough, thawed

1. Preheat oven to 400°.
2. Bring broth to a boil in a large Dutch oven. Add peas and next 5 ingredients (through onions) to pan; cover, reduce heat, and simmer 6 minutes. Add chicken; cook 5 minutes or until chicken is done. Remove chicken and vegetables from broth with a slotted spoon; place in a large bowl.
3. Increase heat to medium. Place all but 1 tablespoon flour in a medium bowl; gradually add milk to bowl, stirring well. Add milk mixture to broth; cook 5 minutes or until thickened, stirring frequently. Stir in chicken mixture, parsley, thyme, salt, and pepper. Spoon mixture into an 11 x 7–inch glass or ceramic baking dish coated with cooking spray.
4. Sprinkle remaining 1 tablespoon flour on a work surface; roll dough into a 13 x 9–inch rectangle. Place dough over chicken mixture, pressing to seal at edges of dish. Cut small slits into dough to allow steam to escape; coat dough lightly with cooking spray. Place dish on a foil-lined baking sheet. Bake at 400° for 16 minutes or until pastry is browned and filling is bubbly. Yield: 8 servings.

CALORIES 388; FAT 13g (sat 2g, mono 3g, poly 7.1g); PROTEIN 21.9g; CARB 45.7g; FIBER 4.4g; CHOL 34mg; IRON 3mg; SODIUM 790mg; CALC 115mg

Turkey Tetrazzini

10 ounces uncooked linguine
2 teaspoons canola oil
1 pound turkey tenderloin, cut into
  bite-sized pieces
¾ teaspoon onion powder, divided
¾ teaspoon freshly ground black
  pepper, divided
½ teaspoon salt, divided
2 tablespoons dry sherry
2 (8-ounce) packages presliced mushrooms

1 cup frozen green peas, thawed
1 cup 2% reduced-fat milk
1 cup light sour cream
⅓ cup grated fresh Parmesan cheese
1 (10¾-ounce) can condensed reduced-
  fat cream of chicken soup
1 (2-ounce) jar diced pimiento, drained
Cooking spray
½ cup panko (Japanese breadcrumbs)
2 tablespoons butter, melted

1. Preheat oven to 450°.
2. Cook pasta according to package directions, omitting salt and fat; drain.
3. Heat oil in a large nonstick skillet over medium-high heat. Sprinkle turkey with ½ teaspoon onion powder, ½ teaspoon pepper, and ¼ teaspoon salt; toss. Add turkey to pan; cook 4 minutes, stirring frequently. Remove from pan.
4. Add remaining ¼ teaspoon onion powder, sherry, and mushrooms to pan. Cover and cook 4 minutes or until mushrooms are tender.
5. Combine peas and next 5 ingredients (through pimiento) in a large bowl. Add remaining ¼ teaspoon pepper, remaining ¼ teaspoon salt, pasta, turkey, and mushroom mixture to soup mixture, tossing gently to combine. Spoon into a 3-quart glass or ceramic baking dish coated with cooking spray.
6. Combine breadcrumbs and butter; toss well. Sprinkle breadcrumb mixture over pasta mixture. Bake at 450° for 12 minutes or until bubbly and thoroughly heated. Yield: 6 servings (serving size: about 1⅔ cups).

CALORIES 479; **FAT** 13.7g (sat 6.4g, mono 2.4g, poly 1g); **PROTEIN** 35.4g; **CARB** 56.6g; **FIBER** 4.1g; **CHOL** 62mg; **IRON** 3.4mg; **SODIUM** 686mg; **CALC** 155mg

Italian Sausage Puttanesca

For less heat, try mild turkey Italian sausage.

8 ounces uncooked penne (tube-shaped pasta)
8 ounces hot turkey Italian sausage
Cooking spray
1 cup chopped onion
1 cup chopped green bell pepper
3 garlic cloves, minced
2 (14.5-ounce) cans no-salt-added whole
   tomatoes, undrained and chopped
¼ cup halved pitted kalamata olives
2 tablespoons tomato paste
1 tablespoon capers, drained
1 teaspoon anchovy paste
¼ cup (1 ounce) finely shredded
   Parmesan cheese

1. Preheat oven to 400°.

2. Cook pasta according to package directions, omitting salt and fat. Drain well.

3. Remove casings from sausage. Place a Dutch oven over medium-high heat; coat pan with cooking spray. Add sausage, onion, bell pepper, and garlic to pan; sauté 8 minutes, stirring to crumble.

4. Add tomatoes, olives, tomato paste, capers, and anchovy paste to pan; bring to a boil. Reduce heat, and simmer 5 minutes. Remove from heat. Add pasta, tossing well to combine. Spoon pasta mixture into an 8-inch square glass or ceramic baking dish or 2-quart casserole coated with cooking spray; sprinkle evenly with cheese. Bake at 400° for 15 minutes or until cheese melts and begins to brown. Yield: 4 servings.

CALORIES 433; FAT 12.3g (sat 3.3g, mono 5.6g, poly 2.2g); PROTEIN 23.1g; CARB 59.7g; FIBER 5.7g; CHOL 56mg; IRON 5.1mg; SODIUM 855mg; CALC 163mg

Sausage and Vegetable Deep-Dish Pizza

Sauce:
Cooking spray
2 cups chopped zucchini
¼ cup chopped onion
1 (8-ounce) package mushrooms, sliced
¼ cup white wine
⅛ teaspoon freshly ground black pepper
2 cups fat-free garlic-and-onion pasta sauce
8 ounces hot turkey Italian sausage
Dough:
2 teaspoons honey
1 package dry yeast (about 2¼ teaspoons)

1 cup warm water (100° to 110°)
11.25 ounces all-purpose flour (about 2½ cups), divided
1 tablespoon yellow cornmeal
½ teaspoon salt
2 teaspoons olive oil
Remaining ingredients:
1½ cups (6 ounces) shredded part-skim mozzarella cheese
½ cup (2 ounces) grated Parmesan cheese

1. To prepare sauce, heat a large saucepan over medium-high heat. Coat pan with cooking spray. Add zucchini, onion, and mushrooms to pan; sauté 7 minutes or until vegetables are lightly browned. Add white wine and pepper; cook 1 minute or until liquid almost evaporates. Stir in sauce. Remove from heat, and cool.

2. Remove casings from Italian sausage. Cook sausage in a large nonstick skillet over medium-high heat until browned, stirring to crumble. Drain and add to sauce.

3. To prepare dough, dissolve honey and yeast in 1 cup warm water in a large bowl; let stand 5 minutes. Weigh or lightly spoon flour into dry measuring cups; level with a knife. Add 10.2 ounces (2¼ cups) flour, cornmeal, and salt to yeast mixture; stir until a soft dough forms. Turn dough out onto a lightly floured surface. Knead until smooth and elastic (about 6 minutes); add enough of remaining flour, 1 tablespoon at a time, to prevent dough from sticking to hands (dough will feel sticky). Place dough in a large bowl coated with cooking spray, turning to coat top. Cover and let rise in a warm place (85°), free from drafts, 45 minutes or until doubled in size. (Gently press two fingers into dough. If indentation remains, dough has risen enough.)

4. Position one oven rack in middle. Position another in lowest position. Preheat to 475°.

5. Brush a 13 x 9–inch metal baking pan with oil. Turn dough out into pan. Gently press dough into bottom and up sides of pan. Lightly spray surface of dough with cooking spray. Cover with plastic wrap; let stand 5 minutes. Remove plastic wrap; discard. Spoon sauce mixture into crust. Bake on bottom rack at 475° for 20 minutes. Remove from oven.

6. Combine cheeses; sprinkle evenly over sauce. Bake on middle rack an additional 15 minutes or until crust is golden brown and cheese melts. Cool 10 minutes on a wire rack. Cut into 6 squares. Yield: 6 servings (serving size: 1 square).

CALORIES 434; **FAT** 12.8g (sat 5.9g, mono 4.1g, poly 1.4g); **PROTEIN** 24.6g; **CARB** 54.2g; **FIBER** 3.9g; **CHOL** 45mg; **IRON** 3.8mg; **SODIUM** 682mg; **CALC** 336mg

Smoky-Spicy Tamale Pies

While ground chipotle chile offers smoky notes, add $1/8$ *teaspoon ground red pepper instead for pure fiery flavor.*

4 ounces ground turkey
$1/2$ cup chopped onion
$1/2$ cup frozen whole-kernel corn, thawed
2 garlic cloves, minced
1 teaspoon chili powder
$1/2$ teaspoon ground cumin
$1/4$ teaspoon ground chipotle chile pepper
1 cup canned organic red kidney beans, rinsed and drained

1 (14.5-ounce) can fire-roasted tomatoes with green chiles, undrained
Cooking spray
1.1 ounces all-purpose flour (about $1/4$ cup)
$1/4$ cup yellow cornmeal
$1/2$ teaspoon baking powder
$1/8$ teaspoon salt
$1/4$ cup fat-free milk
1 large egg white

1. Preheat oven to 375°.

2. Cook turkey in a large nonstick skillet over medium-high heat until browned, stirring to crumble. Add onion, corn, and garlic to pan; sauté 2 minutes. Stir in chili powder, cumin, and chipotle; cook 30 seconds. Add beans and tomatoes to pan, and cook 1 minute. Divide turkey mixture evenly between 2 ($1\frac{1}{2}$-cup) ramekins coated with cooking spray.

3. Weigh or lightly spoon flour into a dry measuring cup; level with a knife. Combine flour, cornmeal, baking powder, and salt, stirring with a whisk. Combine milk and egg white, stirring with a whisk. Add milk mixture to flour mixture; stir just until moist. Spoon batter evenly over turkey mixture. Place ramekins on a baking sheet. Bake at 375° for 25 minutes or until crust is browned. Yield: 2 servings (serving size: 1 pie).

CALORIES 435; FAT 5.8g (sat 1.4g, mono 1.9g, poly 1.3g); PROTEIN 26.2g; CARB 68.9g; FIBER 9.5g; CHOL 45mg; IRON 4.9mg; SODIUM 629mg; CALC 183mg

Speedy Paella, page 134

stovetop & stir-fry

Seitan Stir-Fry with Black Bean Garlic Sauce

Look for seitan—also called wheat gluten—in Asian markets or the refrigerated section of health food or specialty stores. You'll find black bean garlic sauce in the international section of some supermarkets and at Asian markets.

2 cups boiling water
1 ounce dried shiitake mushrooms
2 tablespoons Chinese rice wine or sake
2 tablespoons black bean garlic sauce
2 teaspoons cornstarch
2 tablespoons canola oil, divided
2 cups thinly sliced drained seitan
  (about 8 ounces)

1 tablespoon finely chopped garlic
1 tablespoon finely chopped peeled
  fresh ginger
4 cups (2-inch) cut green beans
  (about 1 pound)
2 cups hot cooked brown rice
¼ teaspoon salt
Cilantro sprigs (optional)

1. Combine 2 cups boiling water and mushrooms in a small bowl; cover and let stand 20 minutes. Drain in a colander over a bowl, reserving ½ cup soaking liquid. Rinse mushrooms; drain well. Discard mushroom stems; thinly slice mushroom caps.

2. Combine reserved liquid, rice wine, black bean garlic sauce, and cornstarch in a small bowl; stir with a whisk, and set mixture aside.

3. Heat 1 tablespoon canola oil in a large nonstick skillet or wok over medium-high heat. Add seitan to pan, and stir-fry 2 minutes or until lightly browned. Place seitan in a medium bowl. Heat remaining 1 tablespoon oil in pan over medium-high heat. Add garlic and ginger to pan; stir-fry 30 seconds. Add mushrooms and beans; cover and cook 3 minutes. Add black bean sauce mixture to pan; cook 1 minute or until sauce slightly thickens. Add seitan to pan; cook 1 minute, stirring occasionally. Combine rice and salt; serve seitan mixture over rice. Garnish with cilantro sprigs, if desired. Yield: 4 servings (serving size: about 1½ cups stir-fry and ½ cup rice).

CALORIES 474; **FAT** 10g (sat 0.8g, mono 4.6g, poly 3.5g); **PROTEIN** 35.5g; **CARB** 60.7g; **FIBER** 9.9g; **CHOL** 0mg; **IRON** 5.3mg; **SODIUM** 818mg; **CALC** 57mg

Lo Mein with Tofu

Although lo mein is traditionally made with Chinese egg noodles, here we substitute whole-wheat linguine. Pan-frying the tofu gives it a crisp exterior.

1 (14-ounce) package firm water-packed tofu, drained and cut crosswise into 4 (1-inch-thick) pieces
8 ounces uncooked whole-wheat linguine
1 teaspoon dark sesame oil
1/2 teaspoon salt, divided
1/4 teaspoon freshly ground black pepper, divided
2 tablespoons canola oil, divided
3 tablespoons oyster sauce
1 1/2 tablespoons mirin (sweet rice wine)
1 1/2 tablespoons lower-sodium soy sauce
1 teaspoon rice vinegar
3/4 cup vertically sliced onion
2 cups shredded cabbage
2 cups peeled, thinly diagonally sliced carrot
2 large garlic cloves, thinly sliced
1 1/2 cups fresh bean sprouts
1/4 cup diagonally cut green onions

1. Place tofu in a single layer on several layers of paper towels. Cover tofu with several more layers of paper towels, and top with a cast-iron skillet or other heavy pan. Let stand 30 minutes. Discard paper towels.
2. Cook pasta in boiling water until al dente; drain. Combine pasta, sesame oil, 1/4 teaspoon salt, and 1/8 teaspoon pepper; toss. Set aside.
3. Sprinkle remaining 1/4 teaspoon salt and remaining 1/8 teaspoon pepper evenly over tofu. Heat 1 tablespoon canola oil in a large cast-iron skillet over medium-high heat. Add tofu to pan; cook 4 minutes on each side or until golden. Remove from pan; cut into bite-sized pieces. Combine oyster sauce and next 3 ingredients (through vinegar) in a small bowl, stirring well.
4. Heat a wok or cast-iron skillet over medium-high heat. Add remaining 1 tablespoon canola oil to pan; swirl to coat. Add onion; stir-fry 2 minutes or until lightly browned. Add cabbage, carrot, and garlic; stir-fry 2 minutes or until cabbage wilts. Reduce heat to medium; stir in tofu and vinegar mixture, tossing to coat. Add pasta and bean sprouts; toss. Cook 2 minutes or until thoroughly heated. Sprinkle with green onions. Yield: 4 servings (serving size: 1¾ cups).

CALORIES 397; **FAT** 15.4g (sat 1.3g, mono 8.8g, poly 4.1g); **PROTEIN** 18.2g; **CARB** 55.1g; **FIBER** 9g; **CHOL** 0mg; **IRON** 4mg; **SODIUM** 736mg; **CALC** 248mg

Garlic-Ginger Shrimp Stir-Fry

Fresh citrus sections add a burst of fresh flavor and sweetness. Short-grain rice cooks up moist, making it easier to eat with chopsticks.

1¼ pounds large shrimp, peeled and deveined
1 teaspoon salt
1 tablespoon dark sesame oil
1½ tablespoons minced peeled fresh ginger
5 garlic cloves, thinly sliced
1½ cups coarsely chopped red bell pepper

3 tablespoons Shaoxing (Chinese rice wine) or dry sherry
2 tablespoons rice vinegar
1 cup orange sections (about 2 large)
3 cups hot cooked short-grain rice
1 cup (1-inch) slices green onions

1. Place shrimp in a bowl, and sprinkle with salt, tossing well. Let stand 10 minutes.
2. Combine oil, ginger, and garlic in a wok or large nonstick skillet. Place over medium-high heat; cook 4 minutes or until ginger and garlic begin to brown. Add shrimp; stir-fry 2 minutes. Add bell pepper; stir-fry 2 minutes. Add wine and vinegar; bring to a simmer. Cook 1 minute or until wine mixture is syrupy. Gently stir in orange sections. Serve over rice, and sprinkle with onions. Yield: 4 servings (serving size: 1½ cups stir-fry and ¾ cup rice).

___

CALORIES 417; FAT 6.5g (sat 1.1g, mono 1.9g, poly 2.6g); PROTEIN 33.4g; CARB 53.8g; FIBER 4.8g; CHOL 215mg; IRON 6.2mg; SODIUM 814mg; CALC 125mg

Speedy Paella *(Pictured on page 126)*

Spanish chorizo, made with smoked pork, is different from Mexican chorizo, which uses fresh pork. If you can't find the Spanish version, substitute kielbasa.

½ cup dry white wine
¼ teaspoon saffron threads, crushed
3 ounces Spanish chorizo sausage, cut into
   ¼-inch-thick slices
1 cup coarsely chopped onion (about 1
   medium)
⅔ cup coarsely chopped red bell pepper
   (about 1 small)
½ teaspoon hot paprika

¼ teaspoon salt
2 garlic cloves, minced
1 cup uncooked short-grain rice
1 cup fat-free, lower-sodium chicken broth
1 (8-ounce) bottle clam juice
1 cup chopped plum tomato
½ cup frozen green peas
12 littleneck clams
½ pound medium shrimp, peeled and deveined

1. Combine wine and saffron threads in a small bowl; let stand 15 minutes.
2. Heat a large cast-iron or nonstick skillet over medium-high heat. Add chorizo to pan; cook 3 minutes, stirring occasionally. Remove chorizo from pan. Add onion and pepper to pan; cook 5 minutes, stirring occasionally. Stir in paprika, salt, and garlic; cook 1 minute. Return chorizo to pan. Add wine mixture, rice, broth, and clam juice; bring to a boil. Cover, reduce heat, and cook 15 minutes or until most of liquid is absorbed. Stir in tomato, peas, clams, and shrimp. Cover and cook 5 minutes or until clams open; discard any unopened shells. Yield: 4 servings (serving size: 1¼ cups rice mixture and 3 clams).

CALORIES 394; **FAT** 10.2g (sat 3.3g, mono 4.1g, poly 1.3g); **PROTEIN** 26.9g; **CARB** 48.6g; **FIBER** 4.4g; **CHOL** 116mg; **IRON** 6.7mg; **SODIUM** 786mg; **CALC** 71mg

Sizzling Shrimp with Corn Relish

Serve over rice for a hearty dinner or over a bed of fresh baby spinach for a lighter meal.

1½ tablespoons fresh lime juice
1 tablespoon fish sauce
½ teaspoon sugar
2 tablespoons canola oil
½ cup chopped shallots
1 tablespoon minced garlic

1 tablespoon minced jalapeño pepper
  (about 1 small)
1½ pounds peeled and deveined
  medium shrimp
1½ cups fresh corn kernels (about 3 ears)
⅓ cup chopped fresh cilantro

1. Combine lime juice, fish sauce, and sugar; set aside.
2. Heat oil in a 14-inch wok over high heat. Add shallots, garlic, and jalapeño to wok; stir-fry 30 seconds or just until shallots begin to brown. Add shrimp to wok; stir-fry 2 minutes. Add corn; stir-fry 1 minute or just until corn is heated and shrimp are done. Stir in juice mixture; sprinkle with chopped cilantro. Yield: 4 servings (serving size: 1 cup).

CALORIES 332; **FAT** 11.2g (sat 1.2g, mono 4.8g, poly 3.6g); **PROTEIN** 37.6g; **CARB** 19.9g; **FIBER** 2.1g; **CHOL** 259mg; **IRON** 4.8mg; **SODIUM** 612mg; **CALC** 101mg

Stir-Fried Shrimp with Garlic and Chile Sauce

A platter of succulent stir-fried orange-pink shrimp symbolizes gold coins (wealth) and good fortune in Chinese tradition.

½ cup fat-free, lower-sodium chicken broth
2 teaspoons cornstarch
1 teaspoon sugar
2 teaspoons Shaoxing (Chinese rice wine) or dry sherry
2 teaspoons lower-sodium soy sauce
¼ teaspoon white pepper
1 tablespoon canola oil

1½ pounds large shrimp, peeled and deveined
2 tablespoons sliced garlic
1½ teaspoons minced peeled fresh ginger
1 jalapeño pepper, seeded and sliced
½ cup (1-inch) slices green onions
½ teaspoon dark sesame oil
Thai bird chile (optional)

1. Combine first 6 ingredients in a small bowl, stirring with a whisk.
2. Heat canola oil in a wok or large skillet over high heat. Add shrimp to pan; stir-fry 1 minute or until shrimp begin to turn pink. Add garlic, ginger, and jalapeño; stir-fry 1 minute. Stir in broth mixture; cook 1 minute or until shrimp are done and sauce is thickened, stirring constantly. Remove from heat; stir in onions and sesame oil. Garnish with a Thai bird chile, if desired. Yield: 4 servings (serving size: 1 cup).

CALORIES 120; FAT 3.5g (sat 0.5g, mono 1.4g, poly 1.2g); PROTEIN 17.7g; CARB 3.4g; FIBER 0.3g; CHOL 129mg; IRON 2.2mg; SODIUM 200mg; CALC 53mg

FYI: Stir-fries are best served sizzling hot straight from the wok or skillet.

Basic Beef Stew with Carrots and Mushrooms

This classic beef stew recipe has all the good things you would expect: tender chunks of beef, carrot, and potato. Yet the cremini mushrooms are a wonderful surprise.

1 tablespoon olive oil, divided
1 pound small cremini mushrooms
Cooking spray
2 cups chopped onion
3 garlic cloves, minced
1½ ounces all-purpose flour (about ⅓ cup)
2 pounds lean beef stew meat, cut into
   bite-sized pieces
¾ teaspoon salt, divided
1 cup dry red wine

1 tablespoon chopped fresh thyme
2 (14-ounce) cans lower-sodium beef broth
1 bay leaf
2 cups (¾-inch) cubed peeled baking potato
   (about 1 pound)
1½ cups (1-inch) slices carrot (about
   12 ounces)
½ teaspoon freshly ground black pepper
Thyme sprigs (optional)

1. Heat 1 teaspoon olive oil in a large Dutch oven over medium-high heat. Add mushrooms, and sauté 5 minutes or until mushrooms begin to brown. Spoon mushrooms into a large bowl. Lightly coat pan with cooking spray. Add onion; sauté 10 minutes or until tender and golden brown. Add garlic; sauté 1 minute. Add onion mixture to mushrooms.
2. Place flour in a shallow bowl or pie plate. Dredge beef in flour, shaking off excess. Heat remaining 2 teaspoons oil in pan over medium-high heat. Add half of beef mixture; sprinkle with ⅛ teaspoon salt. Cook 6 minutes, browning on all sides. Add browned beef to mushroom mixture. Repeat procedure with remaining beef mixture and ⅛ teaspoon salt.
3. Add 1 cup wine to pan, scraping pan to loosen browned bits. Add thyme, broth, and bay leaf; bring to a boil. Stir in beef mixture. Cover, reduce heat to medium-low, and simmer 1 hour or until beef is just tender.
4. Stir in potato and carrot. Simmer, uncovered, 1 hour and 15 minutes or until beef and vegetables are very tender and sauce is thick, stirring occasionally. Stir in remaining ½ teaspoon salt and pepper. Discard bay leaf. Garnish with thyme sprigs, if desired. Yield: 8 servings (serving size: about 1 cup).

CALORIES 303; **FAT** 9.8g (sat 3.2g, mono 4.7g, poly 0.6g); **PROTEIN** 26.4g; **CARB** 26.8g; **FIBER** 2.3g; **CHOL** 71mg; **IRON** 3.9mg; **SODIUM** 494mg; **CALC** 54mg

Sesame Beef Stir-Fry

If presliced beef is not available, ask your butcher to thinly slice flank steak or boneless sirloin steak.

1 tablespoon minced peeled fresh ginger
1 tablespoon minced garlic
2 tablespoons lower-sodium soy sauce
1½ teaspoons dark brown sugar
½ teaspoon crushed red pepper
1 tablespoon dark sesame oil

1 pound presliced stir-fry meat (such as flank or boneless sirloin steak)
8 green onions, cut into 1-inch pieces (white and light green parts only)
4 cups bagged baby spinach leaves
1 tablespoon sesame seeds

1. Combine first 5 ingredients in a small bowl.

2. Heat oil in a wok or skillet over high heat. Add half of beef to pan, and cook 3 minutes or until browned. Remove beef from pan. Repeat procedure with remaining beef. Add onions; cook 1 minute. Add soy sauce mixture; cook 1 minute. Return beef to pan; cook 1 minute. Stir in spinach, and cook 30 seconds. Sprinkle with sesame seeds. Yield: 4 servings (serving size: ¾ cup).

CALORIES 230; **FAT** 11g (sat 3g, mono 4.2g, poly 2.3g); **PROTEIN** 26.5g; **CARB** 6.1g; **FIBER** 1.4g; **CHOL** 37mg; **IRON** 3.3mg; **SODIUM** 356mg; **CALC** 94mg

Stir-Fried Rice Noodles with Beef and Spinach

6 ounces uncooked wide rice sticks
  (rice-flour noodles)
1 tablespoon canola oil
1 cup thinly sliced green onions
²/₃ pound top sirloin steak, cut into thin strips
2 cups sliced shiitake mushroom caps
2 garlic cloves, minced
1 (6-ounce) package fresh baby spinach

2 tablespoons rice vinegar
1 tablespoon fresh lime juice
3 tablespoons lower-sodium soy sauce
2 teaspoons grated peeled fresh ginger
2 teaspoons Sriracha (hot chile sauce)
1 tablespoon dark sesame oil
¼ teaspoon salt
2 teaspoons sesame seeds, toasted

1. Cook noodles according to package directions, omitting salt and fat. Drain and rinse noodles under cold water; drain.

2. Heat canola oil in a large skillet or wok over high heat. Add onions and steak; stir-fry 1 minute. Add mushrooms and garlic; stir-fry 1 minute. Add spinach, and stir-fry 1 minute or until greens wilt.

3. Combine rice vinegar and next 4 ingredients (through Sriracha) in a small bowl, stirring with a whisk. Add vinegar mixture to steak mixture; cook 30 seconds, stirring constantly. Stir in noodles, sesame oil, and salt; cook 1 minute or until noodles are thoroughly heated, tossing to combine. Sprinkle with sesame seeds. Yield: 4 servings (serving size: 1½ cups).

CALORIES 408; FAT 13.2g (sat 2.9g, mono 5.9g, poly 3.1g); PROTEIN 16.7g; CARB 56.1g; FIBER 5g; CHOL 37mg; IRON 5.1mg; SODIUM 616mg; CALC 83mg

---

FYI: Stretch a small amount of sirloin with noodles and fresh vegetables. This not only saves on your grocery bill but also keeps the saturated fat low in this superfast stir-fry.

Smoky Meatballs in Serrano Ham–Tomato Sauce

Use any free time on a weekend to do some of the prep. Cook the meatballs, cool, and freeze in a zip-top plastic bag for up to one month. When you're ready to serve the dish, defrost the meatballs in the refrigerator and sauté the ham. Follow the recipe, adding the ham and thawed meatballs along with the tomatoes to the cooked onion mixture. Manchego is Spain's most famous cheese. It is a golden semihard cheese with a full, buttery flavor. A bold, bright Rioja wine complements the meal.

1 (1½-ounce) slice white bread
1 pound 92% lean ground beef
¼ cup finely chopped onion
2 tablespoons chopped fresh flat-leaf parsley
½ teaspoon kosher salt
½ teaspoon smoked paprika
1½ teaspoons minced garlic
¼ teaspoon freshly ground black pepper
1 large egg
2 teaspoons olive oil, divided
2 ounces serrano ham, finely chopped
Cooking spray

2 cups chopped onion
1¼ cups chopped red bell pepper
1½ teaspoons minced garlic
½ cup dry sherry
1 (28-ounce) can no-salt-added peeled whole tomatoes, undrained and chopped
4 cups hot cooked fettuccine (about 8 ounces uncooked pasta)
¼ cup (1 ounce) finely shredded aged Manchego cheese
Chopped fresh flat-leaf parsley (optional)

1. Place bread in a food processor; pulse 12 times or until coarse crumbs measure ½ cup. Combine breadcrumbs, beef, and next 7 ingredients (through egg) in a bowl. Using wet hands, shape mixture into 20 (about 2 tablespoons each) meatballs. Set aside.

2. Heat 1 teaspoon oil in a large Dutch oven over medium heat. Add ham to pan, and cook 3 minutes or until well browned, stirring frequently. Transfer to a large bowl. Add remaining 1 teaspoon oil to pan. Add meatballs; cook 5 minutes or until browned, turning often. Add meatballs to ham in bowl. Coat pan with cooking spray. Add onion, bell pepper, and 1½ teaspoons garlic to pan; cook 5 minutes or until tender, stirring often. Add sherry to pan; cook 3 minutes or until liquid almost evaporates, scraping pan to loosen browned bits. Add tomatoes and meatball mixture; bring to a boil. Cover, reduce heat, and simmer 30 minutes or until sauce is slightly thickened. Remove from heat. Keep warm.

3. Place 1 cup pasta in each of 4 shallow bowls; top each serving with 5 meatballs, ¾ cup sauce, and 1 tablespoon shredded Manchego cheese. Garnish with additional parsley, if desired. Yield: 4 servings.

CALORIES 559; FAT 17.6g (sat 6.6g, mono 7.2g, poly 1.2g); PROTEIN 38.5g; CARB 61.3g; FIBER 4.7g; CHOL 128mg; IRON 6mg; SODIUM 704mg; CALC 180mg

Bacon, Onion, and Brown Lentil Skillet

Humble brown lentils are fitting for this homey main dish that is economical and quick for a weeknight supper. Pair with corn bread and sautéed Swiss chard or braised collard greens.

6 center-cut bacon slices
1 cup diced onion
1 cup diced carrot
1 cup diced celery
1 teaspoon chopped fresh thyme
6 garlic cloves, minced

3 cups fat-free, lower-sodium chicken broth
1 cup dried brown lentils
1 cup water
2 tablespoons chopped fresh parsley
¼ teaspoon freshly ground black pepper

1. Cook bacon in a large nonstick skillet over medium-high heat until crisp. Remove bacon from pan, reserving 2 teaspoons drippings in pan. Crumble bacon; set aside. Add onion to drippings in pan; sauté 5 minutes or until lightly browned. Add carrot, celery, thyme, and garlic; cook 5 minutes or until crisp-tender. Add broth, lentils, and 1 cup water; bring to a boil. Cover, reduce heat, and simmer 15 minutes or until lentils are just tender. Uncover and increase heat to medium-high; cook 6 minutes or until liquid almost evaporates. Remove from heat; stir in parsley and pepper. Sprinkle with bacon. Yield: 4 servings (serving size: about 1⅓ cups).

CALORIES 278; **FAT** 6.4g (sat 2.3g, mono 2.9g, poly 1g); **PROTEIN** 18.6g; **CARB** 38.5g; **FIBER** 13.8g; **CHOL** 11mg; **IRON** 5.5mg; **SODIUM** 534mg; **CALC** 80mg

Almost-Classic Pork Fried Rice

2 tablespoons peanut oil or olive oil, divided
½ teaspoon kosher salt, divided
½ pound boneless loin pork chops, cut into
  ½-inch pieces
½ cup chopped carrot
½ cup chopped celery
½ cup chopped green onions (white
  part only)
2 tablespoons minced garlic
2 tablespoons minced peeled fresh ginger

3 cups cooked, chilled long-grain brown rice
1 large egg
3 tablespoons mirin (sweet rice wine)
3 tablespoons lower-sodium soy sauce
1 teaspoon dark sesame oil
¼ teaspoon freshly ground black pepper
2 cups fresh bean sprouts
¼ cup canned diced water chestnuts,
  rinsed and drained
1 cup sliced green onion tops

1. Heat 1 tablespoon peanut oil in a large skillet over medium-high heat. Sprinkle ⅛ teaspoon salt over pork. Add pork to pan, and sauté 2 minutes or until browned on all sides. Remove pork from pan. Add carrot and celery to pan; sauté 2 minutes or until lightly browned. Add carrot mixture to pork.

2. Add remaining 1 tablespoon peanut oil to pan, swirling to coat. Stir in green onion bottoms, garlic, and ginger; cook 15 seconds, stirring constantly. Add rice, stirring well to coat rice with oil; cook, without stirring, 2 minutes or until edges begin to brown. Stir rice mixture; cook, without stirring, 2 minutes or until edges begin to brown. Make a well in center of rice mixture. Add egg; stir-fry 30 seconds or until soft-scrambled, stirring constantly.

3. Return pork mixture to pan. Stir in mirin; cook 1 minute or until mirin is absorbed, stirring constantly. Stir in remaining ⅜ teaspoon salt, soy sauce, sesame oil, and pepper. Remove from heat, and stir in bean sprouts and water chestnuts. Sprinkle with green onion tops. Yield: 4 servings (serving size: about 2 cups).

CALORIES 408; FAT 12.4g (sat 2.6g, mono 5.4g, poly 3.6g); PROTEIN 21g; CARB 49.3g; FIBER 6.5g; CHOL 82mg; IRON 2.4mg; SODIUM 627mg; CALC 79mg

FYI: In this more-vegetables-than-meat approach to fried rice, you get a crisp, fresh-tasting alternative to the Chinese classic. The brown rice—with more nutritional benefit than its white counterpart—is so hearty that you don't need as much meat.

Savory Braised-Pork Supper

The high-pressure cooking method works especially well with a less-tender cut such as a pork roast. A tight seal on the pan keeps the liquid and seasonings from escaping, which infuses the meat with moistness and rich flavor.

2 teaspoons Hungarian sweet paprika
1 teaspoon freshly ground black pepper
³/₄ teaspoon salt
¹/₂ teaspoon dried rubbed sage
¹/₂ teaspoon dried thyme
¹/₂ teaspoon dry mustard
1 (3-pound) boneless pork shoulder
  (Boston butt), trimmed

1 tablespoon canola oil
Cooking spray
2¹/₂ cups thinly sliced leek (about 2 large)
4 garlic cloves, minced
1 (14-ounce) can fat-free, lower-sodium
  chicken broth
2 pounds red potatoes, quartered
2 cups (1-inch-thick) slices carrot

1. Combine first 6 ingredients. Rub pork with paprika mixture. Heat oil in a 6-quart pressure cooker coated with cooking spray over medium-high heat. Add pork, browning on all sides. Remove from pan; set aside. Add leek and garlic to pan; sauté 2 minutes. Add broth to pan; bring to a simmer.

2. Return pork to pan; spoon leek mixture over pork. Close lid securely; bring to high pressure over high heat (about 3 minutes). Adjust heat to medium or level needed to maintain high pressure; cook 45 minutes. Remove from heat; place pressure cooker under cold running water. Remove lid; stir in potatoes and carrot. Close lid securely, and bring to high pressure over high heat. Adjust heat to medium or level needed to maintain high pressure; cook 15 minutes. Place cooker under cold running water. Remove lid. Cut pork into ¼-inch-thick slices; discard bone. Yield: 6 servings (serving size: 3 ounces pork and 1⅓ cups vegetables).

CALORIES 363; **FAT** 11.8g (sat 3.6g, mono 4.8g, poly 2.3g); **PROTEIN** 27.6g; **CARB** 36.7g; **FIBER** 4.7g; **CHOL** 76mg; **IRON** 4.9mg; **SODIUM** 572mg; **CALC** 72mg

Pork and Squash Stir-Fry

Chinese black vinegar, available in Asian markets, has a deep, smoky flavor that's slightly sweet; substitute balsamic vinegar, if desired. Serve over hot cooked basmati rice.

1 (2-pound) butternut squash, peeled and cut into ½-inch cubes
2 tablespoons peanut oil
2 tablespoons coarsely grated orange rind
1 tablespoon minced peeled fresh ginger
½ teaspoon crushed red pepper
1 (3-inch) cinnamon stick, broken
1¼ pounds pork tenderloin, trimmed and cut into 2-inch strips

2 tablespoons sugar
3 tablespoons lower-sodium soy sauce
2 tablespoons Chinese black vinegar
2 tablespoons red wine vinegar
1 teaspoon cornstarch
¼ teaspoon salt
1 cup chopped green onions

1. Place squash in a large microwave-safe bowl. Add water to a depth of 1 inch. Cover with plastic wrap; vent. Microwave at HIGH 8 minutes or until tender. Drain and set aside.
2. Heat oil in a large nonstick skillet over medium heat. Add rind, ginger, red pepper, and cinnamon stick pieces; cook 1 minute, stirring constantly. Remove and discard cinnamon stick pieces.
3. Increase heat to medium-high. Add pork to pan, and sauté 4 minutes or until browned. Combine sugar and next 5 ingredients (through salt), stirring with a whisk. Add sugar mixture to pan; cook 2 minutes or until sauce is slightly thickened, stirring constantly. Add squash; toss to coat. Stir in green onions. Yield: 6 servings (serving size: 1 cup).

CALORIES 257; **FAT** 7.9g (sat 1.9g, mono 3.6g, poly 1.9g); **PROTEIN** 21.9g; **CARB** 25.9g; **FIBER** 6.2g; **CHOL** 61mg; **IRON** 2.5mg; **SODIUM** 423mg; **CALC** 84mg

Chicken with Dark Beer

In the South of France, they like their chicken cooked in wine, preferably a rich red, but northerners go for the caramel intensity of dark beer. A spicing of juniper berries and a shot of gin enhance the sweetness of the beer. The traditional accompaniment would be mashed or boiled potatoes. Prepare the chicken ahead and refrigerate it in its sauce up to three days, or freeze for up to one month. Thaw, reheat, and add the yogurt and vinegar before serving.

3 tablespoons all-purpose flour
1/2 teaspoon salt
1/4 teaspoon freshly ground black pepper
2 bone-in chicken breast halves, skinned
2 bone-in chicken thighs, skinned
2 chicken drumsticks, skinned
2 tablespoons butter
1 tablespoon canola oil
3 tablespoons dry gin
3/4 cup chopped celery
3/4 cup chopped carrot

1/2 cup chopped shallots (about 3 medium)
3 juniper berries, crushed
1 (8-ounce) package mushrooms, halved
3 thyme sprigs
3 flat-leaf parsley sprigs
1 bay leaf
1 cup dark beer
1/4 cup plain Greek yogurt
2 teaspoons white wine vinegar
1 tablespoon chopped fresh flat-leaf parsley

1. Combine first 3 ingredients; sprinkle evenly over both sides of chicken. Heat butter and oil in a large, deep skillet over medium-high heat. Add chicken to pan; sauté 5 minutes on each side or until browned. Remove pan from heat. Pour gin into one side of pan; return pan to heat. Ignite gin with a long match; let flames die down. Remove chicken from pan; set aside, and keep warm.

2. Add celery, carrot, shallots, and juniper berries to pan; sauté 5 minutes or until vegetables are tender, stirring occasionally. Add mushrooms. Place thyme, parsley, and bay leaf on a double layer of cheesecloth. Gather edges of cheesecloth together; tie securely. Add cheesecloth bag to pan. Return chicken to pan, nestling into vegetable mixture. Stir in beer; bring to a simmer. Cover, reduce heat, and simmer 45 minutes or until a thermometer inserted in the meaty parts of chicken registers 160°. (Breasts may cook more quickly. Check them after 35 minutes, and remove them when they're done; keep warm.)

3. Discard cheesecloth bag. Remove chicken from pan; keep warm. Place pan over medium heat; stir in yogurt. Cook 1 minute or until thoroughly heated (do not boil, as the yogurt may curdle). Remove from heat; stir in vinegar. Taste and adjust seasoning, if desired. Place 1 chicken breast half or 1 drumstick and 1 thigh on each of 4 plates; top each serving with about ¾ cup sauce and vegetable mixture. Sprinkle with chopped parsley. Yield: 4 servings.

CALORIES 370; **FAT** 16g (sat 6.6g, mono 5g, poly 3g); **PROTEIN** 30.8g; **CARB** 15.1g; **FIBER** 1.4g; **CHOL** 103mg; **IRON** 2mg; **SODIUM** 465mg; **CALC** 55mg

Herbed Chicken and Dumplings

Fluffy herb-flecked dumplings, tender vegetables, and rich dark-meat chicken combine in this soul-satisfying comfort dish. Garnish each serving with a fresh sprig of parsley, if desired. This is a perfect, cozy dinner for two on a chilly night.

Cooking spray
8 ounces skinless, boneless chicken thighs,
   cut into bite-sized pieces
3/4 cup (1/4-inch) diagonally cut celery
1/2 cup (1/4-inch) diagonally cut carrot
1/2 cup chopped onion
1/8 teaspoon dried thyme
3 parsley sprigs

1 bay leaf
3 cups fat-free, lower-sodium chicken broth
2.25 ounces all-purpose flour (about 1/2 cup)
1 tablespoon chopped fresh parsley
1/4 teaspoon baking powder
1/4 teaspoon salt
1/4 cup 1% low-fat milk

1. Heat a large saucepan over medium-high heat. Coat pan with cooking spray. Add chicken to pan; cook 4 minutes, browning on all sides. Remove chicken from pan; keep warm. Add celery and next 5 ingredients (through bay leaf) to pan; sauté 5 minutes or until onion is tender. Return chicken to pan; cook 1 minute. Add broth to pan; bring mixture to a boil. Cover, reduce heat, and simmer 30 minutes.

2. Weigh or lightly spoon flour into a dry measuring cup; level with a knife. Combine flour, chopped parsley, baking powder, and salt in a medium bowl. Add milk, stirring just until moist. Spoon by heaping teaspoonfuls into broth mixture; cover and simmer 10 minutes or until dumplings are done. Discard parsley sprigs and bay leaf. Yield: 2 servings (serving size: 2 cups).

CALORIES 285; **FAT** 5.2g (sat 1.5g, mono 1.9g, poly 1.2g); **PROTEIN** 25g; **CARB** 35.2g; **FIBER** 3.1g; **CHOL** 55mg; **IRON** 3.4mg; **SODIUM** 596mg; **CALC** 133mg

Chicken Fried Rice with Leeks and Dried Cranberries

2 tablespoons olive oil, divided
¾ teaspoon kosher salt, divided
½ pound skinless, boneless chicken thighs, cut into ½-inch pieces
3 cups thinly sliced leek (about 1½ pounds)
¼ teaspoon freshly ground black pepper

3½ cups cooked, chilled long-grain brown rice
1 cup dried cranberries
1 tablespoon chopped fresh sage
¼ cup dry white wine

1. Heat 1 tablespoon oil in a large skillet over medium-high heat. Sprinkle ⅛ teaspoon salt over chicken. Add chicken to pan; sauté 3 minutes or until browned, stirring occasionally. Remove chicken from pan. Add leek, pepper, and remaining ⅝ teaspoon salt to pan; sauté 4 minutes or until leek is tender and golden. Add leek mixture to chicken.
2. Add remaining 1 tablespoon oil to pan, swirling to coat. Add rice, stirring well to coat rice with oil; cook, without stirring, 2 minutes or until edges begin to brown. Stir rice mixture; cook, without stirring, 2 minutes or until edges begin to brown. Stir in chicken mixture, cranberries, and sage. Add wine; cook 2 minutes or until mixture is dry, stirring constantly. Yield: 4 servings (serving size: about 1⅓ cups).

CALORIES 452; FAT 11.1g (sat 1.9g, mono 6.2g, poly 2.1g); PROTEIN 16.6g; CARB 74g; FIBER 6g; CHOL 47.1mg; IRON 3mg; SODIUM 433mg; CALC 70mg

Thai Rice Noodles with Chicken

When shopping in an Asian grocery, look for pad thai noodles designated "XL." At supermarkets, packages will be marked "wide." Check the noodles occasionally as they soak. Take a taste to see when they're ready; they'll be slightly chewy and not too soft.

1/4 cup fresh lime juice, divided

2 (6-ounce) skinless, boneless chicken breast halves, cut into 3/4-inch cubes

8 ounces (1/2-inch-thick) rice noodles

1 tablespoon brown sugar

1 tablespoon water

1 tablespoon fish sauce

1 tablespoon lower-sodium soy sauce

1 1/2 teaspoons sambal oelek (ground fresh chile paste)

1/4 teaspoon salt, divided

4 teaspoons canola oil, divided

3 tablespoons thinly diagonally sliced green onions

1 teaspoon grated peeled fresh ginger

1 teaspoon minced garlic

1/2 cup torn fresh basil leaves

1/4 cup very thinly sliced lemongrass (tough outer stalks removed)

1/4 cup very thinly vertically sliced shallots

1. Combine 2 tablespoons juice and chicken in a bowl. Let stand 15 minutes.

2. Soak noodles in hot water 15 minutes or until somewhat soft but still slightly chewy. Drain well.

3. Combine remaining 2 tablespoons juice, sugar, and next 4 ingredients (through chile paste). Stir in 1/8 teaspoon salt.

4. Heat 1 teaspoon oil in a large wok or skillet over medium-high heat. Remove chicken from juice; discard juice. Add chicken to pan; stir-fry 4 minutes or until chicken is done. Transfer to a large bowl; sprinkle with remaining 1/8 teaspoon salt. Add remaining 1 tablespoon oil to pan. Add green onions, ginger, and garlic; stir-fry 45 seconds or just until golden and fragrant. Add noodles; cook 30 seconds, tossing well. Stir in sugar mixture. Add chicken; cook 30 seconds. Place 1 1/4 cups noodle mixture on each of 4 plates. Top each with 2 tablespoons basil, 1 tablespoon lemongrass, and 1 tablespoon shallots. Yield: 4 servings.

CALORIES 343; FAT 5.5g (sat 0.6g, mono 2.9g, poly 1.6g); PROTEIN 17.5g; CARB 54.4g; FIBER 0.7g; CHOL 34mg; IRON 2.1mg; SODIUM 615mg; CALC 36mg

Roasted Pork and Autumn Vegetables, page 164

one-pot
wonders

Roasted Pork and Autumn Vegetables

(Pictured on page 162)

2 fennel bulbs (about 1½ pounds)
2 small onions
1 tablespoon olive oil, divided
4 cups bite-sized pieces peeled rutabaga
16 baby carrots (about ¾ pound), trimmed
1 (2¼-pound) boneless pork loin roast, trimmed
Cooking spray

2 tablespoons chopped fresh sage
1½ teaspoons kosher salt, divided
¾ teaspoon freshly ground black pepper, divided
¾ cup fat-free, lower-sodium chicken broth
½ cup dry white wine
2 teaspoons Dijon mustard

1. Preheat oven to 400°.

2. Trim stalks from fennel; discard. Cut each bulb into 8 wedges. Peel onions, leaving root intact; cut each into 8 wedges.

3. Heat 1½ teaspoons oil in a large nonstick skillet over medium-high heat. Add fennel and onion; sauté 8 minutes or until lightly browned, stirring frequently. Remove from pan. Add remaining oil, rutabaga, and carrots to pan; sauté 5 minutes or until lightly browned, stirring frequently.

4. Place pork on rack coated with cooking spray; place rack in a shallow roasting pan. Sprinkle pork with sage, 1 teaspoon salt, and ½ teaspoon pepper. Add vegetables; sprinkle with remaining ½ teaspoon salt and remaining ¼ teaspoon pepper.

5. Bake at 400° for 45 minutes or until a thermometer registers 145°. Remove pork and vegetables from pan. Cover, and let stand 10 minutes. Remove rack. Place pan over medium heat; stir in chicken broth, white wine, and mustard, scraping pan to loosen browned bits. Bring to a boil; reduce heat, and simmer 4 minutes, stirring occasionally. Yield: 8 servings (serving size: 3 ounces pork, 1 cup vegetables, and 2 tablespoons sauce).

CALORIES 282; **FAT** 11.5g (sat 3.6g, mono 5.5g, poly 1g); **PROTEIN** 29.9g; **CARB** 14.6g; **FIBER** 4.5g; **CHOL** 78mg; **IRON** 2.2mg; **SODIUM** 539mg; **CALC** 96mg

Red Flannel Hash

This retro classic is skillet cooked, lightened up, easy, and good. A salad is all you need to turn it into a full meal.

2 tablespoons olive oil
8 ounces ground sirloin
1 cup chopped red onion
1 teaspoon kosher salt, divided
1/2 teaspoon freshly ground black pepper
3 garlic cloves, minced
2 cups shredded red cabbage (about 1/2 small head)

2 cups grated beet (3 medium beets)
1/2 cup water
2 tablespoons cider vinegar
1/4 cup plain 2% reduced-fat Greek yogurt
2 tablespoons chopped fresh dill

1. Heat oil in a large skillet over medium-high heat. Add beef to pan, and cook 4 minutes, stirring to crumble. Add onion, ½ teaspoon salt, pepper, and garlic; sauté 5 minutes or until onion is translucent.

2. Add cabbage, beet, ½ cup water, vinegar, and remaining ½ teaspoon salt; cook about 10 minutes or until cabbage begins to wilt and liquid almost evaporates. Spoon 1¼ cups hash into each of 4 serving bowls; top each serving with 1 tablespoon yogurt and 1½ teaspoons dill. Yield: 4 servings.

CALORIES 187; **FAT** 9.8g (sat 2.2g, mono 6g, poly 1g); **PROTEIN** 14.3g; **CARB** 12.7g; **FIBER** 2.9g; **CHOL** 31mg; **IRON** 1.9mg; **SODIUM** 577mg; **CALC** 50mg

Curry-Spiced Noodles

Use only the bulb of the lemongrass stalk, and remove the tough outer leaves before chopping.

8 ounces dry udon noodles (thick, round Japanese wheat noodles) or uncooked spaghetti

4 teaspoons peanut oil, divided

2 cups julienne-cut carrot

2 cups julienne-cut red bell pepper

1 cup julienne-cut green bell pepper

4 cups thinly sliced shiitake mushroom caps (about 8 ounces)

3 tablespoons chopped peeled fresh lemongrass

1 tablespoon grated peeled fresh ginger

1 tablespoon red curry paste

2 teaspoons ground cumin

1 teaspoon ground turmeric

8 garlic cloves, minced

1 cup organic vegetable broth

½ cup water

2 teaspoons lower-sodium soy sauce

¼ teaspoon kosher salt

3 green onions, thinly sliced

⅓ cup fresh cilantro leaves

¼ cup chopped unsalted, dry-roasted cashews

1. Cook noodles according to package directions, omitting salt and fat. Set noodles aside; keep warm.

2. Heat 2 teaspoons peanut oil in a large nonstick skillet over medium-high heat. Add carrot to pan; sauté 2 minutes. Add bell peppers; sauté 2 minutes. Remove carrot mixture from pan.

3. Heat remaining 2 teaspoons oil in pan over medium-high heat; swirl to coat. Add mushrooms; sauté 2 minutes. Add lemongrass and next 5 ingredients (through garlic); cook 1 minute, stirring constantly. Add broth, ½ cup water, soy sauce, and salt. Bring to a boil; cover, reduce heat, and simmer 2 minutes or until slightly thick. Add noodles, carrot mixture, and onions; cook 2 minutes, tossing to combine. Place noodle mixture in each of 4 bowls; top with cilantro and cashews. Yield: 4 servings (serving size: 1½ cups noodle mixture, about 4 teaspoons cilantro, and 1 tablespoon cashews).

CALORIES 402; **FAT** 10.8g (sat 1.7g, mono 4.5g, poly 2.3g); **PROTEIN** 12.7g; **CARB** 66g; **FIBER** 8.5g; **CHOL** 0mg; **IRON** 4.4mg; **SODIUM** 555mg; **CALC** 77mg

Barley Risotto with Eggplant and Tomatoes

6 cups (1/2-inch) diced eggplant
1 pint cherry tomatoes
3 tablespoons olive oil, divided
1/2 teaspoon freshly ground black pepper, divided
5 cups fat-free, lower-sodium chicken broth
2 cups water
1 1/2 cups finely chopped onion

1 cup uncooked pearl barley
2 teaspoons minced garlic
1/2 cup dry white wine
1/4 teaspoon salt
1/2 cup (2 ounces) crumbled soft goat cheese
1/4 cup thinly sliced fresh basil
1/4 cup pine nuts, toasted

1. Preheat oven to 400°.

2. Combine eggplant, tomatoes, 2 tablespoons olive oil, and ¼ teaspoon pepper in a bowl; toss to coat. Arrange mixture in a single layer on a jelly-roll pan. Bake at 400° for 20 minutes or until tomatoes begin to collapse.

3. Combine broth and 2 cups water in a medium saucepan; bring to a simmer (do not boil). Keep warm over low heat.

4. Heat the remaining 1 tablespoon olive oil in a large nonstick skillet over medium-high heat. Add onion; sauté 4 minutes or until browned. Stir in barley and garlic; cook 1 minute. Add wine, and cook 1 minute, stirring constantly. Add 1 cup broth mixture to pan, and bring to a boil, stirring frequently. Cook 5 minutes or until liquid is nearly absorbed, stirring constantly. Add remaining broth mixture, 1 cup at a time, stirring constantly until each portion of broth mixture is absorbed before adding the next (about 40 minutes total). Gently stir in eggplant mixture, remaining ¼ teaspoon pepper, and salt. Top with cheese, basil, and nuts. Yield: 4 servings (serving size: 1¼ cups risotto, 2 tablespoons cheese, 1 tablespoon basil, and 1 tablespoon nuts).

CALORIES 453; **FAT** 20.3g (sat 4.2g, mono 9.9g, poly 4.6g); **PROTEIN** 14.5g; **CARB** 57.5g; **FIBER** 15.5g; **CHOL** 7mg; **IRON** 3.4mg; **SODIUM** 697mg; **CALC** 93mg

Vegetable Korma

1½ tablespoons butter
1 cup chopped onion
1 tablespoon minced peeled fresh ginger
3 garlic cloves, minced
1 tablespoon tomato paste
1½ teaspoons ground cumin
½ teaspoon ground red pepper
¼ teaspoon ground turmeric
⅛ teaspoon ground cinnamon

1 cup frozen shelled edamame (green soybeans)
1 (12-ounce) baking potato, peeled and diced
1 cup fat-free, lower-sodium chicken broth
1 teaspoon all-purpose flour
1 (13.5-ounce) can light coconut milk
3 cups cauliflower florets
2 cups hot cooked long-grain white rice

1. Melt butter in a saucepan over medium-high heat. Add onion, and sauté 2 minutes. Add ginger and garlic; sauté 30 seconds, stirring constantly. Stir in tomato paste and next 4 ingredients (through cinnamon); sauté 1 minute, stirring frequently. Stir in edamame and potato. Combine chicken broth, flour, and milk, stirring until smooth. Add broth mixture to pan, and bring to a boil. Reduce heat, and simmer 8 minutes, stirring occasionally. Stir in cauliflower, and simmer 9 minutes or until vegetables are tender. Serve over rice. Yield: 4 servings (serving size: 1¼ cups vegetable mixture and ½ cup rice).

CALORIES 370; FAT 11.1g (sat 7.1g, mono 2.1g, poly 0.6g); PROTEIN 12.9g; CARB 57.9g; FIBER 7.6g; CHOL 11mg; IRON 4.1mg; SODIUM 238mg; CALC 95mg

Simple Lobster Risotto

Simmering the shells infuses the broth with lobster flavor.

4 cups fat-free, lower-sodium chicken broth
1¹/₂ cups water
3 (5-ounce) American lobster tails

3 tablespoons butter, divided
1 cup uncooked Arborio rice
³/₄ cup frozen green peas, thawed

1. Bring broth and 1½ cups water to a boil in a saucepan. Add lobster; cover and cook 4 minutes. Remove lobster from pan; cool 5 minutes.

2. Remove meat from tails, reserving shells. Chop meat. Place shells in a large zip-top plastic bag. Coarsely crush shells using a meat mallet or heavy skillet. Return crushed shells to broth mixture. Reduce heat to medium-low. Cover; cook 20 minutes.

3. Strain shell mixture through a sieve over a bowl, reserving broth; discard solids. Return broth mixture to saucepan; keep warm over low heat.

4. Heat 1 tablespoon butter in a medium saucepan over medium-high heat. Add rice; cook 2 minutes, stirring constantly. Stir in 1 cup broth mixture; cook 5 minutes or until liquid is nearly absorbed, stirring constantly. Reserve 2 tablespoons broth mixture. Add remaining broth mixture, ½ cup at a time, stirring constantly until each portion is absorbed before adding the next (about 22 minutes total). Remove from heat; stir in lobster, reserved 2 tablespoons broth mixture, 2 tablespoons butter, and green peas. Yield: 4 servings (serving size: 1 cup).

CALORIES 374; **FAT** 10.7g (sat 5.8g, mono 2.6g, poly 0.9g); **PROTEIN** 24.7g; **CARB** 44.4g; **FIBER** 4.1g; **CHOL** 80mg; **IRON** 2mg; **SODIUM** 620mg; **CALC** 63mg

PREP POINTER: Risotto's creaminess is the result of slowly adding and stirring in a hot liquid. The rice should be tender on the outside but slightly firm in the center.

Beer-Braised Beef with Onion, Carrot, and Turnips

Ask your butcher to cut a 1-pound roast for you, or buy a larger one (especially if it's on sale), and freeze the rest for later. Use a dark beer that's not too strong; stout will overpower the other ingredients.

3 tablespoons all-purpose flour
1 1/2 tablespoons canola oil
1 (1-pound) boneless chuck roast, trimmed
1 teaspoon salt, divided
1/2 teaspoon freshly ground black pepper
1 cup fat-free, lower-sodium beef broth
4 garlic cloves, crushed
1 (12-ounce) bottle dark beer

1 bay leaf
3 carrots, peeled and cut diagonally into
   1/2-inch-thick slices
9 ounces small turnips, peeled and cut into
   wedges
1 medium onion, peeled and cut into wedges
1/4 cup chopped fresh flat-leaf parsley

1. Preheat oven to 300°.

2. Place flour in a shallow dish. Heat oil in a Dutch oven over medium-high heat. Sprinkle beef evenly on all sides with 1/2 teaspoon salt and pepper; dredge in flour. Add beef to pan; cook 10 minutes, turning to brown on all sides. Add broth and next 3 ingredients (through bay leaf), scraping pan to loosen browned bits; bring to a boil. Cover and bake at 300° for 1 1/2 hours. Add carrots; cover and cook 25 minutes. Add remaining 1/2 teaspoon salt, turnips, and onion; cover and cook an additional 1 hour and 5 minutes or until vegetables are tender and beef is fork-tender.

3. Remove beef and vegetables from pan; discard bay leaf. Cover beef mixture; keep warm. Let cooking liquid stand 10 minutes. Place a zip-top plastic bag inside a 2-cup glass measure. Pour cooking liquid into bag; let stand 10 minutes (fat will rise to the top). Seal bag; carefully snip off 1 bottom corner of bag. Drain cooking liquid into a medium bowl, stopping before fat layer reaches opening; discard fat. Serve cooking liquid with beef and vegetables. Sprinkle each serving with 1 tablespoon parsley. Yield: 4 servings (serving size: 3 ounces beef, 1 cup vegetables, and about 1/2 cup cooking liquid).

CALORIES 383; FAT 19.7g (sat 6g, mono 9.1g, poly 2.2g); PROTEIN 24.4g; CARB 21g; FIBER 3.6g; CHOL 70mg; IRON 2.9mg; SODIUM 815mg; CALC 68mg

Black Beans and Yellow Rice

4 ounces dried black beans
Cooking spray
4 ounces Spanish chorizo sausage, thinly sliced
6 cups water, divided
1/2 teaspoon salt, divided
1/2 teaspoon freshly ground black pepper, divided
1/4 teaspoon ground cumin

1 1/2 cups chopped onion
1 orange bell pepper, chopped
1 jalapeño pepper, minced
2 garlic cloves, minced
1 cup uncooked long-grain rice
1/4 teaspoon ground turmeric
3 cups chopped fresh tomato
2 tablespoons fresh cilantro leaves

1. Sort and wash beans; place in a bowl. Cover with water to 2 inches above beans; let stand 8 hours. Drain.

2. Heat a large saucepan over medium-high heat. Coat pan with cooking spray. Add chorizo; sauté 3 minutes. Add beans and 4 cups water; bring to a boil. Reduce heat, and simmer 2½ hours or until beans are tender. Stir in ¼ teaspoon salt, ¼ teaspoon black pepper, and cumin.

3. Heat a medium skillet over medium heat. Coat pan with cooking spray. Add onion, bell pepper, jalapeño, and garlic; cook 8 minutes, stirring occasionally. Stir remaining ¼ teaspoon black pepper and onion mixture into bean mixture.

4. Bring remaining 2 cups water to a boil in a small saucepan over medium-high heat. Stir in remaining ¼ teaspoon salt, rice, and turmeric. Cover, reduce heat, and simmer 20 minutes or until liquid evaporates and rice is tender. Spoon ¾ cup rice into each of 4 bowls, and top each serving with about ⅔ cup bean mixture, ¾ cup tomato, and 1½ teaspoons cilantro. Yield: 4 servings.

CALORIES 438; **FAT** 11.6g (sat 4.2g, mono 5.4g, poly 1.2g); **PROTEIN** 17.5g; **CARB** 64.6g; **FIBER** 5.7g; **CHOL** 25mg; **IRON** 4.6mg; **SODIUM** 657mg; **CALC** 40mg

Barley, Wild Rice, and Chicken Pilaf

This recipe has some of the creamy texture of a risotto but requires far less stirring.

½ cup hot water
¼ cup dried porcini mushrooms, chopped
1 tablespoon olive oil
1 cup finely chopped onion (about 1 medium)
3 garlic cloves, minced
¾ cup uncooked pearl barley
¼ cup uncooked wild rice
2 teaspoons chopped fresh thyme

1 (14-ounce) can fat-free, lower-sodium chicken broth
2 cups chopped cooked chicken breast
½ cup (2 ounces) grated fresh Parmesan cheese
¼ cup chopped fresh parsley
¼ teaspoon salt
¼ teaspoon freshly ground black pepper

1. Combine ½ cup hot water and mushrooms; let stand 10 minutes or until mushrooms are tender.

2. Heat in a large nonstick skillet over medium heat. Add onion to pan; cook 1 minute, stirring frequently. Add garlic; cook 30 seconds, stirring frequently. Add barley, rice, and thyme; cook 5 minutes or until lightly browned, stirring frequently. Stir in mushroom mixture and broth. Cover, reduce heat, and simmer 40 minutes or until barley is tender. Stir in chicken and cheese; cook 5 minutes or until thoroughly heated. Stir in parsley, salt, and pepper. Yield: 4 servings (serving size: 1 cup).

CALORIES 409; **FAT** 12.4g (sat 3.9g, mono 5.6g, poly 2g); **PROTEIN** 31.6g; **CARB** 42.8g; **FIBER** 7.7g; **CHOL** 68mg; **IRON** 2.7mg; **SODIUM** 515mg; **CALC** 160mg

Chicken and Sausage Jambalaya

2 teaspoons canola oil
6 ounces reduced-fat smoked sausage, halved lengthwise and cut into ¼-inch slices
½ cup chopped onion
½ cup chopped celery
½ cup chopped green bell pepper
2 garlic cloves, minced
1 cup uncooked long-grain white rice
1 cup water
¼ teaspoon ground red pepper
⅛ teaspoon salt
6 thyme sprigs
1 (14.5-ounce) can fat-free, lower-sodium chicken broth
1 (14.5-ounce) can no-salt-added diced tomatoes, undrained
1 cup shredded skinless, boneless rotisserie chicken breast

1. Heat the oil in a Dutch oven over medium-high heat. Add sausage; sauté 1 minute or until browned. Add onion, celery, bell pepper, and garlic; sauté 6 minutes or until tender. Add rice and next 5 ingredients (through broth); bring to a boil. Cover, reduce heat, and simmer 20 minutes or until rice is done. Remove thyme sprigs; discard. Stir in tomatoes and chicken. Cook 3 minutes or until thoroughly heated. Yield: 4 servings (serving size: about 1¼ cups).

CALORIES 341; **FAT** 5.8g (sat 1.3g, mono 2g, poly 0.9g); **PROTEIN** 19.3g; **CARB** 50.6g; **FIBER** 2.8g; **CHOL** 44mg; **IRON** 3.2mg; **SODIUM** 723mg; **CALC** 59mg

Sweet Potato–Chicken Curry

Serve over hot cooked basmati or jasmine rice, if you wish.

2 teaspoons curry powder
1 teaspoon ground coriander
1 teaspoon ground turmeric
$1/2$ teaspoon salt
$1/2$ teaspoon freshly ground black pepper
$1/4$ teaspoon ground red pepper
1 bay leaf
$1^1/2$ teaspoons olive oil
$1^1/2$ pounds skinless, boneless chicken breast, cut into 1-inch pieces
$1^1/2$ cups vertically sliced onion

$1^1/2$ teaspoons minced peeled fresh ginger
2 garlic cloves, minced
1 (14-ounce) can fat-free, lower-sodium chicken broth
1 (14.5-ounce) can diced tomatoes, undrained
2 cups cubed peeled sweet potato
$3/4$ cup canned chickpeas (garbanzo beans), rinsed and drained
$1/2$ cup frozen green peas
1 tablespoon fresh lemon juice
Parsley sprigs (optional)

1. Combine first 7 ingredients.
2. Heat oil in a large Dutch oven over medium-high heat. Add chicken, and sauté 5 minutes or until browned, stirring occasionally. Remove chicken from pan. Reduce heat to medium. Add onion to pan; cook 10 minutes, stirring frequently. Increase heat to medium-high; return chicken to pan. Cook 1 minute. Stir in ginger and garlic; cook 1 minute, stirring constantly. Add curry powder mixture; cook 2 minutes, stirring constantly. Add broth and tomatoes; bring to a boil. Cover, reduce heat, and simmer 1 hour. Stir in potato and chickpeas. Cook, uncovered, 30 minutes. Add peas; cook 5 minutes. Remove from heat; stir in lemon juice. Discard bay leaf. Garnish with parsley sprigs, if desired. Yield: 7 servings (serving size: about 1 cup).

CALORIES 196; FAT 3.9g (sat 0.9g, mono 1.6g, poly 0.8g); PROTEIN 23g; CARB 16.9g; FIBER 3.5g; CHOL 54mg; IRON 1.9mg; SODIUM 467mg; CALC 46mg

Spinach and Butternut Lasagna, page 184

vegetarian

Spinach and Butternut Lasagna *(Pictured on page 182)*

3 cups 2% reduced-fat milk
1 ounce all-purpose flour (about 1/4 cup)
2 tablespoons butter
1/3 cup minced shallots
1 1/4 teaspoons salt, divided
1/2 teaspoon freshly ground black pepper, divided
8 cups (3/4-inch) cubed peeled butternut squash (about 2 1/4 pounds)
1 tablespoon balsamic vinegar
4 teaspoons olive oil, divided
Cooking spray

1 teaspoon chopped fresh or 1/4 teaspoon dried thyme
1/4 teaspoon crushed red pepper
4 garlic cloves, minced
3 (6-ounce) packages fresh baby spinach
9 cooked lasagna noodles (8 ounces uncooked noodles)
1 cup (4 ounces) grated Asiago cheese, divided
1 cup (4 ounces) grated fresh Parmigiano-Reggiano cheese, divided

1. Cook milk in a small, heavy saucepan over medium-high heat to 180° or until tiny bubbles form around edge (do not boil). Remove from heat, and keep warm.
2. Weigh or lightly spoon flour into a dry measuring cup; level with a knife. Melt butter in a medium nonstick saucepan over medium heat. Add shallots; cook 2 minutes or until tender. Reduce heat; add flour to pan, and cook 5 minutes or until smooth and golden, stirring constantly. Remove from heat; add about 2 tablespoons warm milk to flour mixture, stirring constantly with a whisk. Gradually add remaining warm milk, about 1/2 cup at a time, until mixture is smooth, stirring constantly with a whisk. Stir in 1/2 teaspoon salt and 1/4 teaspoon black pepper. Bring to a boil; reduce heat, and cook until smooth and thickened. Remove from heat. Cover surface of milk mixture with plastic wrap; set aside.
3. Preheat oven to 425°. Place squash in a large bowl. Add vinegar; toss to coat. Add 1 tablespoon oil; toss to coat. Arrange squash in a single layer on a jelly-roll pan coated with cooking spray. Sprinkle with 1/2 teaspoon salt, remaining 1/4 teaspoon black pepper, and thyme. Bake at 425° for 30 minutes, stirring after 15 minutes.
4. Combine remaining 1 teaspoon oil, red pepper, and garlic in a Dutch oven over medium heat; cook 2 minutes, stirring constantly. Add spinach, 1 bag at a time; cook until wilted, stirring frequently. Add remaining 1/4 teaspoon salt; cook until liquid evaporates, stirring frequently.
5. Reduce oven temperature to 350°. Spoon 1/3 cup milk mixture into a 13 x 9–inch baking pan coated with cooking spray. Arrange 3 noodles over mixture; top with spinach mixture, 2/3 cup milk mixture, 1/2 cup Asiago, and 1/4 cup Parmigiano-Reggiano. Arrange 3 noodles over cheese; top with squash mixture, 2/3 cup milk mixture, remaining 1/2 cup Asiago, and 1/4 cup Parmigiano-Reggiano. Arrange remaining 3 noodles over cheese; spread remaining 1/2 cup milk mixture over noodles. Sprinkle with remaining 1/2 cup Parmigiano-Reggiano. Bake at 350° for 30 minutes or until bubbly. Let stand 15 minutes. Yield: 8 servings (serving size: 1 piece).

CALORIES 445; **FAT** 15g (sat 8.1g, mono 4.2g, poly 0.7g); **PROTEIN** 20.7g; **CARB** 61.5g; **FIBER** 7.3g; **CHOL** 36mg; **IRON** 4.8mg; **SODIUM** 758mg; **CALC** 599mg

Gemelli with Roasted Fennel and Sun-Dried Tomatoes

Substitute fusilli, cavatappi, or penne rigate for the gemelli. To save time, cook the pasta while the fennel bakes.

2 large fennel bulbs (about 2¼ pounds)
Cooking spray
2 tablespoons olive oil, divided
½ teaspoon salt, divided
½ teaspoon freshly ground black pepper, divided
¾ pound uncooked gemelli (short tube-shaped pasta)

¾ cup (3 ounces) crumbled feta cheese
½ cup drained oil-packed sun-dried tomatoes
¼ cup chopped fresh parsley
3 tablespoons chopped fresh basil
2 teaspoons grated lemon rind

1. Preheat oven to 425°.
2. Trim tough outer leaves from fennel. Cut fennel bulbs in half crosswise; discard cores. Cut bulbs into ½-inch-thick pieces. Place fennel pieces in a large roasting pan. Coat fennel with cooking spray. Add 1 tablespoon oil, ¼ teaspoon salt, and ¼ teaspoon pepper; toss to coat. Bake at 425° for 20 minutes. Stir fennel; bake an additional 10 minutes or until tender.
3. Cook pasta according to package directions, omitting salt and fat. Drain, reserving 2 tablespoons pasta cooking water. Return pasta to pan. Add reserved pasta cooking water, fennel, remaining 1 tablespoon oil, remaining ¼ teaspoon salt, remaining ¼ teaspoon pepper, feta, and remaining ingredients; toss well. Yield: 4 servings (serving size: 2 cups).

CALORIES 496; FAT 15.2g (sat 4.8g, mono 7.4g, poly 1.9g); PROTEIN 17g; CARB 76.6g; FIBER 7.4g; CHOL 19mg; IRON 4.4mg; SODIUM 636mg; CALC 195mg

Marmalade French Toast Casserole

Grapefruit or mixed-fruit marmalade can stand in for orange marmalade. Serve the casserole with honey or pancake syrup warmed with orange rind and a splash of orange juice (add 1 teaspoon grated rind and 2 tablespoons juice per ½ cup syrup).

3 tablespoons butter, softened
1 (16-ounce) loaf sourdough French bread,
cut into 24 (½-inch-thick) slices
Cooking spray
1 (12-ounce) jar orange marmalade
2¾ cups 1% low-fat milk

⅓ cup sugar
1 teaspoon vanilla extract
¼ teaspoon ground nutmeg
6 large eggs
⅓ cup finely chopped walnuts

1. Spread softened butter on one side of each bread slice. Arrange 12 bread slices, buttered sides down, slightly overlapping in a single layer in a 13 x 9–inch glass or ceramic baking dish coated with cooking spray. Spread marmalade evenly over bread; top with remaining 12 bread slices, buttered sides up.
2. Combine milk and next 4 ingredients (through eggs), stirring with a whisk. Pour egg mixture over bread. Cover and refrigerate 8 hours or overnight.
3. Preheat oven to 350°.
4. Sprinkle casserole with chopped walnuts. Bake at 350° for 45 minutes or until golden. Let stand 5 minutes before serving. Yield: 12 servings (serving size: 1 piece).

CALORIES 293; **FAT** 9g (sat 3.2g, mono 2.2g, poly 2.3g); **PROTEIN** 9.1g; **CARB** 46.4g; **FIBER** 1.6g; **CHOL** 116mg; **IRON** 2.2mg; **SODIUM** 315mg; **CALC** 132mg

---

PREP POINTER: You can assemble this easy casserole in less than 15 minutes. Store it in the refrigerator overnight. Or prep in the morning as a breakfast-for-dinner option with veggie sausage links or patties.

Artichoke, Spinach, and Feta Stuffed Shells

To fill the shells, simply spoon the cheese mixture into a heavy-duty zip-top plastic bag; squeeze out the air. Snip a 1-inch hole in one corner of the bag, and pipe the filling into the shells.

1 teaspoon dried oregano
¼ cup chopped pepperoncini peppers
1 (28-ounce) can no-salt-added crushed tomatoes
1 (8-ounce) can no-salt-added tomato sauce
1 cup (4 ounces) shredded provolone cheese, divided
1 cup (4 ounces) crumbled feta cheese
½ cup (4 ounces) fat-free cream cheese, softened

¼ teaspoon freshly ground black pepper
1 (9-ounce) package frozen artichoke hearts, thawed and chopped
½ (10-ounce) package frozen chopped spinach, thawed, drained, and squeezed dry
2 garlic cloves, minced
20 cooked jumbo pasta shells (about 8 ounces uncooked pasta)
Cooking spray

1. Preheat oven to 375°.

2. Combine first 4 ingredients in a medium saucepan. Place over medium heat; cook 12 minutes or until slightly thick, stirring occasionally. Remove from heat; set aside.

3. Combine ½ cup provolone and next 6 ingredients (through garlic) in a medium bowl. Spoon or pipe about 1½ tablespoons cheese mixture into each pasta shell; place stuffed shells in a 13 x 9–inch glass or ceramic baking dish coated with cooking spray. Spoon tomato mixture over shells; sprinkle with remaining ½ cup provolone. Bake at 375° for 25 minutes or until thoroughly heated and cheese melts. Yield: 5 servings (serving size: 4 stuffed shells).

CALORIES 434; **FAT** 12.7g (sat 7.6g, mono 2.9g, poly 0.7g); **PROTEIN** 23.8g; **CARB** 54.1g; **FIBER** 8.6g; **CHOL** 39mg; **IRON** 4.8mg; **SODIUM** 684mg; **CALC** 491mg

Ratatouille with Tofu

This dish epitomizes the fusion of French and Asian cuisines. Serve with rice noodles. Offer the extra Pesto Coulis as a dipping sauce with crusty French bread; it's also nice tossed with hot rice or pasta.

Cooking spray
1 cup finely chopped carrot
1/2 cup finely chopped onion
1/4 cup chopped fresh basil
2 teaspoons chopped fresh thyme
2 teaspoons minced garlic (about 4 cloves)
2 cups finely chopped reduced-fat firm tofu, drained (about 11 ounces)
2 cups diced eggplant

1 cup diced zucchini
1 cup chopped plum tomato
4 teaspoons Pesto Coulis
2 (14-ounce) cans no-salt-added tomato sauce
1 teaspoon ground cumin
1/2 teaspoon salt
1/8 teaspoon freshly ground black pepper

1. Heat a large Dutch oven over medium-high heat. Coat pan with cooking spray. Add carrot to pan; sauté 6 minutes. Add onion, basil, thyme, and garlic; sauté 4 minutes. Add tofu, eggplant, and zucchini; sauté 4 minutes. Add tomato, Pesto Coulis, and tomato sauce; bring to a boil. Reduce heat, and simmer 30 minutes, stirring occasionally. Stir in cumin, salt, and pepper. Yield: 4 servings (serving size: 1½ cups).

CALORIES 201; FAT 5.6g (sat 0.6g, mono 3.4g, poly 0.7g); PROTEIN 12.4g; CARB 28.5g; FIBER 7.7g; CHOL 0mg; IRON 4.3mg; SODIUM 379mg; CALC 235mg

Pesto Coulis:

1 cup fresh parsley leaves (about 1 bunch)
1 cup fresh basil leaves (about 1 bunch)

1/2 cup chopped green onions
1/2 cup extra-virgin olive oil

1. Place all ingredients in a food processor. Pulse until smooth. Yield: ¾ cup (serving size: 1 teaspoon).

CALORIES 28; FAT 3g (sat 0.4g, mono 2.2g, poly 0.3g); PROTEIN 0.1g; CARB 0.3g; FIBER 0.1g; CHOL 0mg; IRON 0.2mg; SODIUM 1mg; CALC 5mg

Baked Mac and Cheese

3 cups (12 ounces) uncooked penne
  (tube-shaped pasta)
1 (12-ounce) carton 2% low-fat cottage cheese
½ cup (2 ounces) finely shredded sharp
  cheddar cheese
½ cup (2 ounces) grated fresh Parmesan
  cheese, divided

½ teaspoon salt
⅛ teaspoon freshly ground black pepper
Cooking spray
3 tablespoons panko (Japanese
  breadcrumbs)
1 tablespoon minced fresh flat-leaf parsley

1. Preheat oven to 375°.

2. Cook pasta according to package directions, omitting salt and fat. Drain; place in a large bowl.

3. Place cottage cheese in a food processor; process until smooth. Combine cottage cheese, cheddar cheese, ¼ cup Parmesan cheese, salt, and pepper. Add cheese mixture to pasta, and stir well. Spoon mixture into an 11 x 7–inch glass or ceramic baking dish coated with cooking spray.

4. Combine remaining ¼ cup Parmesan, panko, and parsley in a small bowl. Sprinkle evenly over pasta mixture. Bake at 375° for 10 minutes.

5. Preheat broiler (do not remove dish from oven).

6. Broil pasta 1 minute or until top browns. Yield: 6 servings (serving size: about 1⅓ cups).

CALORIES 329; FAT 7.4g (sat 4.4g, mono 0.8g, poly 0.1g); PROTEIN 19.1g; CARB 47g; FIBER 1.9g; CHOL 21mg; IRON 2mg; SODIUM 455mg; CALC 275mg

> **SIMPLE SIDE:** Serve this creamy mac and cheese with a spinach salad graced with vertically sliced red onion and cherry tomato halves. Drizzle with a simple vinaigrette.

Spicy Stir-Fried Tofu with Snow Peas, Peanut Butter, and Mushrooms

This colorful meatless entrée is a superfast skillet dinner.

1 (14-ounce) package extra-firm tofu, drained and cut into 1-inch cubes
2 teaspoons canola oil
3/4 pound snow peas, trimmed
1 cup red bell pepper strips
3/4 cup water, divided
1/2 cup sliced green onions
2 teaspoons minced peeled fresh ginger

2 garlic cloves, minced
3 cups sliced shiitake mushrooms (about 8 ounces)
2 tablespoons reduced-sodium tamari
2 tablespoons creamy peanut butter
1 teaspoon cornstarch
2 teaspoons Sriracha (hot chile sauce)
1/4 teaspoon salt

1. Place tofu cubes on several layers of paper towels. Cover with additional layers of paper towels; let stand 5 minutes.

2. Heat oil in a large nonstick skillet over medium-high heat. Add tofu to pan; cook 7 minutes or until lightly browned, gently turning occasionally. Remove from pan; keep warm. Add snow peas, bell pepper, 1/4 cup water, onions, ginger, and garlic to pan; stir-fry 3 minutes. Add mushrooms, and stir-fry 2 minutes.

3. Combine remaining 1/2 cup water, tamari, peanut butter, cornstarch, Sriracha, and salt in a small bowl; stir well. Add tamari mixture and tofu to pan; cook 1 minute or until thickened, stirring constantly. Yield: 4 servings (serving size: 1½ cups).

CALORIES 212; **FAT** 8.7g (sat 1.4g, mono 3.7g, poly 3g); **PROTEIN** 13.1g; **CARB** 21.5g; **FIBER** 4.7g; **CHOL** 0mg; **IRON** 3.6mg; **SODIUM** 639mg; **CALC** 84mg

Cheese Pie with Peppers

In addition to feta, this version of a Greek specialty uses readily available cheeses such as extra-sharp cheddar and blue.

2¼ ounces semolina or pasta flour (about ½ cup)
1½ cups chopped green bell pepper
1 tablespoon finely chopped seeded jalapeño pepper
1½ cups fat-free milk, divided
1 cup plain fat-free yogurt
1 cup (4 ounces) crumbled feta cheese
1 cup (4 ounces) shredded reduced-fat extra-sharp cheddar cheese

¼ cup (1 ounce) crumbled blue cheese
½ teaspoon salt
¼ teaspoon freshly ground black pepper
2 large egg whites
8 (18 x 14–inch) sheets frozen phyllo dough, thawed
Cooking spray

1. Preheat oven to 400°.

2. Weigh or lightly spoon flour into a dry measuring cup; level with a knife. Set aside.

3. Heat a large nonstick skillet over medium-high heat. Add bell pepper and jalapeño; sauté 5 minutes. Stir in flour; remove from heat. Set aside 2 tablespoons milk. Gradually add remaining milk to pan, stirring well with a whisk. Stir in yogurt; bring to a boil. Remove from heat; stir 2 minutes or until thick. Cool 5 minutes. Stir in cheeses, salt, black pepper, and egg whites.

4. Working with 1 phyllo sheet at a time (cover remaining dough to keep from drying), place 2 phyllo sheets in a 13 x 9–inch metal baking pan coated with cooking spray; gently press sheets into bottom and sides of pan, allowing ends to extend over edges of pan. Coat top sheet with cooking spray. Fold 1 phyllo sheet in half crosswise, and place on sheets in bottom of pan. Coat with cooking spray. Top with 1 phyllo sheet, gently pressing sheet into bottom and sides of pan; coat with cooking spray. Spread cheese mixture evenly over top of phyllo. Fold 1 phyllo sheet in half crosswise; gently press on cheese mixture in pan. Coat with cooking spray. Top with remaining 3 phyllo sheets, coating each sheet with cooking spray. Cut ends of sheets extending over pan. Fold edges of phyllo to form a rim; flatten rim with fork. Cut 4 slits with a sharp knife in top of phyllo, and brush with reserved 2 tablespoons milk. Bake at 400° for 22 minutes. Reduce oven temperature to 375° (do not remove pie from oven); bake for 20 minutes or until browned. Remove from oven; let stand 15 minutes. Yield: 8 servings (serving size: 1 piece).

CALORIES 243; **FAT** 8.7g (sat 5.2g, mono 1.7g, poly 0.4g); **PROTEIN** 13.3g; **CARB** 27.6g; **FIBER** 1.4g; **CHOL** 27mg; **IRON** 1.5mg; **SODIUM** 641mg; **CALC** 292mg

Fontina and Mascarpone Baked Pasta

The nuttiness of fontina and the creaminess of mascarpone create a unique updated version of mac and cheese. If your supermarket doesn't stock mascarpone cheese, substitute full-fat cream cheese. For a dinner party, bake the pasta in individual gratin dishes for 15 minutes. Add gourmet greens tossed with raspberry vinaigrette to complete the menu. A basic mac and cheese has endless possibilities. Improvise with any pasta and cheese you have on hand.

1 pound uncooked penne (tube-shaped pasta)
1 ounce all-purpose flour (about ¼ cup)
3 cups fat-free milk
2 cups (8 ounces) shredded fontina cheese
¼ cup (2 ounces) mascarpone cheese
¾ teaspoon salt

¼ teaspoon freshly ground black pepper
Cooking spray
3 (1-ounce) slices white bread
1 tablespoon butter
1 small garlic clove, minced
1½ tablespoons chopped fresh parsley

1. Cook pasta according to package directions, omitting salt and fat. Drain; keep warm.
2. Preheat oven to 350°.
3. Weigh or lightly spoon flour into a dry measuring cup; level with a knife. Combine flour and milk in a large saucepan over medium heat, stirring with a whisk. Cook 10 minutes or until thick, stirring constantly with a whisk. Remove from heat; add cheeses, stirring with a whisk until smooth. Stir in salt and black pepper. Add cooked pasta, stirring to coat. Spoon pasta mixture into a 13 x 9–inch glass or ceramic baking dish coated with cooking spray.
4. Tear bread slices into several pieces. Place bread in a food processor, and process until fine crumbs measure 1½ cups.
5. Melt butter in a small skillet over medium heat. Add minced garlic, and cook 30 seconds. Remove from heat. Stir in breadcrumbs until well combined. Sprinkle breadcrumb mixture evenly over pasta mixture. Bake at 350° for 25 minutes or until bubbly. Sprinkle with chopped parsley. Yield: 8 servings (serving size: 1¼ cups).

CALORIES 423; **FAT** 14.3g (sat 8.2g, mono 3.7g, poly 0.7g); **PROTEIN** 19.3g; **CARB** 54.6g; **FIBER** 2.1g; **CHOL** 46mg; **IRON** 2.4mg; **SODIUM** 550mg; **CALC** 298mg

Broccoli and Three-Cheese Casserole

Fresh broccoli remains crisp-tender in this recipe, though you can substitute any leftover cooked vegetables you have on hand. Assemble the casserole up to eight hours in advance; cover and refrigerate.

2 cups cooked white rice
6 tablespoons (1½ ounces) grated fresh
  Parmesan cheese, divided
¾ teaspoon salt, divided
½ teaspoon dried fines herbes
3 large egg whites
Cooking spray
½ cup (2 ounces) shredded fontina cheese
4 cups coarsely chopped broccoli florets
  (about 1 bunch)

1 cup finely chopped onion
¼ cup (1 ounce) shredded reduced-fat
  extra-sharp cheddar cheese
¾ cup egg substitute
¾ cup 1% low-fat milk
¼ teaspoon freshly ground black pepper
2 (1-ounce) slices firm white bread

1. Preheat oven to 400°.
2. Combine rice, ¼ cup Parmesan cheese, ¼ teaspoon salt, fines herbes, and egg whites. Press mixture into an 11 x 7–inch glass or ceramic baking dish coated with cooking spray. Sprinkle fontina evenly over rice mixture.
3. Cook broccoli in boiling water 4 minutes or until tender; drain well.
4. Heat a large nonstick skillet over medium heat. Add onion to pan; cook 4 minutes or until tender, stirring occasionally. Stir in broccoli. Spoon broccoli mixture evenly over rice mixture. Top with cheddar cheese.
5. Combine egg substitute, milk, remaining ½ teaspoon salt, and black pepper in a small bowl, and stir well with a whisk. Pour egg mixture over the broccoli mixture.
6. Place bread in a food processor; pulse 10 times or until coarse crumbs measure 1¼ cups. Combine breadcrumbs and remaining 2 tablespoons Parmesan cheese. Sprinkle breadcrumb mixture evenly over broccoli. Bake at 400° for 23 minutes or until set. Yield: 6 servings.

CALORIES 242; **FAT** 7.6g (sat 4g, mono 1.6g, poly 0.9g); **PROTEIN** 16.3g; **CARB** 27.8g; **FIBER** 2.5g; **CHOL** 20mg; **IRON** 2.2mg; **SODIUM** 613mg; **CALC** 259mg

Soba Salad with Soy-Wasabi Vinaigrette

Curly soba noodles, found in the international or ethnic aisle of your grocery store, impart a neutral flavor that works well in this quick and easy Asian-inspired entrée. Wasabi is also called Japanese horseradish.

1 garlic clove
6 ounces uncooked Japanese curly noodles (chucka soba)
1 cup frozen shelled edamame (green soybeans)
4 ounces snow peas, trimmed and halved crosswise (about 1½ cups)
4 ounces whole baby carrots, quartered lengthwise
3 tablespoons rice vinegar
3 tablespoons lower-sodium soy sauce
1 tablespoon dark sesame oil
1 tablespoon wasabi paste
½ cup thinly sliced radishes

1. Mince garlic; let stand 10 minutes.
2. Cook noodles according to package directions, omitting salt and fat. Drain and rinse noodles under cold water; drain well.
3. Steam edamame, peas, and carrots 4 minutes or until crisp-tender. Drain and plunge vegetables into ice water; drain.
4. Combine garlic, vinegar, soy sauce, sesame oil, and wasabi in a large bowl; stir with a whisk. Add noodles, vegetable mixture, and radishes; toss gently to coat. Serve immediately. Yield: 4 servings (serving size: about 1½ cups).

CALORIES 274; **FAT** 6g (sat 0.7g, mono 1.6g, poly 2.2g); **PROTEIN** 9.2g; **CARB** 41.6g; **FIBER** 4g; **CHOL** 0mg; **IRON** 2mg; **SODIUM** 740mg; **CALC** 47mg

FYI: In addition to their satisfying textures, steamed vegetables retain more water-soluble nutrients than their boiled counterparts.

Brie and Egg Strata

Try this for your next weekend brunch. The night before, assemble and layer the casserole without the egg mixture (steps one and two); cover and refrigerate. Combine the egg mixture (step three), and refrigerate in a separate container. In the morning, pour the egg mixture over the bread mixture; allow the strata to stand for 30 minutes before baking. Substitute a French baguette or sourdough loaf for the ciabatta, if desired. Freeze the Brie for about 15 minutes to make chopping easier.

2 teaspoons olive oil
2 cups chopped onion
1 1/2 cups diced unpeeled Yukon gold potato (1 large)
1 cup chopped red bell pepper
1 cup halved grape tomatoes
1 teaspoon salt, divided
3/4 pound ciabatta, cut into 1-inch cubes, toasted
Cooking spray
4 ounces Brie cheese, rind removed and chopped
1 cup egg substitute
2 large eggs
1 teaspoon herbes de Provence
1/4 teaspoon freshly ground black pepper
3 cups 1% low-fat milk
2 tablespoons chopped fresh parsley

1. Heat oil in a large nonstick skillet over medium-high heat. Add onion, potato, and bell pepper; sauté 4 minutes or until tender. Stir in tomatoes; sauté 2 minutes. Stir in 1/2 teaspoon salt. Combine onion mixture and bread.

2. Place half of bread mixture in a 13 x 9–inch glass or ceramic baking dish coated with cooking spray. Sprinkle with half of Brie. Top with remaining bread mixture and remaining Brie.

3. Place egg substitute and eggs in a medium bowl. Add remaining 1/2 teaspoon salt, herbes de Provence, and pepper. Add milk, stirring with a whisk until well blended. Pour egg mixture over bread mixture. Let stand 30 minutes.

4. Preheat oven to 350°.

5. Bake at 350° for 50 minutes or until set. Sprinkle with parsley. Serve immediately. Yield: 12 servings (serving size: 1 piece).

CALORIES 205; **FAT** 6.9g (sat 2.7g, mono 3g, poly 0.8g); **PROTEIN** 10.8g; **CARB** 26.1g; **FIBER** 1.7g; **CHOL** 47mg; **IRON** 2mg; **SODIUM** 534mg; **CALC** 120mg

Cumin-Spiced Chickpeas and Carrots on Couscous

½ cup organic vegetable broth
1 tablespoon grated lemon rind
3 tablespoons fresh lemon juice
1 tablespoon tomato paste
2 (15½-ounce) cans chickpeas
  (garbanzo beans), rinsed and drained
3 tablespoons canola oil, divided
1 cup chopped red bell pepper
1 cup matchstick-cut carrots
1 jalapeño pepper, finely chopped
1 teaspoon cumin seeds
¼ teaspoon salt
¼ teaspoon freshly ground black pepper
¼ teaspoon ground allspice
⅛ teaspoon ground red pepper
6 garlic cloves, minced
4 cups warm cooked couscous
½ cup fresh cilantro leaves
Lemon wedges (optional)

1. Combine first 4 ingredients, stirring with a whisk.
2. Dry chickpeas thoroughly in a single layer on paper towels. Heat 2 tablespoons oil in a large skillet over high heat. Add chickpeas to pan, and stir-fry 3 minutes or until lightly browned. Remove chickpeas from pan with a slotted spoon; wipe pan clean with a paper towel. Add remaining 1 tablespoon oil to pan, and swirl to coat. Add bell pepper, carrots, and jalapeño to pan, and stir-fry 2 minutes or until vegetables are slightly tender. Add cumin seeds and next 5 ingredients (through garlic) to pan, and stir-fry 30 seconds. Add reserved broth mixture and chickpeas. Bring to a boil, and remove from heat. Serve over couscous, and top with cilantro. Garnish with lemon wedges, if desired. Yield: 4 servings (serving size: 1 cup couscous, about ¾ cup chickpea mixture, and 2 tablespoons cilantro).

CALORIES 420; **FAT** 12.8g (sat 0.9g, mono 6.7g, poly 3.2g); **PROTEIN** 12.7g; **CARB** 64.5g; **FIBER** 8.8g; **CHOL** 0mg; **IRON** 2.6mg; **SODIUM** 586mg; **CALC** 66mg

WINE NOTE: Pair with a chenin blanc to temper the fiery peppers.

Green Curry with Bok Choy

½ cup chopped fresh cilantro
2 tablespoons chopped peeled fresh ginger
2 teaspoons ground coriander
2 teaspoons ground cumin
8 garlic cloves, peeled
3 small serrano chiles, seeded
2 large shallots, coarsely chopped
4 cups chopped broccoli florets
2 cups (½-inch-thick) sliced baby bok choy
2 teaspoons dark sesame oil
4 teaspoons sugar

1 tablespoon lower-sodium soy sauce
¾ teaspoon kosher salt
1 (13.5-ounce) can light coconut milk
1 (14-ounce) package water-packed organic firm tofu, drained and cut into ¾-inch cubes
¼ cup fresh lime juice
2 cups hot cooked long-grain white rice
¼ cup small basil leaves
2 tablespoons mint leaves

1. Place first 7 ingredients in a food processor; process until smooth.

2. Cook broccoli florets in boiling water in a large Dutch oven 3 minutes or until crisp-tender. Remove broccoli from water with a slotted spoon; drain and rinse with cold water. Drain; set aside. Return water to a boil. Add bok choy to pan; cook 1 minute. Drain; rinse with cold water. Drain; set aside.

3. Heat Dutch oven over medium-high heat. Add oil to pan; swirl to coat. Add cilantro mixture to pan; sauté 1 minute, stirring constantly. Add sugar and next 3 ingredients (through milk) to pan; bring to a boil. Add tofu; cover, reduce heat, and simmer 6 minutes or until slightly thick. Add broccoli, bok choy, and juice; cook 1 minute or until heated, tossing to combine. Place ½ cup rice in each of 4 bowls; spoon 1½ cups tofu mixture over each serving. Sprinkle 1 tablespoon basil and 1½ teaspoons mint over each serving. Yield: 4 servings.

CALORIES 338; **FAT** 12.8g (sat 5.3g, mono 2.2g, poly 4.1g); **PROTEIN** 16.6g; **CARB** 44.2g; **FIBER** 4.1g; **CHOL** 0mg; **IRON** 5mg; **SODIUM** 566mg; **CALC** 333mg

Roasted Vegetables with Onion–Pine Nut Topping over Chickpea Couscous

The slightly sweet topping offsets plain couscous and heightens the natural sweetness of the roasted root vegetables.

Vegetables:
1½ pounds sweet potato, peeled and cut into bite-sized pieces
¾ pound parsnips, peeled and cut into bite-sized pieces
3 carrots, peeled and cut crosswise into 2-inch pieces (about 9 ounces)
1½ tablespoons extra-virgin olive oil
2 teaspoons Ras el Hanout
½ teaspoon kosher salt

Couscous:
1¼ cups organic vegetable broth
1 cup uncooked couscous

½ teaspoon kosher salt
¼ cup chopped fresh mint
1 (15-ounce) can no-salt-added chickpeas (garbanzo beans), rinsed and drained

Topping:
1 tablespoon extra-virgin olive oil
1 yellow onion, cut into ¼-inch-thick slices, separated into rings
¼ cup pine nuts
¼ cup golden raisins
1 teaspoon ground cinnamon
1 tablespoon honey

1. Preheat oven to 475°.

2. To prepare vegetables, combine first 5 ingredients in a large bowl; stir in ½ teaspoon salt. Place potato mixture in a single layer on a baking sheet. Bake at 475° for 30 minutes or until vegetables are golden brown, stirring once.

3. To prepare couscous, bring broth to a boil in a medium saucepan. Stir in couscous and ½ teaspoon salt. Remove from heat; cover and let stand 5 minutes. Fluff with a fork; gently stir in mint and chickpeas. Keep warm.

4. To prepare topping, heat 1 tablespoon oil in a medium skillet over medium heat. Add onion to pan; cook 12 minutes or until tender and golden brown, stirring occasionally. Add pine nuts and raisins; cook 2 minutes. Stir in cinnamon; cook 30 seconds. Stir in honey; remove from heat. Spoon about ⅔ cup couscous onto each of 6 plates. Divide vegetables evenly among servings; top each with 2 tablespoons topping. Yield: 6 servings.

CALORIES 521; **FAT** 13.7g (sat 1.5g, mono 7.4g, poly 3.8g); **PROTEIN** 11.7g; **CARB** 90.5g; **FIBER** 13.9g; **CHOL** 0mg; **IRON** 3.5mg; **SODIUM** 753mg; **CALC** 135mg

Ras el Hanout:

2¹⁄₂ teaspoons kosher salt
2 teaspoons ground cumin
2 teaspoons ground ginger
2 teaspoons freshly ground black pepper
1¹⁄₂ teaspoons ground cinnamon
1 teaspoon ground coriander

1 teaspoon ground red pepper
1 teaspoon ground allspice
1 teaspoon saffron threads, crushed
¹⁄₂ teaspoon ground cloves
¹⁄₄ teaspoon freshly ground nutmeg

1. Combine all ingredients in a small bowl. Store in an airtight container for up to 1 month. Yield: ¼ cup (serving size: ¼ teaspoon).

CALORIES 2; FAT 0.1g (sat 0g, mono 0g, poly 0g); PROTEIN 0.1g; CARB 0.3g; FIBER 0.1g; CHOL 0mg; IRON 0.1mg; SODIUM 98mg; CALC 3mg

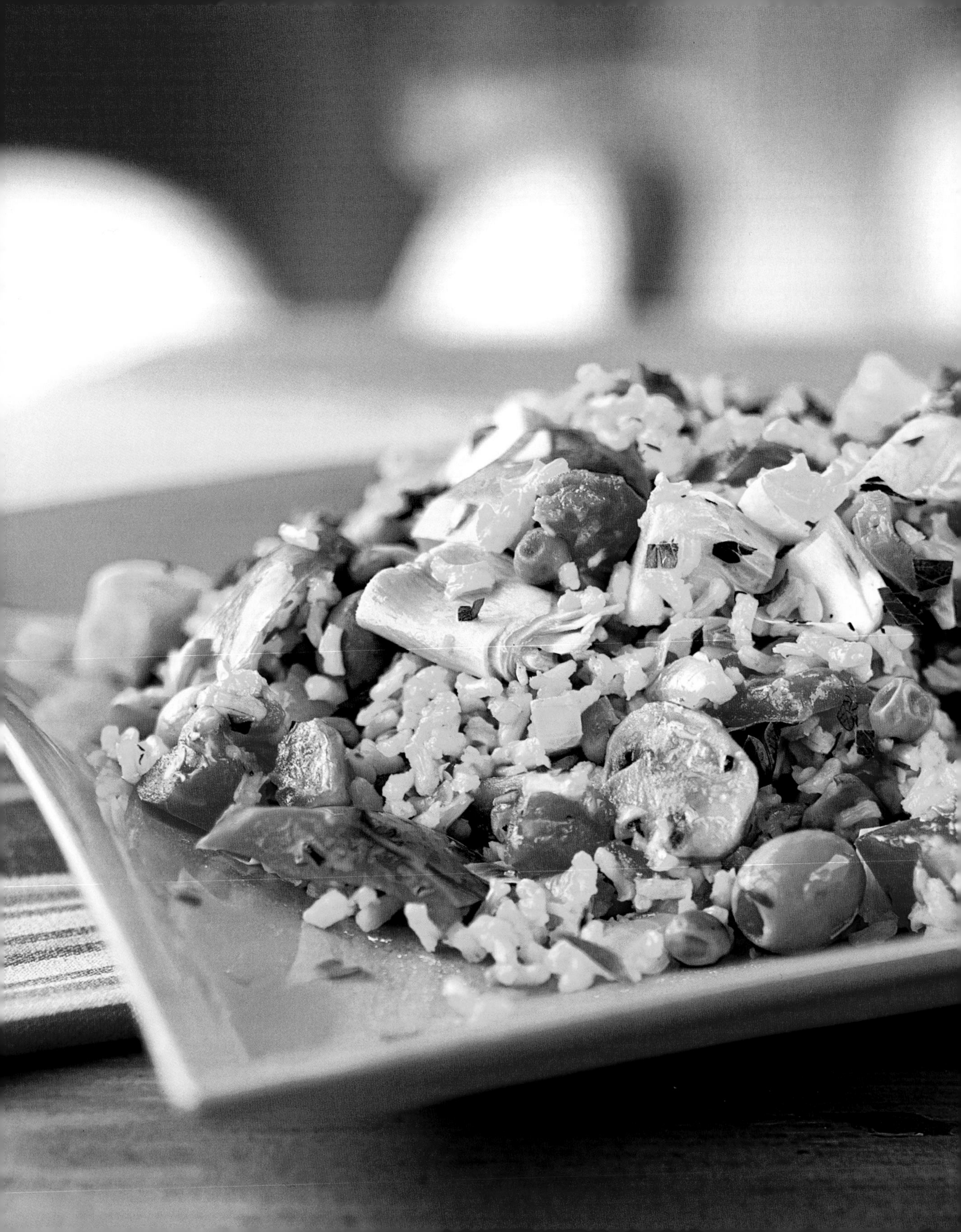

Quick Vegetarian Paella

This Spanish classic is simple to prepare and easily doubled to serve a crowd. Artichokes, bell peppers, mushrooms, and olives cooked with nutty brown rice make this a hearty one-dish meal. Saffron lends an exotic flavor.

2 tablespoons extra-virgin olive oil
2 cups chopped onion
2 cups (1-inch) chopped green bell pepper
1 cup sliced cremini mushrooms
2 garlic cloves, minced
3 cups uncooked quick-cooking brown rice
2 cups fat-free, lower-sodium vegetable broth
1 cup water
1 teaspoon saffron threads, crushed, or
  ground turmeric

1/2 teaspoon dried thyme
2 cups chopped tomato
1 cup frozen green peas
1/2 cup pimiento-stuffed olives, chopped
2 tablespoons chopped fresh flat-leaf parsley
1/4 teaspoon freshly ground black pepper
1 (14-ounce) can artichoke hearts, drained
  and coarsely chopped
Chopped fresh flat-leaf parsley (optional)

1. Heat olive oil in a stockpot over medium-high heat. Add onion, bell pepper, mushrooms, and garlic; sauté 5 minutes. Stir in rice and next 4 ingredients (through thyme); bring to a boil. Cover, reduce heat, and simmer 10 minutes.

2. Stir in tomato, green peas, olives, 2 tablespoons parsley, black pepper, and artichoke hearts. Cook 3 minutes or until rice is tender and mixture is thoroughly heated. Garnish with additional chopped fresh parsley, if desired. Yield: 5 servings (serving size: about 2 cups).

CALORIES 350; **FAT** 8.9g (sat 1g, mono 5.1g, poly 0.9g); **PROTEIN** 10.8g; **CARB** 62g; **FIBER** 7.2g; **CHOL** 0mg; **IRON** 3.4mg; **SODIUM** 686mg; **CALC** 78mg

Tempeh and Green Bean Stir-Fry with Peanut Sauce

Tempeh is a high-protein soy product that originated in Indonesia; substitute extra-firm tofu, if desired.

Peanut sauce:
¼ cup water
1 tablespoon brown sugar
3 tablespoons natural-style, chunky peanut butter
1 teaspoon Sriracha (hot chile sauce)
1 teaspoon lower-sodium soy sauce

Stir-fry:
2 teaspoons brown sugar
5 teaspoons lower-sodium soy sauce
1 teaspoon Sriracha

4 garlic cloves, chopped
1 tablespoon plus 2 teaspoons sesame oil, divided
1 (8-ounce) package organic tempeh, cut into ⅓-inch strips
2 cups thinly sliced carrot
1 cup (2-inch) strips red bell pepper
1 pound green beans, trimmed
½ cup water
¾ cup thinly sliced green onions, divided
6 ounces mung bean sprouts

1. To prepare peanut sauce, combine first 5 ingredients in a medium bowl, stirring well with a whisk. Set aside.

2. To prepare stir-fry, combine 2 teaspoons sugar and next 3 ingredients (through garlic) in a small bowl, stirring with a whisk.

3. Heat a large heavy skillet over medium-high heat. Add 1 tablespoon sesame oil to pan, swirling to coat. Add tempeh and half of soy sauce mixture; stir-fry 5 minutes or until tempeh is golden brown. Remove tempeh mixture from pan; keep warm. Add remaining 2 teaspoons oil to pan, swirling to coat. Add carrot, bell pepper, and green beans to pan; stir-fry 3 minutes. Add ½ cup water; reduce heat to medium. Cover and simmer 5 minutes or until beans are crisp-tender. Stir in remaining half of soy sauce mixture, tempeh mixture, half of onions, and bean sprouts; cook 2 minutes or until sprouts are tender. Serve with peanut sauce and remaining half of onions. Yield: 4 servings (serving size: 2 cups tempeh mixture, 2 tablespoons peanut sauce, and 1½ tablespoons green onions).

CALORIES 357; **FAT** 18.3g (sat 2.9g, mono 7.1g, poly 6.7g); **PROTEIN** 18.4g; **CARB** 35.2g; **FIBER** 8.2g; **CHOL** 0mg; **IRON** 4mg; **SODIUM** 353mg; **CALC** 158mg

Lemon Chicken
Orzo Soup, page 283

soups & stews

African Ground Nut Stew with Sour Cream–Chive Topping

Peanuts are also called ground nuts to distinguish them from tree nuts. They're a staple in African cuisine. For more intense heat, use a full teaspoon of crushed red pepper. Garnish with chives, if desired.

1 cup fat-free sour cream
¼ cup minced fresh chives
2 teaspoons canola oil
1¼ cups thinly sliced yellow onion
¾ cup chopped red bell pepper
3 garlic cloves, minced
1 cup chopped unsalted, dry-roasted peanuts
½ teaspoon salt

½ to 1 teaspoon crushed red pepper
4 cups (1-inch) cubed peeled sweet potatoes (about 1½ pounds)
2½ cups quartered small red potatoes (about 1 pound)
2½ cups organic vegetable broth
1 (28-ounce) can no-salt-added diced tomatoes, undrained

1. Combine sour cream and chives in a small bowl; cover. Refrigerate 2 hours.
2. Heat canola oil in a Dutch oven over medium-high heat. Add sliced onion and bell pepper; sauté 3 minutes or until tender. Add garlic; sauté 30 seconds. Stir in peanuts, salt, and crushed red pepper; sauté 2 minutes. Add potatoes, vegetable broth, and tomatoes; bring to a boil. Cover, reduce heat, and simmer 1 hour and 10 minutes or until potatoes are tender. Place 1⅔ cups stew into each of 6 bowls; top each serving with about 2½ tablespoons sour cream mixture. Yield: 6 servings.

CALORIES 417; **FAT** 14g (sat 1.9g, mono 7g, poly 4.4g); **PROTEIN** 14.1g; **CARB** 62g; **FIBER** 10g; **CHOL** 6.7mg; **IRON** 2.5mg; **SODIUM** 565mg; **CALC** 180mg

Calabaza and Poblano Stew

Redolent of honey, cinnamon, and aniseed, this stew highlights mild but exotic flavors that are typically associated with European cuisine but also commonly used in Mexico. Calabaza is a pumpkin-like winter squash. If you prefer a smoother consistency, use a potato masher to break up the squash. Crema mexicana looks like and has a tang similar to that of sour cream but is thinner and richer, like heavy cream.

5 poblano chiles (about 1 pound)
1 teaspoon aniseed
1 (3-inch) cinnamon stick, broken
1 tablespoon peanut oil
3½ cups chopped onion
4 garlic cloves, minced
10 cups (2-inch) pieces peeled calabaza or butternut squash (about 3 pounds)

4 cups vegetable broth
2 cups water
3 tablespoons honey
½ teaspoon salt
6 tablespoons crema mexicana
½ cup roasted pumpkinseed kernels

1. Preheat broiler.

2. Cut poblano chiles in half; discard seeds and membranes. Place chile halves, skin sides up, on a foil-lined baking sheet; flatten with hand. Broil 5 minutes or until blackened. Place in a paper bag; fold to close tightly. Let stand 15 minutes. Peel chiles; discard skins. Chop chiles.

3. Place aniseed and cinnamon in a spice or coffee grinder; process until finely ground.

4. Heat oil in a large Dutch oven over medium-high heat. Add onion to pan; sauté 5 minutes or until browned. Add garlic; sauté 1 minute. Add cinnamon mixture to pan; sauté 1 minute. Add chopped chiles, squash, broth, 2 cups water, honey, and salt; bring to a boil. Reduce heat, and simmer 30 minutes or until squash is tender. Ladle stew into individual bowls.

5. Drizzle each serving with crema mexicana; sprinkle with pumpkinseeds. Yield: 8 servings (serving size: 1½ cups stew, about 2 teaspoons crema mexicana, and 1 tablespoon pumpkinseeds).

CALORIES 266; **FAT** 10.4g (sat 2.6g, mono 2.7g, poly 3.4g); **PROTEIN** 9g; **CARB** 40.7g; **FIBER** 8.4g; **CHOL** 8mg; **IRON** 4mg; **SODIUM** 669mg; **CALC** 118mg

Lentil-Barley Soup

2 teaspoons canola oil
1 cup sliced leek
3 cups organic vegetable broth
1 cup water
¾ cup beer
1 cup chopped carrot
1 cup chopped celery
½ cup chopped parsnip
¼ cup chopped fresh celery leaves
¼ cup chopped fresh dill
¼ cup uncooked pearl barley
½ teaspoon freshly ground black pepper
¼ teaspoon dried thyme
2 bay leaves
½ cup dried lentils
⅛ teaspoon salt

1. Heat oil in a Dutch oven over medium-high heat. Add leek to pan; sauté 2 minutes. Add broth, 1 cup water, and beer; bring to a boil. Add chopped carrot and next 8 ingredients (through bay leaves); return to a boil. Cover, reduce heat, and simmer 15 minutes. Stir in lentils; cover and cook 30 minutes. Discard bay leaves.

2. Place 1½ cups broth mixture in a blender. Remove center piece of blender lid (to allow steam to escape); secure blender lid on blender. Place a clean towel over opening in blender lid (to avoid splatters). Blend until smooth. Return pureed mixture to pan, and stir in salt. Return mixture to a boil; cover, reduce heat, and simmer 10 minutes or until thoroughly heated, stirring occasionally. Yield: 4 servings (serving size: about 1⅓ cups).

CALORIES 300; **FAT** 4.7g (sat 2.2g, mono 1.5g, poly 0.8g); **PROTEIN** 11.8g; **CARB** 53.6g; **FIBER** 15.7g; **CHOL** 0mg; **IRON** 6.6mg; **SODIUM** 593mg; **CALC** 63mg

> **FYI:** Consider doubling this soup, and refrigerate or freeze the leftovers. You'll be glad you did.

Ribollita (Italian Bread Soup)

3 cups (1-inch) cubed hearty Italian country
   bread (about 6 ounces)
Cooking spray
3 tablespoons extra-virgin olive oil, divided
1 cup chopped onion
1/4 cup chopped celery
1 tablespoon minced garlic
6 cups water, divided
6 cups (1-inch) chopped kale
6 cups chopped Savoy cabbage
4 cups chopped broccoli rabe (rapini)
2 cups (1-inch) cubed peeled Yukon gold or
   red potato

1 cup thinly sliced carrot
1 (14.5-ounce) can whole plum tomatoes,
   undrained and chopped
2 (15-ounce) cans cannellini beans or other
   white beans, rinsed, drained, and divided
3/4 teaspoon salt
1/2 teaspoon dried thyme
1/2 teaspoon dried oregano
1/4 teaspoon crushed red pepper
1/2 cup (2 ounces) shaved or grated
   Parmigiano-Reggiano cheese

1. Preheat oven to 375°.

2. Place 3 cups bread on a baking sheet, and lightly coat with cooking spray. Bake at 375° for 15 minutes or until toasted, stirring occasionally. Remove from oven; cool.

3. Heat 1 tablespoon olive oil in a large stockpot or Dutch oven over medium-high heat. Add onion and celery to pan; sauté 5 minutes. Add garlic, and sauté 1 minute. Add 5 cups water and next 6 ingredients (through tomatoes). Cover, reduce heat, and simmer 20 minutes or until greens are wilted, stirring occasionally. Mash 1 can of beans. Add mashed beans and remaining 1 cup water to pan; bring to a boil. Reduce heat, and simmer 35 minutes or until potato and carrot are tender.

4. Stir in bread, remaining can of beans, salt, thyme, oregano, and red pepper; bring to a boil. Reduce heat, and simmer 10 minutes. Remove from heat; cover and let stand 10 minutes. Ladle about 1½ cups soup into each of 8 bowls. Sprinkle each serving with 1 tablespoon cheese, and drizzle each with ¾ teaspoon oil. Yield: 8 servings.

CALORIES 305; FAT 8.7g (sat 2.8g, mono 4.3g, poly 1g); PROTEIN 11.7g; CARB 45.6g; FIBER 10.7g; CHOL 4.4mg; IRON 4.1mg; SODIUM 693mg; CALC 161mg

Garbanzo Beans and Greens

Substitute escarole or another hearty green, such as collards, if you don't like kale. Serve with torn baguette bread to soak up all the tasty juices.

2 center-cut bacon slices
1 cup chopped carrot
1/2 cup chopped onion
2 garlic cloves, minced
1 teaspoon paprika
1/4 teaspoon kosher salt
1/2 teaspoon ground cumin
1/2 teaspoon crushed red pepper

2 1/2 cups fat-free, lower-sodium chicken broth
1 cup water
2 (15-ounce) cans organic chickpeas (garbanzo beans), rinsed and drained
4 cups chopped kale
1/2 cup plain 2% reduced-fat Greek yogurt
4 lemon wedges (optional)

1. Cook bacon in a Dutch oven over medium heat until crisp. Remove bacon from pan using a slotted spoon. Add carrot and onion to drippings in pan, and cook 4 minutes, stirring occasionally. Add garlic, and cook 1 minute, stirring constantly. Add paprika, salt, cumin, and red pepper; cook 30 seconds, stirring constantly. Stir in chicken broth, 1 cup water, and beans; bring to a boil. Reduce heat, and simmer 20 minutes, stirring occasionally.
2. Add kale to bean mixture. Cover and simmer 10 minutes or until kale is tender, stirring occasionally. Ladle about 1¼ cups bean mixture into each of 4 bowls, and top each serving with 2 tablespoons yogurt. Top each with ½ slice bacon, and serve with lemon wedges, if desired. Yield: 4 servings.

CALORIES 216; **FAT** 4.2g (sat 0.9g, mono 0.2g, poly 0.1g); **PROTEIN** 15.1g; **CARB** 33.7g; **FIBER** 6g; **CHOL** 4mg; **IRON** 4mg; **SODIUM** 595mg; **CALC** 197mg

Curried Chickpea Stew with Brown Rice Pilaf

This curry hails from the Punjab region of India. The cardamom pods puff up to almost twice their size and float to the top, so they're easy to find and discard before serving. In just one serving, you get close to 10 grams of fiber, thanks to brown rice, chickpeas, tomatoes, and plenty of onion.

Pilaf:

1 tablespoon canola oil
1 cup finely chopped onion
1 cup uncooked brown rice
$\frac{1}{2}$ teaspoon ground turmeric
3 cardamom pods, crushed
1 (3-inch) cinnamon stick
1 garlic clove, minced
$1\frac{2}{3}$ cups water
1 bay leaf

Stew:

1 tablespoon canola oil
2 cups chopped onion
1 tablespoon grated peeled fresh ginger
1 teaspoon ground cumin
1 teaspoon ground coriander
$\frac{3}{4}$ teaspoon ground turmeric
$\frac{1}{4}$ teaspoon ground red pepper
4 garlic cloves, minced
3 cardamom pods, crushed
1 (3-inch) cinnamon stick
$2\frac{1}{2}$ cups water
1 cup diced carrot
$\frac{1}{4}$ teaspoon kosher salt
1 (15-ounce) can chickpeas (garbanzo beans), rinsed and drained
1 (14.5-ounce) can fire-roasted crushed tomatoes, undrained
$\frac{1}{2}$ cup plain fat-free yogurt
$\frac{1}{4}$ cup chopped fresh cilantro

1. To prepare pilaf, heat 1 tablespoon oil in a large nonstick skillet over medium heat. Add 1 cup onion; cook 6 minutes or until golden, stirring frequently. Add rice and next 4 ingredients (through 1 garlic clove); cook 1 minute, stirring constantly. Add 1⅔ cups water and bay leaf; bring to a boil. Cover, reduce heat, and simmer 45 minutes. Let stand 5 minutes. Discard cardamom, cinnamon, and bay leaf. Keep warm.

2. To prepare stew, heat 1 tablespoon oil in a large Dutch oven over medium-high heat. Add 2 cups onion; sauté 6 minutes or until golden. Add ginger and next 7 ingredients (through cinnamon stick); cook 1 minute, stirring constantly. Add 2½ cups water, carrot, salt, chickpeas, and tomatoes; bring to a boil. Cover, reduce heat, and simmer 20 minutes or until carrot is tender and sauce is slightly thick. Discard cardamom and cinnamon stick.

3. Place 1 cup pilaf in each of 4 bowls; spoon 1¼ cups stew over rice. Top each serving with 2 tablespoons yogurt and 1 tablespoon cilantro. Yield: 4 servings.

CALORIES 431; **FAT** 9.6g (sat 1g, mono 5.1g, poly 2.9g); **PROTEIN** 11.9g; **CARB** 77.9g; **FIBER** 9.6g; **CHOL** 1mg; **IRON** 3.1mg; **SODIUM** 626mg; **CALC** 121mg

Three-Bean Chili with Vegetables

Chipotle chiles add a subtle smokiness and a touch of spicy heat. Cook this hearty, kid-friendly dish up to two days ahead. Thin it with a little water when reheating, if necessary.

1½ tablespoons canola oil
2 cups chopped onion
⅔ cup chopped carrot
4 garlic cloves, minced
4 cups water
2 cups frozen whole-kernel corn
1 cup chopped red bell pepper (about 1 large)
1 cup chopped zucchini
2 tablespoons chili powder
2 teaspoons dried oregano
2 teaspoons ground cumin
¾ teaspoon salt
2 (28-ounce) cans crushed tomatoes
2 (16-ounce) cans pinto beans, rinsed and drained

2 (16-ounce) cans kidney beans, rinsed and drained
2 (15-ounce) cans black beans, rinsed and drained
1 (6-ounce) can no-salt-added tomato paste
1½ tablespoons rice vinegar
1½ teaspoons to 1 tablespoon finely chopped chipotle chile, canned in adobo sauce
1 cup reduced-fat sour cream
1 cup (4 ounces) shredded reduced-fat cheddar cheese
1 cup chopped fresh cilantro

1. Heat oil in a large stockpot over medium-high heat. Add onion, carrot, and garlic; sauté 5 minutes. Stir in 4 cups water and next 12 ingredients (through tomato paste); bring to a boil. Cover, reduce heat, and simmer about 25 minutes or until carrot is tender, stirring occasionally. Stir in vinegar and chipotle. Top each serving with sour cream, cheese, and cilantro. Yield: 16 servings (serving size: 1¼ cups chili, 1 tablespoon sour cream, 1 tablespoon cheese, and 1 tablespoon cilantro).

CALORIES 211; FAT 6.1g (sat 2.4g, mono 1.5g, poly 0.9g); PROTEIN 10.3g; CARB 34.6g; FIBER 8.8g; CHOL 11mg; IRON 3.5mg; SODIUM 708mg; CALC 159mg

Quick Vegetarian Chili with Avocado Salsa

Quick-cooking barley provides a convenient way to get more whole grains in your diet. It also makes a nice textural contrast to the beans.

2 teaspoons canola oil
1 cup chopped onion
1 cup chopped red bell pepper
2 teaspoons chili powder
1 teaspoon ground cumin
1 teaspoon dried oregano
3 garlic cloves, minced
1 (4.5-ounce) can chopped green chiles
²/₃ cup uncooked quick-cooking barley
¼ cup water

1 (15-ounce) can black beans, drained
1 (14.5-ounce) can no-salt-added diced
  tomatoes, undrained
1 (14.5-ounce) can vegetable broth
3 tablespoons chopped fresh cilantro
6 tablespoons reduced-fat sour cream
6 lime wedges
18 baked tortilla chips
Avocado Salsa

1. Heat canola oil in a Dutch oven over medium-high heat. Add onion and bell pepper, and sauté 3 minutes. Add chili powder, cumin, oregano, garlic, and green chiles; cook 1 minute. Stir in barley, ¼ cup water, black beans, tomatoes, and broth; bring to a boil. Cover, reduce heat, and simmer 20 minutes or until barley is tender. Stir in cilantro. Serve with sour cream, lime wedges, tortilla chips, and Avocado Salsa. Yield: 6 servings (serving size: 1 cup chili, 1 tablespoon sour cream, 1 lime wedge, 3 tortilla chips, and about 2½ tablespoons Avocado Salsa).

CALORIES 274; **FAT** 6.7g (sat 1.7g, mono 2.9g, poly 1.2g); **PROTEIN** 9g; **CARB** 46.8g; **FIBER** 9.1g; **CHOL** 8mg; **IRON** 2mg; **SODIUM** 734mg; **CALC** 108mg

Avocado Salsa:

½ cup finely chopped peeled avocado
⅓ cup chopped seeded tomato
2 tablespoons finely chopped onion
1 tablespoon finely chopped seeded jalapeño
  pepper

1 tablespoon chopped fresh cilantro
1 tablespoon fresh lime juice
⅛ teaspoon salt

1. Combine all ingredients; toss. Serve immediately. Yield: 1 cup (serving size: about 2½ tablespoons).

CALORIES 59; **FAT** 5.2g (sat 0.8g, mono 3.2g, poly 0.7g); **PROTEIN** 0.8g; **CARB** 3.7g; **FIBER** 1.9g; **CHOL** 0mg; **IRON** 0.5mg; **SODIUM** 54mg; **CALC** 6mg

Chunky Vegetarian Chili

This quick and easy soup is not too spicy, which makes it a good choice to pack in a thermos.

1 tablespoon canola oil
2 cups chopped onion
1/2 cup chopped yellow bell pepper
1/2 cup chopped green bell pepper
2 garlic cloves, minced
1 tablespoon brown sugar
1 1/2 tablespoons chili powder
1 teaspoon ground cumin
1 teaspoon dried oregano
1/2 teaspoon salt

1/2 teaspoon freshly ground black pepper
2 (16-ounce) cans stewed tomatoes, undrained
2 (15-ounce) cans black beans, rinsed and drained
1 (15-ounce) can kidney beans, rinsed and drained
1 (15-ounce) can pinto beans, rinsed and drained

1. Heat oil in a Dutch oven over medium-high heat. Add onion, bell peppers, and garlic; sauté 5 minutes or until tender. Add sugar and remaining ingredients, and bring to a boil. Reduce heat; simmer 30 minutes. Yield: 8 servings (serving size: 1 cup).

CALORIES 248; **FAT** 2.3g (sat 0.2g, mono 1.1g, poly 0.5g); **PROTEIN** 12.3g; **CARB** 42.7g; **FIBER** 12.1g; **CHOL** 0mg; **IRON** 4.4mg; **SODIUM** 695mg; **CALC** 130mg

Mushroom Stew with Spaetzle

Spaetzle are small German noodles or dumplings. Here, we pair them with a thick gravy made with three types of mushrooms.

⅓ cup dried porcini mushrooms (about
  ⅜ ounce)
4.5 ounces all-purpose flour (about 1 cup)
¼ teaspoon salt
3 tablespoons 1% low-fat milk
2 large eggs
2 quarts water
½ cup boiling water
1 tablespoon canola oil
1½ cups chopped onion
2 garlic cloves, minced
7 cups (½-inch) sliced cremini mushrooms
  (about 14 ounces)

10 ounces button mushrooms, halved
2 tablespoons all-purpose flour
1 tablespoon paprika
¼ cup red wine
1½ cups organic vegetable broth
½ cup chopped fresh flat-leaf parsley,
  divided
2 teaspoons balsamic vinegar
¼ teaspoon salt
¼ teaspoon freshly ground black pepper

1. Combine porcini mushrooms and ½ cup boiling water in a small bowl; cover and let stand 30 minutes. Drain mushroom mixture in a colander over a bowl, reserving ¼ cup liquid. Rinse and chop mushrooms.

2. Weigh or lightly spoon 4.5 ounces (about 1 cup) flour into a dry measuring cup, and level with a knife. Sift together flour and ¼ teaspoon salt. Combine milk and eggs in a medium bowl; stir with a whisk. Add flour mixture to egg mixture, stirring until well combined. Let stand 10 minutes.

3. Bring 2 quarts water to a boil in a large saucepan. Hold a colander with large holes (about ¼ inch in diameter) over boiling water; spoon about ½ cup dough into colander. Press dough through holes with a rubber spatula (droplets will form spaetzle), and set colander aside. Cook 3 minutes or until done (spaetzle will rise to the surface). Remove with a slotted spoon; drain in a strainer (spaetzle will stick to a paper towel). Repeat procedure with remaining dough.

4. Heat oil in a Dutch oven over medium-high heat. Add onion and garlic to pan; sauté 2 minutes. Add reserved porcini mushrooms, cremini mushrooms, and button mushrooms to pan; sauté 15 minutes or until moisture almost evaporates. Stir in 2 tablespoons flour and paprika. Add wine to pan; cook 1 minute or until liquid is absorbed. Stir in reserved mushroom liquid and broth; bring to a boil. Reduce heat, and simmer 15 minutes, stirring occasionally. Add ¼ cup parsley, vinegar, ¼ teaspoon salt, and pepper to pan; cook 1 minute. Add spaetzle to pan; cook 2 minutes or until thoroughly heated. Garnish with remaining ¼ cup parsley. Yield: 4 servings (serving size: about 1½ cups stew and 1 tablespoon parsley).

CALORIES 300; FAT 7g (sat 1.2g, mono 3.3g, poly 1.5g); PROTEIN 12.8g; CARB 45.7g; FIBER 5.1g; CHOL 106mg; IRON 4.3mg; SODIUM 571mg; CALC 76mg

Creamy Root Vegetable Stew with Gruyère Crostini

1 tablespoon olive oil
1 cup chopped onion
3 tablespoons chopped garlic
1 tablespoon chopped fresh rosemary, divided
2½ cups (¾-inch) diced peeled Yukon gold potato (about 1 pound)
2¼ cups (¾-inch) diced peeled rutabaga (about ¾ pound)
2 cups (¾-inch) diced peeled turnip
1¼ cups (¾-inch) diced peeled parsnip (about ½ pound)

2 cups organic vegetable broth
2 cups water
2 tablespoons heavy whipping cream
½ teaspoon freshly ground black pepper
¼ teaspoon salt
8 (⅛-inch) slices diagonally cut French bread baguette
½ cup shredded Gruyère cheese

1. Heat olive oil in a Dutch oven over medium heat. Add onion to pan; cook 5 minutes or until tender, stirring occasionally. Add garlic and 2 teaspoons rosemary; cook 1 minute, stirring occasionally. Stir in potato and next 5 ingredients (through 2 cups water). Bring to a simmer; cook, covered, 20 minutes or until vegetables are tender.

2. Place 3 cups vegetable mixture in a blender. Remove center piece of blender lid (to allow steam to escape); secure blender lid on blender. Place a clean towel over opening in blender lid (to avoid splatters). Blend until smooth. Return pureed mixture to pan. Stir in cream, pepper, and salt.

3. Preheat broiler.

4. Arrange bread slices on a baking sheet. Sprinkle each bread slice with 1 tablespoon shredded cheese, and top evenly with remaining 1 teaspoon rosemary. Broil 1 minute or until cheese melts. Yield: 4 servings (serving size: 2 cups stew and 2 crostini).

CALORIES 383; **FAT** 12.8g (sat 5.2g, mono 5.2g, poly 1.7g); **PROTEIN** 11g; **CARB** 57.7g; **FIBER** 7.5g; **CHOL** 26mg; **IRON** 2.5mg; **SODIUM** 639mg; **CALC** 246mg

Baked Potato Soup

A simple white sauce of flour and reduced-fat milk is the base for this super creamy soup. To save time, bake the potatoes, shred the cheese, chop the onions, and cook the bacon in advance.

4 baking potatoes (about 2½ pounds)
3 ounces all-purpose flour (about ⅔ cup)
6 cups 2% reduced-fat milk
1 cup (4 ounces) shredded reduced-fat
   extra-sharp cheddar cheese, divided
1 teaspoon salt

½ teaspoon freshly ground black pepper
1 cup reduced-fat sour cream
¾ cup chopped green onions
6 bacon slices, cooked and crumbled
Cracked black pepper (optional)

1. Preheat oven to 400°.

2. Pierce potatoes with a fork; bake at 400° for 1 hour or until tender. Cool. Peel potatoes; coarsely mash.

3. Weigh or lightly spoon flour into a dry measuring cup; level with a knife. Place flour in a Dutch oven, and gradually add milk, stirring with a whisk until blended. Cook over medium heat until thick and bubbly (about 8 minutes). Add mashed potatoes, ¾ cup cheese, salt, and ½ teaspoon black pepper, stirring until cheese melts. Remove from heat.

4. Stir in sour cream. Cook over low heat 10 minutes or until thoroughly heated (do not let mixture boil). Ladle 1½ cups soup into each of 8 bowls. Sprinkle each serving with 1½ teaspoons cheese, 1½ tablespoons onions, and about 1 tablespoon bacon. Garnish with cracked pepper, if desired. Yield: 8 servings.

CALORIES 329; FAT 10.8g (sat 5.9g, mono 3.5g, poly 0.7g); PROTEIN 13.6g; CARB 44.5g; FIBER 2.8g; CHOL 38mg; IRON 1.1mg; SODIUM 587mg; CALC 407mg

Curried Potatoes and Squash

Substitute vegetable broth for the chicken broth, if you prefer a vegetarian dish. Serve with warm flatbread to soak up the flavorful juices.

2 tablespoons butter
1 cup chopped onion
1¹/₂ tablespoons grated peeled fresh ginger
4 garlic cloves, minced
3 cups (¹/₂-inch) cubed peeled baking potato (about 1¹/₂ pounds)
3 cups (¹/₂-inch) cubed peeled butternut squash (about 1¹/₄ pounds)
¹/₂ teaspoon salt
¹/₂ teaspoon ground cumin
¹/₂ teaspoon ground red pepper
1 (14.5-ounce) can whole tomatoes, undrained and chopped
1 (14-ounce) can fat-free, lower-sodium chicken broth
³/₄ cup light coconut milk
1 cup frozen green peas, thawed
¹/₂ cup thinly diagonally sliced green onions (about 4 medium)

1. Melt butter in a large skillet over medium-high heat. Add onion to pan, and cook 4 minutes, stirring occasionally. Add ginger and garlic; sauté 1 minute. Add potato and next 4 ingredients (through pepper); sauté 1 minute. Stir in tomatoes and broth; bring to a boil. Cover and cook 5 minutes.
2. Stir in coconut milk and peas; bring to a simmer. Cook, uncovered, 12 minutes or until squash is tender, stirring occasionally. Sprinkle with green onions. Yield: 4 servings (serving size: 1¾ cups).

CALORIES 356; **FAT** 8.8g (sat 5.9g, mono 1.6g, poly 0.5g); **PROTEIN** 10.5g; **CARB** 66g; **FIBER** 9.3g; **CHOL** 15mg; **IRON** 4.9mg; **SODIUM** 668mg; **CALC** 166mg

Butternut Squash–Leek Soup

Butternut squash is one of the most beloved vegetables of the fall harvest. This simple soup really lets the flavor of the squash shine through.

1 whole garlic head
4 teaspoons olive oil
6 cups thinly sliced leek (about 4 large)
4 cups (³/₄-inch) cubed peeled butternut
   squash (about 1 medium)

2 cups water
2 cups fat-free, lower-sodium chicken broth
½ teaspoon salt
½ teaspoon freshly ground black pepper

1. Preheat oven to 350°.

2. Remove white papery skin from garlic head (do not peel or separate cloves). Wrap head in foil. Bake at 350° for 1 hour; cool 10 minutes. Separate cloves; squeeze to extract garlic pulp. Discard skins.

3. Heat oil in a large saucepan over medium-high heat. Add leek; sauté 5 minutes or until tender. Stir in garlic, squash, 2 cups water, broth, salt, and black pepper; bring to a boil. Reduce heat, and simmer 10 minutes or until squash is tender. Place half of squash mixture in a blender. Remove center piece of blender lid (to allow steam to escape); secure blender lid on blender. Place a clean towel over opening in blender lid (to avoid splatters). Blend until smooth. Pour pureed soup into a bowl. Repeat procedure with remaining squash mixture. Yield: 6 servings (serving size: about 1 cup).

CALORIES 167; FAT 3.5g (sat 0.5g, mono 2.2g, poly 0.6g); PROTEIN 4.1g; CARB 33.5g; FIBER 5.3g; CHOL 0mg; IRON 3.3mg; SODIUM 351mg; CALC 144mg

> **BUYING TIP:** Look for precut butternut squash in the produce section of your grocery store. Not all stores have it, but if yours does, it is definitely a worthy timesaver.

French Onion and Apple Soup

Add a green salad to complete the meal.

3 tablespoons unsalted butter
15 cups sliced yellow onion (about 4 pounds)
3/4 teaspoon freshly ground black pepper
1 Honeycrisp or Pink Lady apple, peeled, quartered, and cut into julienne strips
3 thyme sprigs
2 bay leaves
1/2 cup Madeira wine or dry sherry

6 cups lower-sodium beef broth
1/2 cup apple cider
1 tablespoon sherry vinegar
10 (1/2-ounce) slices sourdough bread, cut into 1-inch cubes
2 cups (8 ounces) grated Gruyère or Swiss cheese
Fresh thyme leaves (optional)

1. Melt butter in a Dutch oven over medium heat. Add sliced onion to pan, and cook 5 minutes, stirring frequently. Continue cooking 50 minutes or until deep golden brown, stirring occasionally. Add pepper, apple, thyme sprigs, and bay leaves; cook 3 minutes or until apple softens. Add wine; cook 2 minutes, scraping pan to loosen browned bits. Add beef broth and cider; bring to a boil. Reduce heat, and simmer 45 minutes. Discard bay leaves; stir in vinegar.
2. Preheat broiler.
3. Arrange bread cubes in a single layer on a jelly-roll pan, and broil 2 minutes or until toasted, turning after 1 minute.
4. Preheat oven to 500°.
5. Ladle 1 cup of the soup into each of 10 ovenproof soup bowls. Divide croutons evenly among bowls; top each serving with about 3 tablespoons cheese. Place bowls on jelly-roll pan. Bake at 500° for 8 minutes or until cheese melts. Garnish with thyme leaves, if desired. Yield: 10 servings.

CALORIES 254; FAT 11g (sat 6.4g, mono 3.1g, poly 0.7g); PROTEIN 11.1g; CARB 29.2g; FIBER 4.1g; CHOL 33mg; IRON 1.1mg; SODIUM 426mg; CALC 278mg

Summer Squash and Corn Chowder

Enjoy soup in the summertime when you make this satisfying chowder with the season's produce. Top with cheese and bacon for kid appeal.

2 applewood-smoked bacon slices
¾ cup sliced green onions, divided
¼ cup chopped celery
1 pound yellow summer squash, chopped
1 pound frozen white and yellow baby corn
   kernels, thawed and divided
2¼ cups 1% low-fat milk, divided

1 teaspoon chopped fresh thyme
½ teaspoon salt
¼ teaspoon freshly ground black pepper
⅛ teaspoon salt
¼ cup (1 ounce) shredded extra-sharp
   cheddar cheese

1. Cook bacon in a large Dutch oven over medium-high heat until crisp. Remove bacon from pan, reserving 2 teaspoons drippings in pan. Crumble bacon, and set aside. Add ½ cup onions, celery, and squash to drippings in pan; sauté 8 minutes or until vegetables are tender.
2. Reserve 1 cup corn; set aside. Place remaining corn and 1 cup milk in a blender; process until smooth. Add remaining 1¼ cups milk, thyme, ½ teaspoon salt, and pepper to blender; process just until combined. Add pureed mixture and reserved 1 cup corn to pan. Reduce heat to medium; cook 5 minutes or until thoroughly heated, stirring constantly. Stir in ⅛ teaspoon salt. Ladle about 1½ cups soup into each of 4 bowls; top each serving with about 1 tablespoon bacon, 1 tablespoon remaining onions, and 1 tablespoon cheese. Yield: 4 servings.

CALORIES 285; **FAT** 9.4g (sat 3.9g, mono 3.4g, poly 1.2g); **PROTEIN** 13.3g; **CARB** 37.8g; **FIBER** 5.4g; **CHOL** 20mg; **IRON** 1.3mg; **SODIUM** 605mg; **CALC** 260mg

Saffron Fish Stew with White Beans

Be sure to choose a sustainable fish, such as wild-caught Pacific flounder or wild-caught Alaskan halibut.

1 tablespoon extra-virgin olive oil
1 cup prechopped onion
1 teaspoon ground fennel
½ teaspoon ground coriander
2 garlic cloves, crushed
1 thyme sprig
½ teaspoon grated orange rind
¼ teaspoon saffron threads, crushed
1½ cups water

1½ cups clam juice
1 (14.5-ounce) can diced tomatoes, undrained
¼ teaspoon salt
1 (1-pound) flounder fillet, cut into (2-inch) pieces
1 (14-ounce) can Great Northern beans, rinsed and drained
Fresh thyme leaves

1. Heat olive oil in a large Dutch oven over medium-high heat. Add onion, fennel, coriander, garlic, and thyme sprig; sauté 5 minutes. Stir in rind and saffron; add 1½ cups water, clam juice, and tomatoes. Bring to a boil; reduce heat, and simmer 5 minutes. Stir in salt, fish, and beans; cook 5 minutes. Top with thyme leaves. Yield: 4 servings (serving size: 2 cups).

CALORIES 249; **FAT** 5.1g (sat 0.9g, mono 2.8g, poly 0.9g); **PROTEIN** 27.9g; **CARB** 23g; **FIBER** 5.7g; **CHOL** 57mg; **IRON** 2.2mg; **SODIUM** 569mg; **CALC** 101mg

FLAVOR HITS: Fragrant Middle Eastern spices imbue this simple weeknight meal with exotic flavor. Fennel has a light licorice taste. Coriander's heady spice underscores the dish.

Classic Bouillabaisse with Rouille-Topped Croutons

We use red snapper in this dish, but cod, haddock, halibut, or other fresh white fish fillets will work. Rouille (roo-EE) is traditionally spicy; add 1/4 teaspoon ground red pepper, if you like.

Rouille:
2/3 cup chopped bottled roasted red bell peppers
3 tablespoons reduced-fat mayonnaise

Croutons:
4 ounces sourdough bread baguette, cut diagonally into 6 slices
1 garlic clove, halved

Bouillabaisse:
1 tablespoon olive oil
1 cup chopped onion (about 1 medium)
2 garlic cloves, minced
3/4 cup chopped plum tomato (about 2)

1/2 teaspoon saffron threads, lightly crushed
3 1/2 cups (3/4-inch) cubed red potato (about 1 pound)
2 1/2 cups thinly sliced fennel bulb (about 8 ounces)
3 cups clam juice
1 (14-ounce) can lower-sodium chicken broth
24 littleneck clams
24 mussels, scrubbed and debearded
12 ounces large shrimp, peeled and deveined
1 (1-pound) red snapper fillet, cut into 12 (2-inch) pieces
6 tablespoons chopped fresh parsley

1. Preheat oven to 400°.

2. To prepare rouille, place bell pepper and mayonnaise in a blender or food processor, and process until smooth.

3. To prepare croutons, arrange baguette slices in a single layer on a baking sheet; bake slices at 400° for 8 minutes or until toasted. Rub one side of each crouton with cut side of garlic clove halves; discard garlic clove halves.

4. To prepare bouillabaisse, heat oil in a large Dutch oven over medium heat. Add onion and garlic to pan; cook 8 minutes or until tender. Add tomato; cook 3 minutes. Add saffron; cook 30 seconds. Add potato, fennel, clam juice, and broth; bring to a boil. Cover, reduce heat, and simmer 10 minutes or until potato is almost done. Increase heat to medium. Add clams; cover and simmer 5 minutes. Add mussels; cover and simmer 3 minutes. Add shrimp and fish; cover and simmer 5 minutes or until shells open, shrimp is done, and fish flakes easily when tested with a fork or until desired degree of doneness. Discard any unopened shells.

5. Ladle 2 cups seafood mixture into each of 6 shallow bowls. Spread each crouton with about 1 tablespoon rouille. Place 1 crouton on top of each serving; sprinkle each serving with 1 tablespoon parsley. Yield: 6 servings.

CALORIES 403; **FAT** 10.7g (sat 1.7g, mono 2.9g, poly 2.5g); **PROTEIN** 43.6g; **CARB** 33.2g; **FIBER** 4.9g; **CHOL** 149mg; **IRON** 11.1mg; **SODIUM** 762mg; **CALC** 146mg

Southwest Shrimp and Corn Chowder

Even though we've taken some shortcuts with frozen potatoes and canned corn, this soup has full flavor and richness and can be prepared in less than 30 minutes.

2 tablespoons butter

1 cup chopped green onions

1/2 cup chopped red bell pepper

2 tablespoons finely chopped serrano chile (about 1 small)

1 (4.5-ounce) can chopped green chiles, undrained

3 tablespoons all-purpose flour

1 1/2 cups 2% reduced-fat milk

1 1/2 cups fat-free, lower-sodium chicken broth

1 1/2 cups frozen Southern-style hash brown potatoes, thawed, diced

1/2 teaspoon salt

1/2 teaspoon ground cumin

1 (15.25-ounce) can whole-kernel corn with sweet peppers, drained

1 pound peeled and deveined small shrimp

2 tablespoons chopped fresh cilantro

1. Melt butter in a large Dutch oven over medium-high heat. Add onions, bell pepper, and serrano chile to pan; cook 2 minutes or until tender, stirring frequently. Add canned chiles to pan; cook 1 minute. Add flour to pan; cook 1 minute, stirring constantly. Stir in milk and next 5 ingredients (through corn); bring to a boil. Cook 5 minutes or until slightly thick. Stir in shrimp; cook 1 minute or until shrimp are done. Remove from heat; stir in cilantro. Yield: 6 servings (serving size: about 1 cup).

CALORIES 212; FAT 6.7g (sat 3.4g, mono 1.5g, poly 0.7g); PROTEIN 19.3g; CARB 18.3g; FIBER 2.2g; CHOL 130mg; IRON 2.5mg; SODIUM 702mg; CALC 131mg

Spicy Tortilla Soup with Shrimp and Avocado

Chipotle chile and fire-roasted tomatoes lend a smoky flavor to the soup.

1 tablespoon olive oil
1 cup prechopped onion
⅓ cup prechopped celery
⅓ cup chopped carrot
1 tablespoon minced chipotle chile, canned in adobo sauce
1 teaspoon ground cumin
1 teaspoon chili powder
2 teaspoons minced garlic
4 cups fat-free, lower-sodium chicken broth
1 (15-ounce) can white hominy, rinsed and drained

1 (15-ounce) can no-salt-added fire-roasted diced tomatoes, undrained
12 ounces peeled and deveined medium shrimp
1 tablespoon fresh lime juice
⅛ teaspoon salt
½ cup lightly crushed baked tortilla chips (about 1 ounce)
1 cup diced peeled avocado (about ½ pound)
2 tablespoons fresh cilantro leaves (optional)

1. Heat oil in a Dutch oven over medium-high heat. Add onion and next 6 ingredients (through garlic); cook 6 minutes or until carrot is crisp-tender, stirring occasionally. Add broth, hominy, and tomatoes; bring to a boil. Cover and cook 6 minutes, stirring occasionally. Add shrimp; cook 2 minutes or until shrimp are done.

2. Remove from heat; stir in juice and salt. Ladle shrimp mixture into each of 4 bowls; top with chips and avocado. Garnish with cilantro, if desired. Yield: 4 servings (serving size: about 1¾ cups soup, 2 tablespoons chips, and ¼ cup avocado).

CALORIES 357; FAT 13.9g (sat 2.3g, mono 7.6g, poly 2.5g); PROTEIN 25.9g; CARB 32.7g; FIBER 7g; CHOL 130mg; IRON 3.7mg; SODIUM 570mg; CALC 97mg

Shrimp and Okra Gumbo

Thanks to savory spices and a quick-cooking roux, this gumbo saves you time (and calories) while keeping the rich flavor. Server over grits, if desired.

2 tablespoons canola oil, divided
3 tablespoons all-purpose flour
10 tablespoons fat-free, lower-sodium chicken broth
1 cup chopped onion
4 ounces smoked ham, chopped
1 cup chopped green bell pepper
2/3 cup diced celery
1/2 teaspoon dried thyme
3 garlic cloves, minced
1/2 pound fresh okra pods, sliced

1/4 cup water
1/2 teaspoon ground red pepper
1/2 teaspoon paprika
1/2 teaspoon freshly ground black pepper
1/4 teaspoon salt
1/4 teaspoon ground allspice
1 (28-ounce) can no-salt-added diced tomatoes, drained
3/4 pound peeled and deveined large shrimp
2 tablespoons chopped fresh flat-leaf parsley

1. Heat 1 tablespoon oil in a large saucepan over medium-high heat. Add flour; cook 1 minute or until lightly browned, stirring constantly with a whisk. Add broth; stir with a whisk until thick. Pour into a bowl; set aside. Wipe pan clean with paper towels.

2. Heat remaining 1 tablespoon oil in pan over medium heat. Add onion and ham; cook 10 minutes, stirring occasionally. Add bell pepper and next 4 ingredients (through okra); cook 5 minutes or until vegetables are almost tender, stirring occasionally. Add broth mixture, 1/4 cup water, and next 6 ingredients (through tomatoes). Bring to a boil; reduce heat, and simmer 10 minutes or until vegetables are tender. Stir in shrimp; cook 4 minutes or until shrimp are done. Sprinkle with parsley. Yield: 4 servings (serving size: 1½ cups gumbo and 1½ teaspoons parsley).

CALORIES 298; FAT 10.5g (sat 1.4g, mono 5g, poly 2.9g); PROTEIN 26.6g; CARB 26.1g; FIBER 7.1g; CHOL 143mg; IRON 4mg; SODIUM 755mg; CALC 160mg

Bacon-Corn Chowder with Shrimp

This soup can also serve six as a first course instead of an entrée.

6 center-cut bacon slices, chopped

1 cup prechopped onion

½ cup prechopped celery

1 teaspoon chopped fresh thyme

1 garlic clove, minced

4 cups fresh or frozen corn kernels, thawed

2 cups fat-free, lower-sodium chicken broth

¾ pound peeled and deveined medium shrimp

⅓ cup half-and-half

¼ teaspoon freshly ground black pepper

⅛ teaspoon salt

1. Heat a large Dutch oven over medium-high heat. Add bacon to pan; sauté 4 minutes or until bacon begins to brown. Remove one-third of bacon. Drain on paper towels. Add onion and next 3 ingredients (through minced garlic) to pan, and sauté 2 minutes. Add corn, and cook 2 minutes, stirring occasionally. Add broth; bring to a boil, and cook 4 minutes.

2. Place 2 cups corn mixture in a blender. Remove center piece of blender lid (to allow steam to escape), and secure lid on blender. Place a clean towel over opening in blender lid (to avoid splatters). Blend until smooth. Return pureed corn mixture to pan. Stir in shrimp; cook 2 minutes or until shrimp are done. Stir in half-and-half, pepper, and salt. Crumble reserved bacon over soup. Yield: 4 servings (serving size: about 1⅔ cups).

CALORIES 294; **FAT** 7g (sat 2.7g, mono 1.3g, poly 1.2g); **PROTEIN** 26.8g; **CARB** 34.8g; **FIBER** 4.3g; **CHOL** 14mg; **IRON** 3.1mg; **SODIUM** 547mg; **CALC** 94mg

Clam Chowder

Add oyster crackers and a romaine and tomato salad for an easy weeknight dinner.

1½ cups chopped onion, divided
½ cup unoaked chardonnay
3½ pounds littleneck clams
1 (8-ounce) bottle clam juice
1 bay leaf
1 tablespoon butter
1 bacon slice, chopped
3 cups diced red potato

½ cup chopped celery
⅛ teaspoon ground red pepper
3 tablespoons all-purpose flour
⅓ cup water
¾ cup half-and-half
¾ cup 2% reduced-fat milk
2 tablespoons chopped fresh chives
1 teaspoon chopped fresh thyme

1. Combine ½ cup onion, wine, and next 3 ingredients (through bay leaf) in a Dutch oven over medium-high heat; bring to a boil. Cover and cook 2 minutes or until clams open; discard any unopened shells. Strain through a cheesecloth-lined sieve over a bowl, reserving cooking liquid and clams. Remove meat from clams; chop. Discard shells.
2. Wipe pan clean. Melt butter in pan. Add bacon; sauté 3 minutes. Stir in remaining 1 cup onion, potato, celery, and red pepper; sauté 4 minutes. Stir in flour; cook 1 minute. Stir in reserved cooking liquid and ⅓ cup water; bring to a boil. Cover and reduce heat; simmer 30 minutes, stirring occasionally. Stir in clams, half-and-half, and milk; cook 1 minute or until heated. Stir in chives and thyme. Yield: 4 servings (serving size: 1¼ cups).

CALORIES 337; **FAT** 11.1g (sat 6.1g, mono 1.4g, poly 2.1g); **PROTEIN** 24.3g; **CARB** 34.9g; **FIBER** 3.1g; **CHOL** 78mg; **IRON** 20.6mg; **SODIUM** 310mg; **CALC** 204mg

Meatball Soup

In Mexico, albóndigas (meatballs) are sometimes made using rice as the binding agent, as they are here. Other times, the rice is in the soup.

2 teaspoons coriander seeds
1½ teaspoons cumin seeds
4 whole cloves
1 (3-inch) cinnamon stick, broken
½ cup uncooked long-grain white rice
2 tablespoons grated fresh onion
¾ teaspoon salt, divided
1 pound ground round
1 large egg white
1 garlic clove, minced
Cooking spray
3 cups chopped green cabbage

2 cups chopped onion
1 cup sliced carrot
½ cup chopped celery
1 tablespoon chili powder
1½ tablespoons drained chopped chipotle chile, canned in adobo sauce
2 (14-ounce) cans fat-free, lower-sodium chicken broth
1 (14.5-ounce) can fire-roasted whole tomatoes, undrained and chopped
1½ cups cubed peeled baking potato

1. Cook coriander seeds and cumin seeds in a large Dutch oven over medium heat 1 minute or until toasted and fragrant. Place toasted seeds, cloves, and cinnamon in a spice or coffee grinder; process until finely ground.

2. Combine 2 teaspoons cinnamon mixture, rice, grated onion, ½ teaspoon salt, beef, egg white, and garlic in a large bowl; set remaining cinnamon mixture aside. Shape beef mixture into 24 (1-inch) meatballs.

3. Heat pan over medium heat. Coat pan with cooking spray. Add cabbage, chopped onion, carrot, and celery to pan; cook 8 minutes, stirring frequently. Add remaining cinnamon mixture, chili powder, and chipotle; cook 1 minute, stirring constantly. Stir in remaining ¼ teaspoon salt, broth, and tomatoes; bring to a boil. Reduce heat to simmer. Add meatballs; cover and cook 15 minutes. Add potato; cook, uncovered, over medium heat 20 minutes or until potato is tender. Yield: 6 servings (serving size: 1⅔ cups).

CALORIES 330; FAT 12.4g (sat 4.6g, mono 5.2g, poly 0.6g); PROTEIN 20.6g; CARB 34.5g; FIBER 4.9g; CHOL 51mg; IRON 4mg; SODIUM 780mg; CALC 97mg

Green Chile Chili

Serve this tangy chili with corn bread or corn muffins.

1 tablespoon canola oil
12 ounces ground sirloin
1½ cups chopped onion
1 tablespoon chili powder
1 teaspoon hot paprika
5 garlic cloves, minced
1 (12-ounce) bottle dark beer
½ cup salsa verde

1 (4-ounce) can diced green chiles, undrained
1 (15-ounce) can no-salt-added tomatoes,
  undrained and crushed
1 (15-ounce) can organic kidney beans,
  rinsed and drained
¼ cup (1 ounce) shredded sharp cheddar
  cheese
1 green onion, sliced

1. Heat oil in a large Dutch oven over medium-high heat. Add beef; cook 5 minutes or until no longer pink, stirring to crumble. Add chopped onion, chili powder, and paprika; cook 4 minutes, stirring occasionally. Add garlic; sauté 1 minute.

2. Stir in beer; bring to a boil. Cook 15 minutes or until liquid almost evaporates. Add salsa and next 3 ingredients (through beans); bring to a boil. Reduce heat, and simmer 30 minutes, stirring occasionally. Ladle 1¼ cups chili into each of 4 bowls, and top each serving with 1 tablespoon cheese. Sprinkle with green onion. Yield: 4 servings.

CALORIES 310; **FAT** 10.6g (sat 3.3g, mono 1.5g, poly 4.4g); **PROTEIN** 24.1g; **CARB** 25.1g; **FIBER** 4.3g; **CHOL** 52mg; **IRON** 4.8mg; **SODIUM** 575mg; **CALC** 95mg

Chili con Carne

A traditional Texas-style chili, this stew packs a smoky punch from mildly spicy poblanos and a hot chipotle chile. Rinsing the chipotle mellows the heat; skip that step for more fire.

8 poblano chiles
3 pounds boneless chuck roast, trimmed
   and cut into 1/2-inch cubes
1 1/2 teaspoons salt
1/2 teaspoon freshly ground black pepper
3 tablespoons all-purpose flour
2 tablespoons olive oil, divided
3 cups chopped onion
4 garlic cloves, minced

3 cups chopped seeded peeled plum tomato
   (about 10 medium)
1 tablespoon dried oregano
1 tablespoon ground cumin
1 chipotle chile, canned in adobo sauce
6 tablespoons shredded reduced-fat cheddar
   cheese
3 tablespoons chopped fresh cilantro

1. Preheat broiler.

2. Place poblanos on a foil-lined baking sheet; broil 8 minutes or until charred, turning after 6 minutes. Place poblanos in a paper bag; fold to close tightly. Let stand 15 minutes. Peel chiles, and cut into 1-inch pieces.

3. Sprinkle beef with salt and black pepper; dredge in flour. Heat 1 tablespoon olive oil in a Dutch oven over medium-high heat. Add half of beef to pan; cook 5 minutes, turning to brown on all sides. Remove from pan. Repeat procedure with remaining oil and beef.

4. Reduce heat to medium. Add onion to pan; cook 12 minutes, stirring occasionally. Add garlic; cook 3 minutes, stirring frequently. Return beef to pan. Stir in tomato, oregano, and cumin; bring to a simmer. Cover and cook 1 hour, stirring occasionally. Stir in poblanos; simmer 45 minutes or until beef is tender, stirring occasionally. Rinse, seed, and chop chipotle. Stir in chipotle. Sprinkle with cheese and cilantro. Yield: 10 servings (serving size: about 1 cup chili, about 2 teaspoons cheese, and about 1 teaspoon cilantro).

CALORIES 269; **FAT** 9.7g (sat 3.1g, mono 4.6g, poly 0.9g); **PROTEIN** 33.1g; **CARB** 11.9g; **FIBER** 2.1g; **CHOL** 63mg; **IRON** 3.7mg; **SODIUM** 517mg; **CALC** 115mg

Beef and Pinto Bean Chili

For a three-alarm chili, leave the seeds and membranes in the jalapeños. The sour cream has a cooling effect, but you can seed the peppers or use less for a milder result.

Cooking spray
1 pound boneless chuck roast, trimmed
    and cut into 1-inch pieces
3/8 teaspoon salt, divided
2 tablespoons canola oil
4 cups chopped onion (about 2 medium)
1/4 cup minced jalapeño pepper (about
    2 large)
10 garlic cloves, minced
1 (12-ounce) bottle beer
1 tablespoon paprika
1 tablespoon ground cumin

2 tablespoons tomato paste
3 cups fat-free, lower-sodium beef broth
1 (28-ounce) can peeled whole tomatoes,
    drained and chopped
1 (15-ounce) can pinto beans, rinsed and
    drained
1/2 cup thinly sliced radish
1 avocado, peeled and chopped
6 tablespoons small fresh cilantro leaves
6 tablespoons sour cream
6 lime wedges

1. Heat a Dutch oven over high heat. Coat pan with cooking spray. Sprinkle beef evenly with ⅛ teaspoon salt. Add beef to pan; cook 5 minutes, turning to brown on all sides. Remove from pan. Heat oil in pan over high heat. Add onion and jalapeño; cook 8 minutes or until lightly browned, stirring occasionally. Add garlic; sauté 1 minute. Stir in beer, scraping pan to loosen browned bits; bring to a boil. Cook until liquid almost evaporates (about 10 minutes), stirring occasionally. Stir in paprika, cumin, and tomato paste; cook 1 minute, stirring frequently. Add broth, tomatoes, beans, and beef; bring to a boil. Reduce heat, and simmer 1½ hours or until mixture is thick and beef is very tender, stirring occasionally. Stir in remaining ¼ teaspoon salt.

2. Ladle 1 cup chili into each of 6 bowls. Divide radish and avocado evenly among bowls. Top each serving with 1 tablespoon cilantro and 1 tablespoon sour cream. Serve with lime wedges. Yield: 6 servings.

CALORIES 421; FAT 23g (sat 6.8g, mono 10.9g, poly 2.6g); PROTEIN 21.6g; CARB 30.4g; FIBER 8.5g; CHOL 53mg; IRON 4.1mg; SODIUM 565mg; CALC 123mg

Barley and Beef Soup

Make this soup the night before to allow time for its flavors to develop. Pour hot servings into a thermos to take for lunch, or reheat individual portions in the microwave as needed.

Cooking spray
2 cups chopped onion (about 1 large)
1 pound chuck steak, trimmed and cut into
 ½-inch cubes
1½ cups chopped carrot (about 4)
1 cup chopped celery (about 4 stalks)
5 garlic cloves, minced

1 cup uncooked pearl barley
5 cups fat-free, lower-sodium beef broth
2 cups water
½ cup no-salt-added tomato puree
½ teaspoon kosher salt
¼ teaspoon freshly ground black pepper
2 bay leaves

1. Heat a large Dutch oven over medium heat. Coat pan with cooking spray. Add onion and beef to pan; cook 10 minutes or until onion is tender and beef is browned, stirring occasionally. Add carrot and celery to pan; cook 5 minutes, stirring occasionally. Stir in garlic; cook 30 seconds. Stir in barley and remaining ingredients, and bring to a boil. Cover, reduce heat, and simmer 40 minutes or until barley is done and vegetables are tender. Discard bay leaves. Yield: 6 servings (serving size: 1¾ cups).

CALORIES 275; FAT 5g (sat 1.6g, mono 2.3g, poly 0.5g); PROTEIN 21.8g; CARB 36g; FIBER 8g; CHOL 43mg; IRON 3.1mg; SODIUM 649mg; CALC 57mg

SIMPLE SIDES: Serve this hearty soup with warm, crusty bread or whole-wheat crackers to round out your meal.

Beef and Butternut Chili

Cooking spray
1 tablespoon canola oil, divided
1½ pounds boneless chuck roast, trimmed
  and cut into ½-inch cubes
¾ teaspoon salt
1½ cups chopped onion
½ cup chopped green bell pepper
2 tablespoons tomato paste
1 tablespoon minced garlic
2 teaspoons diced jalapeño pepper
⅔ cup dry red wine
1½ teaspoons ground ancho chile pepper
1 teaspoon dried oregano
½ teaspoon ground red pepper
¼ teaspoon ground cumin
¼ teaspoon ground coriander
⅛ teaspoon ground cinnamon
1 (28-ounce) can whole tomatoes, undrained
  and chopped
1 (15-ounce) can no-salt-added kidney beans,
  rinsed and drained
2 cups (½-inch) cubed peeled butternut
  squash
1 cup coarsely chopped carrot
6 tablespoons reduced-fat sour cream
2 tablespoons fresh cilantro leaves

1. Heat a large Dutch oven over medium-high heat. Coat pan with cooking spray. Add 1 teaspoon oil; swirl to coat. Sprinkle beef with salt. Add beef to pan; cook 8 minutes, turning to brown on all sides. Remove beef.

2. Add remaining 2 teaspoons oil to pan. Add onion and bell pepper; sauté 3 minutes. Add tomato paste, garlic, and jalapeño; sauté 2 minutes. Add wine; bring to a boil, scraping pan to loosen browned bits. Cook 2 minutes. Return beef to pan.

3. Stir in ancho chile pepper and next 7 ingredients (through kidney beans), and bring to a boil. Cover, reduce heat to medium, and simmer gently 1 hour. Add butternut squash and carrot, and simmer 1 hour or until beef is tender. Ladle 1⅓ cups chili into each of 6 bowls, and top each with 1 tablespoon sour cream and 1 teaspoon cilantro. Yield: 6 servings.

CALORIES 308; **FAT** 9.9g (sat 3.3g, mono 3.6g, poly 1g); **PROTEIN** 28.4g; **CARB** 25.5g; **FIBER** 5.8g; **CHOL** 55mg; **IRON** 4.7mg; **SODIUM** 606mg; **CALC** 138mg

Beef Tagine with Butternut Squash

Take your basic beef stew to the next level by making this simple, fragrant tagine featuring butternut squash. Serve with couscous, if desired.

2 teaspoons paprika
1 teaspoon ground cinnamon
³/₄ teaspoon salt
¹/₂ teaspoon ground ginger
¹/₂ teaspoon crushed red pepper
¹/₄ teaspoon freshly ground black pepper
1 (1-pound) beef shoulder roast or petite tender roast, trimmed and cut into 1-inch cubes

1 tablespoon olive oil
4 shallots, quartered
4 garlic cloves, chopped
¹/₂ cup fat-free, lower-sodium chicken broth
1 (14.5-ounce) can no-salt-added diced tomatoes, undrained
3 cups (1-inch) cubed peeled butternut squash (about 1 pound)
¹/₄ cup chopped fresh cilantro

1. Combine first 6 ingredients in a medium bowl. Add beef; toss well to coat.

2. Heat oil in a Dutch oven over medium-high heat. Add beef mixture and shallots; cook 4 minutes or until browned, stirring occasionally. Add garlic; cook 1 minute, stirring frequently. Stir in broth and tomatoes; bring to a boil. Cook 5 minutes. Add squash; cover, reduce heat, and simmer 15 minutes or until squash is tender. Sprinkle with cilantro. Yield: 4 servings (serving size: 1½ cups).

CALORIES 283; **FAT** 9.5g (sat 2g, mono 4.8g, poly 0.5g); **PROTEIN** 25.6g; **CARB** 25.7g; **FIBER** 4.8g; **CHOL** 67mg; **IRON** 4.6mg; **SODIUM** 617mg; **CALC** 103mg

Italian Beef Stew

7 teaspoons olive oil, divided
1½ cups chopped onion
½ cup chopped carrot
1 tablespoon minced garlic
2 pounds boneless chuck roast, trimmed and
  cut into cubes
¼ cup all-purpose flour
¾ teaspoon salt, divided
½ teaspoon freshly ground black pepper
1 cup dry red wine
3¾ cups chopped seeded peeled plum
  tomato (about 2 pounds)

1½ cups lower-sodium beef broth
½ cup water
2 teaspoons chopped fresh oregano
2 teaspoons chopped fresh thyme
1 bay leaf
1 (8-ounce) package cremini mushrooms,
  quartered
¾ cup (¼-inch-thick) slices carrot
2 tablespoons chopped fresh basil
1 tablespoon chopped fresh flat-leaf parsley

1. Heat 1 teaspoon oil in a Dutch oven over medium-high heat. Add onion and chopped carrot; cook 8 minutes, stirring occasionally. Add garlic; sauté 45 seconds. Remove onion mixture from pan.

2. Add 1 tablespoon oil to pan. Sprinkle beef with flour, ½ teaspoon salt, and pepper; toss. Add half of beef mixture to pan, browning on all sides. Remove from pan. Repeat procedure with remaining oil and beef mixture.

3. Add wine to pan, and bring to a boil, scraping pan to loosen browned bits. Cook until reduced to ⅓ cup (about 5 minutes). Return beef and onion mixture to pan. Add tomato and next 6 ingredients (through mushrooms); bring to a boil. Cover, reduce heat, and simmer 45 minutes, stirring occasionally. Uncover, and stir in sliced carrot. Simmer, uncovered, 1 hour or until meat is very tender, stirring occasionally. Discard bay leaf. Stir in remaining ¼ teaspoon salt, basil, and parsley. Yield: 8 servings (serving size: 1 cup).

CALORIES 334; **FAT** 13g (sat 3.9g, mono 0.8g, poly 6.6g); **PROTEIN** 40.6g; **CARB** 12.2g; **FIBER** 2.4g; **CHOL** 86mg; **IRON** 4.1mg; **SODIUM** 387mg; **CALC** 51mg

PREP TIP: Avoid making these mistakes: boiling versus simmering the stew, or skimping on the first steps that build deep flavor.

Guinness Lamb Stew

If you can't find Guinness, or if you don't like it, substitute another dark beer.

8 teaspoons olive oil, divided
2 cups chopped onion
1 tablespoon chopped fresh thyme
1½ teaspoons chopped fresh rosemary
3 tablespoons all-purpose flour
2½ pounds boneless leg of lamb, trimmed and cut into 1-inch cubes
1 teaspoon salt, divided
¾ teaspoon freshly ground black pepper, divided

2 cups Guinness Stout
1 tablespoon tomato paste
3 cups fat-free, lower-sodium beef broth
1 bay leaf
2 cups cubed peeled Yukon gold potato
2 cups 1-inch-thick diagonally sliced carrot
8 ounces baby turnips, peeled and quartered
1 tablespoon whole-grain Dijon mustard
⅓ cup chopped fresh parsley

1. Heat 2 teaspoons oil in a large Dutch oven over medium-high heat. Add onion, thyme, and rosemary; cook 5 minutes, stirring occasionally. Place onion mixture in a large bowl. Place flour in a shallow dish. Sprinkle lamb evenly with ½ teaspoon salt and ½ teaspoon pepper. Dredge lamb in flour, and shake off excess. Heat 1 tablespoon oil in pan over medium-high heat. Add half of lamb mixture to pan; cook 6 minutes, turning to brown on all sides. Add browned lamb to onion mixture. Repeat procedure with remaining lamb and remaining 1 tablespoon oil.

2. Add beer to pan; bring to a boil, scraping pan to loosen browned bits. Cook until reduced to 1 cup (about 5 minutes). Return onion mixture and lamb to pan. Stir in tomato paste; cook 30 seconds. Add broth and bay leaf; bring to a boil. Cover, reduce heat, and simmer 1 hour and 15 minutes, stirring occasionally. Uncover and stir in potato, carrot, and turnips. Simmer, uncovered, 1½ hours or until meat and vegetables are tender. Stir in remaining ½ teaspoon salt, remaining ¼ teaspoon pepper, and mustard. Discard bay leaf. Ladle about 1 cup stew into each of 7 bowls; sprinkle evenly with parsley. Yield: 7 servings.

CALORIES 430; FAT 22.9g (sat 8.3g, mono 11g, poly 2g); PROTEIN 26.3g; CARB 24.2g; FIBER 3.4g; CHOL 83mg; IRON 3.3mg; SODIUM 702mg; CALC 50mg

Lamb Tagine

Serve this Moroccan-style lamb stew with hot cooked couscous.

Cooking spray
1 (1-pound) boneless leg of lamb roast, trimmed and cut into ½-inch cubes
¾ teaspoon kosher salt, divided
1½ cups chopped onion
1 teaspoon ground cumin
½ teaspoon ground cinnamon

½ teaspoon ground red pepper
6 garlic cloves, coarsely chopped
2 tablespoons honey
1 tablespoon tomato paste
½ cup dried apricots, quartered
1 (14-ounce) can fat-free, lower-sodium beef broth

1. Heat a Dutch oven over medium-high heat. Coat pan with cooking spray. Sprinkle lamb evenly with ½ teaspoon salt. Add lamb to pan; cook 4 minutes, turning to brown on all sides. Remove from pan. Add onion to pan; cook 4 minutes, stirring frequently. Add remaining ¼ teaspoon salt, cumin, and next 3 ingredients (through garlic); sauté 1 minute. Stir in honey and tomato paste; cook 30 seconds, stirring frequently. Return lamb to pan. Add apricots and broth; bring to a boil. Cover, reduce heat, and simmer 1 hour or until lamb is tender, stirring occasionally. Yield: 4 servings (serving size: 1 cup).

CALORIES 395; FAT 17.8g (sat 8.3g, mono 7g, poly 0.8g); PROTEIN 28.3g; CARB 30g; FIBER 3.2g; CHOL 90mg; IRON 3.7mg; SODIUM 617mg; CALC 71mg

Pork Posole

Serve with warm whole-wheat flour tortillas.

1 tablespoon olive oil
12 ounces boneless pork shoulder (Boston butt), trimmed and cut into 1/2-inch pieces
1 cup chopped onion
4 garlic cloves, minced
1 1/2 teaspoons ground cumin
1/2 teaspoon ground red pepper

1/2 cup beer
2 cups fat-free, lower-sodium chicken broth
1/2 cup salsa verde
1 (28-ounce) can hominy, drained
1/4 cup fresh cilantro leaves
4 radishes, sliced
4 lime wedges

1. Heat oil in a Dutch oven over medium-high heat. Add pork; cook 5 minutes, turning to brown on all sides. Remove pork from pan. Add onion to pan; cook 4 minutes, stirring occasionally. Add garlic, and sauté 1 minute. Return pork to pan; stir in cumin and pepper. Add beer, and bring to a boil. Cook until liquid almost evaporates (about 9 minutes).
2. Add broth, salsa, and hominy to pan; bring to a boil. Cover, reduce heat, and simmer 1 hour and 10 minutes or until pork is very tender, stirring occasionally. Ladle 1½ cups soup into each of 4 bowls. Top each serving with 1 tablespoon cilantro and 1 sliced radish. Serve with lime wedges. Yield: 4 servings.

CALORIES 315; **FAT** 11.5g (sat 2.8g, mono 5.6g, poly 1.6g); **PROTEIN** 21.2g; **CARB** 30.4g; **FIBER** 6.1g; **CHOL** 57mg; **IRON** 3.6mg; **SODIUM** 736mg; **CALC** 77mg

FYI: Hominy makes a great foil for the hearty pork, spices, salsa, radishes, onion, and lime. With canned hominy, this dish takes a fraction of the time needed for traditional posole.

Quick Chicken Noodle Soup

Heat the broth mixture in the microwave to jump-start the cooking. Meanwhile, sauté the aromatic ingredients in your soup pot to get this dish under way. Though we like the shape of fusilli, you can also make this soup with wide egg noodles, rotini, or even orzo.

2 cups water
1 (32-ounce) carton fat-free, lower-sodium
  chicken broth
1 tablespoon olive oil
1/2 cup prechopped onion
1/2 cup prechopped celery
1/2 teaspoon salt

1/2 teaspoon freshly ground black pepper
1 medium carrot, chopped
6 ounces uncooked fusilli (short twisted
  spaghetti)
2 1/2 cups shredded skinless, boneless
  rotisserie chicken breast
2 tablespoons chopped fresh flat-leaf parsley

1. Combine 2 cups water and chicken broth in a microwave-safe dish, and microwave at HIGH 5 minutes.

2. While broth mixture heats, heat oil in a large saucepan over medium-high heat. Add onion, celery, salt, pepper, and carrot; cook 3 minutes or until almost tender, stirring frequently. Add hot broth mixture and pasta; bring to a boil. Cook 7 minutes or until pasta is almost al dente. Stir in chicken; cook 1 minute or until thoroughly heated. Stir in parsley. Yield: 6 servings (serving size: about 1 cup).

CALORIES 237; **FAT** 4.8g (sat 1g, mono 2.4g, poly 0.9g); **PROTEIN** 22.9g; **CARB** 23.9g; **FIBER** 1.7g; **CHOL** 50mg; **IRON** 1.8mg; **SODIUM** 589mg; **CALC** 28mg

Superfast Chicken Posole

1 tablespoon olive oil
1 teaspoon dried oregano
3/4 teaspoon ground cumin
1/2 teaspoon chili powder
2 garlic cloves, minced
1 (8-ounce) package prechopped onion and celery mix
4 canned tomatillos, drained and coarsely chopped
2 (14-ounce) cans fat-free, lower-sodium chicken broth
1 (15-ounce) can white hominy, rinsed and drained
2 cups chopped skinless, boneless rotisserie chicken breast
1 tablespoon fresh lime juice
1/4 teaspoon salt
1/4 teaspoon freshly ground black pepper
1/2 ripe peeled avocado, diced
4 radishes, thinly sliced
Fresh cilantro leaves (optional)

1. Heat olive oil in a large saucepan over medium-high heat. Add oregano and next 4 ingredients (through onion and celery mix); sauté 2 minutes. Stir in tomatillos; cook 1 minute. Add broth and hominy; cover and bring to a boil. Uncover and cook 8 minutes. Stir in chicken; cook 1 minute or until heated. Remove from heat; stir in lime juice, salt, and pepper. Ladle into each of 4 bowls. Top with avocado and radish. Garnish with cilantro, if desired. Yield: 4 servings (serving size: 1½ cups soup, 2 tablespoons avocado, and 1 radish).

CALORIES 290; FAT 11.2g (sat 2.2g, mono 5.9g, poly 2g); PROTEIN 28.2g; CARB 20.2g; FIBER 4.5g; CHOL 60mg; IRON 2.4mg; SODIUM 452mg; CALC 62mg

Chicken and Parsnip Soup

1½ teaspoons olive oil
¾ cup thinly diagonally sliced parsnip
  (2 parsnips)
¾ cup thinly sliced shallots (2 shallots)
1 (4-ounce) package gourmet mushroom
  blend
1 garlic clove, minced
2½ cups fat-free, lower-sodium chicken broth
1 cup water

1 cup chickpeas (garbanzo beans), rinsed
  and drained
1 cup shredded skinless, boneless rotisserie
  chicken breast
½ teaspoon freshly ground black pepper
¼ teaspoon salt
⅛ teaspoon hot sauce
1 thyme sprig
2 tablespoons chopped fresh parsley

1. Heat olive oil in a medium saucepan over medium-high heat. Add parsnip, shallots, mushrooms, and garlic; sauté 3 minutes. Add broth and next 7 ingredients (through thyme); bring to a simmer, and cook 10 minutes or until parsnip is tender. Remove from heat; stir in parsley. Yield: 4 servings (serving size: 1⅓ cups).

CALORIES 204; **FAT** 4.1g (sat 0.8g, mono 1.9g, poly 0.9g); **PROTEIN** 17.4g; **CARB** 25.3g; **FIBER** 5.1g; **CHOL** 30mg; **IRON** 2.3mg; **SODIUM** 607mg; **CALC** 62mg

SIMPLE SUBS: If you don't have shallots, you may substitute half a cup of sliced onion instead. Button mushrooms will also make a good substitute for the gourmet mushroom blend.

Broccoli and Chicken Noodle Soup

If the broccoli florets are large, break them into smaller pieces at the stalk; they'll cook more quickly. Count on having dinner on the table in about 40 minutes, and serve this soup the moment it's done for the best results. In fact, you'll find it gets thicker with time. Thin any leftover soup with a little chicken broth or milk to attain the desired consistency.

Cooking spray
2 cups chopped onion
1 cup presliced mushrooms
1 garlic clove, minced
3 tablespoons butter
1.1 ounces all-purpose flour (about ¼ cup)
4 cups 1% low-fat milk
1 (14-ounce) can fat-free, lower-sodium
   chicken broth

4 ounces uncooked vermicelli, broken into
   2-inch pieces
2 cups (8 ounces) shredded light processed
   cheese
4 cups (1-inch) cubed cooked chicken breast
3 cups small broccoli florets (8 ounces)
1 cup half-and-half
1 teaspoon freshly ground black pepper
¾ teaspoon salt

1. Heat a Dutch oven over medium-high heat. Coat pan with cooking spray. Add onion, mushrooms, and garlic to pan; cook 5 minutes or until liquid evaporates, stirring occasionally. Reduce heat to medium; add butter to mushroom mixture, stirring until butter melts. Sprinkle mushroom mixture with flour; cook 2 minutes, stirring occasionally. Gradually add milk and broth, stirring constantly with a whisk; bring to a boil. Reduce heat to medium-low; cook 10 minutes or until slightly thick, stirring constantly. Add pasta to pan; cook 10 minutes. Add cheese to pan, and stir until cheese melts. Add chicken and remaining ingredients to pan; cook 5 minutes or until broccoli is tender and soup is thoroughly heated. Yield: 10 servings (serving size: 1 cup).

CALORIES 317; FAT 12.3g (sat 6.8g, mono 2.9g, poly 0.9g); PROTEIN 27.5g; CARB 23.8g; FIBER 1.9g; CHOL 74mg; IRON 1.6mg; SODIUM 723mg; CALC 179mg

Lemon Chicken Orzo Soup *(Pictured on page 214)*

Chicken noodle soup is probably the top comfort food of all time. You'll need to start a day ahead to prepare the tasty homemade broth.

1 (4-pound) whole chicken
2 carrots, peeled and cut into 1-inch pieces
2 celery stalks, cut into 1-inch pieces
1 medium onion, peeled and sliced
6 garlic cloves, crushed
4 flat-leaf parsley sprigs
2 teaspoons black peppercorns
2 bay leaves
6 cups water
1⅓ cups chopped carrot

1¼ cups chopped onion
1 cup chopped celery
2 teaspoons salt
8 ounces uncooked orzo (rice-shaped pasta)
¼ cup chopped fresh flat-leaf parsley
2½ teaspoons grated lemon rind
¼ cup fresh lemon juice
Lemon slices (optional)
Coarsely cracked black pepper (optional)

1. Remove and discard giblets and neck from chicken. Place chicken in a large Dutch oven. Add 2 chopped carrots, 2 chopped celery stalks, and next 5 ingredients (through bay leaves) to pan. Add 6 cups water; bring to a simmer. Reduce heat, and simmer 45 minutes.
2. Remove chicken from pan; place chicken in a bowl. Chill 15 minutes. Discard skin; remove chicken from bones, discarding bones. Chop chicken into bite-sized pieces; cover and chill. Strain broth mixture through a sieve into a large bowl; discard solids. Cool broth mixture to room temperature. Cover and chill 8 to 24 hours. Skim fat from surface, and discard.
3. Add enough water to broth to equal 9 cups; place broth mixture in a large Dutch oven. Add 1⅓ cups carrot, 1¼ cups onion, 1 cup celery, and salt to pan; bring to a boil. Cover, reduce heat, and simmer 15 minutes or until vegetables are tender. Add reserved chicken, and simmer 3 minutes or until thoroughly heated. Keep warm.
4. Cook pasta according to package directions, omitting salt and fat. Add pasta to pan with chicken and broth mixture; stir in parsley, rind, and juice. Garnish each serving with lemon slices and cracked black pepper, if desired. Yield: 8 servings (serving size: about 1¾ cups).

CALORIES 235; **FAT** 5.2g (sat 1.3g, mono 1.8g, poly 1.1g); **PROTEIN** 21.3g; **CARB** 24.6g; **FIBER** 2.3g; **CHOL** 53mg; **IRON** 1.1mg; **SODIUM** 679mg; **CALC** 39mg

Coconut–Red Curry Hot Pot with Braised Chicken and Mushrooms

2 cups fat-free, lower-sodium chicken broth
¾ cup chopped peeled fresh lemongrass
6 Kaffir lime leaves, torn
5 (¼-inch) slices fresh galangal
1½ tablespoons red curry paste
1 (4-ounce) package presliced exotic mushroom blend (such as shiitake, cremini, and oyster)
8 ounces skinless, boneless chicken breast, cut into bite-sized pieces

1 (13.5-ounce) can light coconut milk
1 tablespoon Thai fish sauce
2 teaspoons brown sugar
⅓ cup thinly diagonally cut green onions
2 tablespoons fresh lime juice
6 tablespoons coarsely chopped fresh cilantro, divided
3 ounces uncooked wide rice noodles

1. Bring broth to a boil in a medium saucepan over medium-high heat; stir in lemongrass, lime leaves, and galangal. Reduce heat, and simmer 5 minutes. Remove from heat; let stand 30 minutes. Strain through a sieve over a bowl; discard solids. Return broth to pan; add curry paste, stirring with a whisk. Bring to a simmer over medium-high heat. Add mushrooms; cook 2 minutes or until tender. Stir in chicken; cook 3 minutes or until chicken is done. Add coconut milk, stirring well to combine. Stir in fish sauce and sugar, stirring until sugar dissolves. Remove from heat; stir in onions, juice, and ¼ cup cilantro.
2. Cook noodles according to package directions; drain. Add noodles to coconut milk mixture. Ladle 1 cup soup into each of 6 bowls; sprinkle evenly with remaining 2 tablespoons cilantro. Yield: 6 servings.

CALORIES 221; **FAT** 5.4g (sat 4.4g, mono 0.2g, poly 0.2g); **PROTEIN** 17.2g; **CARB** 27.3g; **FIBER** 1g; **CHOL** 33mg; **IRON** 1.8mg; **SODIUM** 681mg; **CALC** 20mg

SIMPLE SUBS: If you can't find Kaffir lime leaves, use an extra ¼ cup chopped peeled fresh lemongrass. No galangal? Use regular sliced fresh ginger in its place.

Coconut-Curry Chicken Soup

The aroma, color, texture, and combination of flavors make Thai cuisine delicious. Coconut milk gives this soup a creamy, smooth texture. The soup also reheats well. Cook and shred the chicken before you start the recipe.

4 cups water
3 cups fresh spinach leaves
1/2 pound snow peas, trimmed and cut in half crosswise
1 (5³/4-ounce) package pad thai noodles (wide rice stick noodles)
1 tablespoon canola oil
1/4 cup thinly sliced shallots
2 teaspoons red curry paste
1¹/2 teaspoons curry powder
1/2 teaspoon ground turmeric
1/2 teaspoon ground coriander

2 garlic cloves, minced
6 cups lower-sodium chicken broth
1 (13.5-ounce) can light coconut milk
2¹/2 cups shredded cooked chicken breast (about 1 pound)
1/2 cup chopped green onions
2 tablespoons sugar
2 tablespoons fish sauce
1/2 cup chopped fresh cilantro
4 small hot red chiles, seeded and chopped, or 1/4 teaspoon crushed red pepper
7 lime wedges

1. Bring 4 cups water to a boil in a large saucepan. Add spinach and peas to pan; cook 30 seconds. Remove vegetables from pan with a slotted spoon; place in a large bowl. Add noodles to pan; cook 3 minutes. Drain; add noodles to spinach mixture in bowl.
2. Heat oil in pan over medium-high heat. Add shallots and next 5 ingredients (through garlic) to pan; sauté 1 minute. Add broth to pan; bring to a boil. Add coconut milk to pan; reduce heat, and simmer 5 minutes. Add chicken, onions, sugar, and fish sauce to pan; cook 2 minutes. Pour chicken mixture over noodle mixture in bowl. Stir in chopped cilantro and chiles. Serve with lime wedges. Yield: 7 servings (serving size: 2 cups soup and 1 lime wedge).

CALORIES 277; FAT 8.4g (sat 4g, mono 1.9g, poly 1g); PROTEIN 22.6g; CARB 28.4g; FIBER 2.1g; CHOL 47mg; IRON 2.1mg; SODIUM 694mg; CALC 64mg

Chicken and White Bean Soup

Cannellini beans, native to Tuscany, work beautifully in this rustic soup because they hold their shape after simmering in the flavorful broth. Serve with a crusty Italian bread, such as ciabatta, and a salad of bitter greens.

2 smoked bacon slices, chopped
12 ounces skinless, boneless chicken thighs,
    trimmed and cut into 2-inch pieces
1/2 cup chopped onion
1 garlic clove, minced
1 cup chopped plum tomato
2 tablespoons chopped fresh oregano
1/4 teaspoon freshly ground black pepper

2 cups water
2 cups fat-free, lower-sodium chicken broth
2/3 cup uncooked orzo (rice-shaped pasta)
1 (15-ounce) can organic white beans, rinsed
    and drained
2 tablespoons chopped fresh flat-leaf parsley
1 tablespoon white wine vinegar
1/4 teaspoon salt

1. Cook bacon in a large saucepan over medium heat 7 minutes or until crisp. Remove bacon from pan, reserving drippings in pan; set bacon aside.

2. Add chicken to drippings in pan; sauté 6 minutes. Remove chicken from pan. Add onion and garlic to pan; cook 4 minutes or until tender. Add tomato, oregano, and pepper; cook 1 minute, stirring constantly. Return bacon and chicken to pan. Stir in 2 cups water and broth, scraping pan to loosen browned bits. Bring to a boil. Add orzo to pan, and cook 9 minutes or until al dente. Add beans; cook 2 minutes or until heated. Remove from heat; stir in chopped parsley, vinegar, and salt. Yield: 4 servings (serving size: 1¼ cups).

CALORIES 335; **FAT** 9.9g (sat 2.8g, mono 2.5g, poly 1.5g); **PROTEIN** 26g; **CARB** 35.4g; **FIBER** 5.1g; **CHOL** 61mg; **IRON** 3.2mg; **SODIUM** 530mg; **CALC** 64mg

Sweet and Spicy Chicken and White Bean Stew

Lemongrass lends a hint of citrus.

2 tablespoons canola oil
½ teaspoon ground cardamom
⅛ teaspoon ground cloves
3 garlic cloves, minced
2 cups finely chopped onion
½ teaspoon chili powder
½ teaspoon ground coriander
¼ teaspoon ground turmeric
1 (15.5-ounce) can cannellini beans or other white beans, undrained
¾ pound skinless, boneless chicken breast, cut into bite-sized pieces
1 cup light coconut milk
½ cup water
1 tablespoon chopped peeled fresh lemongrass (about 1 stalk)
1 (14.5-ounce) can fire-roasted diced tomatoes, undrained
1 (8-ounce) baking potato, cut into ½-inch cubes
¼ cup chopped fresh cilantro
Cilantro leaves (optional)

1. Heat oil in a Dutch oven over medium-high heat. Add cardamom, cloves, and garlic to pan; cook 30 seconds, stirring constantly. Add onion; sauté 8 minutes or until tender. Add chili powder, coriander, and turmeric; cook 30 seconds. Add beans and chicken; stir to coat. Add milk, ½ cup water, lemongrass, tomatoes, and potato to pan. Cover, reduce heat, and simmer 30 minutes or until potato is tender. Stir in chopped cilantro. Garnish with cilantro leaves, if desired. Yield: 4 servings (serving size: 1¾ cups stew and 1 tablespoon cilantro).

CALORIES 364; FAT 11.7g (sat 3.7g, mono 4.4g, poly 2.8g); PROTEIN 27.3g; CARB 37.5g; FIBER 6.7g; CHOL 49mg; IRON 3.8mg; SODIUM 544mg; CALC 82mg

Chicken Verde Stew with Hominy

2 Anaheim chiles
Cooking spray
1 1/2 pounds tomatillos
1/4 cup finely chopped fresh cilantro
1 1/2 teaspoons ground cumin
1 teaspoon dried oregano
2 cups fat-free, lower-sodium chicken broth, divided
2 tablespoons olive oil, divided
1 1/2 cups finely chopped onion
1/2 cup chopped carrot
1/2 cup chopped celery
1/2 cup chopped red bell pepper
3 tablespoons all-purpose flour
4 teaspoons finely chopped garlic
1 pound skinless, boneless chicken thighs, cut into 1 1/2-inch pieces
3/4 teaspoon kosher salt, divided
1/2 teaspoon freshly ground black pepper, divided
1 (29-ounce) can golden hominy, rinsed and drained
6 tablespoons reduced-fat sour cream
Fresh cilantro leaves (optional)

1. Preheat broiler to high.
2. Halve, stem, and seed chiles. Place chiles, skin side up, on a foil-lined baking sheet coated with cooking spray; broil 5 minutes or until charred. Place chiles in a paper bag; fold to close tightly. Let stand 15 minutes. Peel and discard skins. Arrange tomatillos on prepared baking sheet, and broil 14 minutes or until blackened, turning once. Place chiles, tomatillos, 1/4 cup cilantro, cumin, and oregano in a blender. Add 1 cup broth; process until smooth.
3. Heat 2 teaspoons olive oil in a large Dutch oven over medium-high heat. Add onion, carrot, celery, and bell pepper to pan; sauté 2 minutes, stirring occasionally. Stir in flour; cook 2 minutes, stirring frequently. Add garlic, and sauté 30 seconds. Place onion mixture in a large bowl.
4. Sprinkle chicken with 1/2 teaspoon salt and 1/4 teaspoon black pepper. Heat 2 teaspoons olive oil in pan over medium-high heat. Add half of chicken; sauté 3 minutes. Add browned chicken to onion mixture. Repeat procedure with remaining chicken and remaining 2 teaspoons oil. Combine remaining 1 cup broth, tomatillo mixture, onion mixture, and hominy in pan over medium-high heat, and bring to a boil. Cover, reduce heat, and simmer 45 minutes, stirring occasionally. Stir in remaining 1/4 teaspoon salt and 1/4 teaspoon black pepper. Ladle 1 2/3 cups stew into each of 6 bowls; top each with 1 tablespoon sour cream. Garnish with cilantro, if desired. Yield: 6 servings.

CALORIES 322; FAT 14.1g (sat 3.6g, mono 6.3g, poly 2.7g); PROTEIN 18.7g; CARB 30.9g; FIBER 6.3g; CHOL 56mg; IRON 2.9mg; SODIUM 651mg; CALC 69mg

Chicken and Okra Stew

This Haitian version of Southern Brunswick stew is fierier, thanks to the habanero. If you don't want it quite as spicy, use a minced seeded jalapeño.

4 teaspoons canola oil, divided
2 pounds skinless, boneless chicken thighs, quartered
1 habanero pepper
1½ cups chopped green bell pepper
1 cup finely chopped onion
⅔ cup finely chopped celery
2½ cups chopped plum tomato

2 tablespoons chopped fresh parsley
1 tablespoon chopped fresh oregano
1 teaspoon salt
1 teaspoon freshly ground black pepper
⅛ teaspoon ground cloves
1 (14-ounce) can fat-free, lower-sodium chicken broth
1 pound fresh okra pods, cut into 1-inch pieces

1. Heat 2 teaspoons oil in a Dutch oven over medium-high heat. Add half of chicken to pan; cook 6 minutes, browning on all sides. Remove chicken from pan. Repeat with remaining chicken; remove from pan.
2. Cut habanero in half. Seed one half of pepper, and leave seeds in other half. Mince both pepper halves. Heat remaining 2 teaspoons oil in pan over medium-high heat. Add minced habanero, bell pepper, onion, and celery; cook 5 minutes or until tender, stirring occasionally. Add tomato; cook 3 minutes or until tomato softens. Add parsley and next 5 ingredients (through broth); bring to a boil. Return chicken to pan; cover, reduce heat, and simmer 10 minutes. Add okra; cover and simmer 15 minutes or until okra is just tender. Yield: 6 servings (serving size: 1⅓ cups).

CALORIES 269; FAT 9.4g (sat 1.8g, mono 3.7g, poly 2.5g); PROTEIN 33g; CARB 13.4g; FIBER 4.8g; CHOL 126mg; IRON 2.8mg; SODIUM 692mg; CALC 106mg

Brunswick Stew

From 19th-century Virginia, this stew originally included squirrel meat (we opt for chicken here). Our version uses flour to give it body. Garnish with fresh thyme sprigs.

Cooking spray
1 cup chopped red bell pepper
3/4 cup chopped yellow onion
1/2 cup chopped celery
1 tablespoon peanut oil
1 tablespoon all-purpose flour
1 pound skinless, boneless chicken thighs, cut into 1/2-inch pieces
2 cups fat-free, lower-sodium chicken broth
2 tablespoons no-salt-added tomato paste

1 teaspoon dried thyme
1/2 teaspoon salt
1/2 teaspoon hot pepper sauce
1 (10-ounce) package frozen whole-kernel corn, thawed
1 (10-ounce) package frozen baby lima beans, thawed
6 (1-ounce) slices Italian bread, toasted
2 garlic cloves, halved

1. Heat a large Dutch oven over medium-high heat. Coat pan with cooking spray. Add bell pepper, onion, and celery to pan; cook 5 minutes, stirring occasionally. Add oil to pan. Combine flour and chicken in a medium bowl, tossing to coat. Add chicken to pan; cook 2 minutes or until lightly browned. Gradually stir in chicken broth; bring to a boil. Cook 1 minute or until slightly thick, stirring constantly. Add tomato paste and next 5 ingredients (through lima beans) to pan. Cover, reduce heat, and simmer 30 minutes.
2. Rub bread slices with cut sides of garlic; discard garlic. Serve bread with stew. Yield: 6 servings (serving size: 1 cup stew and 1 slice bread).

CALORIES 319; FAT 9.2g (sat 2.2g, mono 3.5g, poly 2.6g); PROTEIN 22.4g; CARB 38g; FIBER 5.8g; CHOL 50mg; IRON 3.2mg; SODIUM 596mg; CALC 58mg

Quick and Easy Turkey-Vegetable Soup

The mild cheese complements this slightly spicy soup that's ideal for a weeknight supper.

Cooking spray
1 cup finely chopped celery (about 2 stalks)
1/2 cup finely chopped onion
1 1/2 teaspoons minced garlic
1 1/2 pounds ground turkey breast
3 cups water
1 cup sliced carrot (about 2 large)
1/2 cup frozen French-cut green beans
1/2 cup frozen whole-kernel corn
1 1/2 teaspoons ground cumin

1 teaspoon chili powder
2 bay leaves
2 beef-flavored dry bouillon cubes, chopped
1 (15-ounce) can kidney beans, rinsed and drained
1 (14.5-ounce) can diced tomatoes and green chiles, undrained
6 tablespoons shredded Monterey Jack cheese

1. Heat a Dutch oven over medium-high heat. Coat pan with cooking spray. Add celery, onion, garlic, and turkey to pan; cook 5 minutes or until turkey is browned, stirring to crumble. Add 3 cups water and remaining ingredients except cheese to pan; bring to a boil. Cover, reduce heat, and simmer 20 minutes or until vegetables are tender. Discard bay leaves. Ladle 1½ cups soup into each of 6 bowls; top each serving with 1 tablespoon cheese. Yield: 6 servings.

CALORIES 261; FAT 4.5g (sat 1.9g, mono 0.8g, poly 0.2g); PROTEIN 33.3g; CARB 21.1g; FIBER 6g; CHOL 52mg; IRON 2.5mg; SODIUM 714mg; CALC 118mg

White Bean and Turkey Chili

This crowd-pleasing white-bean chili calls for canned beans and chicken broth, making prep convenient.

1 tablespoon canola oil
2 cups diced yellow onion (about 2 medium)
1½ tablespoons chili powder
1 tablespoon minced garlic
1½ teaspoons ground cumin
1 teaspoon dried oregano
3 (15.8-ounce) cans Great Northern beans, rinsed and drained
4 cups fat-free, lower-sodium chicken broth

3 cups chopped cooked turkey
½ cup diced seeded plum tomato (about 1)
⅓ cup chopped fresh cilantro
2 tablespoons fresh lime juice
½ teaspoon salt
½ teaspoon freshly ground black pepper
8 lime wedges (optional)
Parsley sprigs (optional)

1. Heat oil in a large Dutch oven over medium-high heat. Add onion; sauté 10 minutes or until tender and golden. Add chili powder, garlic, and cumin; sauté 2 minutes. Add oregano and beans; cook 30 seconds. Add broth; bring to a simmer. Cook 20 minutes.
2. Place 2 cups bean mixture in a blender or food processor, and process until smooth. Return pureed mixture to pan. Add turkey, and cook 5 minutes or until thoroughly heated. Remove from heat. Add tomato, cilantro, juice, salt, and pepper, stirring well. Garnish with lime wedges and parsley, if desired. Yield: 8 servings (serving size: about 1 cup).

CALORIES 286; **FAT** 6g (sat 1.2g, mono 2.1g, poly 1.6g); **PROTEIN** 32.4g; **CARB** 24.3g; **FIBER** 5.5g; **CHOL** 85mg; **IRON** 4.8mg; **SODIUM** 435mg; **CALC** 105mg

Mexican Turkey Stew

Usually an ingredient in moles, roasted pumpkinseed kernels add another layer of nutty flavor to this posole-style broth. Look for them in specialty markets and health-food stores. Substitute ancho chile powder if guajillo is unavailable.

3 large Anaheim chiles, halved lengthwise and seeded
2 teaspoons canola oil
Cooking spray
1½ cups chopped onion
4 garlic cloves, minced
2 tablespoons ground guajillo chile pepper
1½ teaspoons dried oregano
4 cups water
3 cups fat-free, lower-sodium chicken broth

1 (15-ounce) can golden or white hominy, drained
4 cups shredded cooked turkey breast
⅓ cup chopped fresh cilantro
¼ teaspoon salt
½ cup roasted unsalted pumpkinseed kernels
½ cup thinly sliced radishes
½ cup thinly sliced green onions
½ cup (2 ounces) crumbled queso fresco
Lime wedges (optional)

1. Preheat broiler.
2. Place pepper halves, skin side up, on a foil-lined baking sheet. Broil 6 minutes or until blackened. Place in a paper bag, and fold to close tightly. Let stand 15 minutes. Peel and chop; set aside.
3. Heat oil in a large Dutch oven coated with cooking spray over medium heat. Add onion to pan; cook 6 minutes, stirring occasionally. Add garlic; cook 1 minute, stirring occasionally. Add guajillo and oregano; cook 1 minute, stirring constantly. Stir in 4 cups water, broth, and hominy; bring to a boil. Reduce heat, and simmer, uncovered, 10 minutes. Stir in Anaheim chiles and turkey; cook 2 minutes. Stir in cilantro and salt; cook 3 minutes. Ladle about 1⅓ cups soup into each of 8 bowls. Top each serving with 1 tablespoon pumpkinseed kernels, 1 tablespoon radishes, 1 tablespoon green onions, and 1 tablespoon cheese. Serve with lime wedges, if desired. Yield: 8 servings.

CALORIES 213; **FAT** 6.8g (sat 2.3g, mono 1.9g, poly 1.6g); **PROTEIN** 25.4g; **CARB** 13.5g; **FIBER** 3.2g; **CHOL** 56mg; **IRON** 1.7mg; **SODIUM** 483mg; **CALC** 88mg

Company Pot Roast, page 321

slow cooker

Chickpea Chili

1 cup dried chickpeas
2 quarts boiling water
2 tablespoons olive oil, divided
1½ cups chopped onion
5 garlic cloves, minced
1 tablespoon tomato paste
1½ teaspoons ground cumin
1 teaspoon kosher salt
½ teaspoon ground red pepper
½ teaspoon ground cinnamon
¼ teaspoon ground turmeric

2½ cups fat-free, lower-sodium chicken broth
½ cup water
⅔ cup sliced pimiento-stuffed olives
½ cup golden raisins
1 (28-ounce) can whole tomatoes,
   undrained and crushed
4 cups chopped peeled butternut squash
1 cup frozen green peas, thawed
6 cups hot cooked couscous
8 lime wedges
¼ cup chopped fresh cilantro

1. Place chickpeas in a saucepan; add 2 quarts boiling water. Cover and let stand 1 hour; drain. Place chickpeas in a 6-quart electric slow cooker.
2. Heat 1 tablespoon oil in a large skillet over medium-high heat. Add onion; cook 4 minutes, stirring occasionally. Add garlic; sauté 1 minute. Stir in tomato paste and next 5 ingredients (through turmeric); sauté 30 seconds. Add onion mixture to slow cooker. Add broth and next 4 ingredients (through tomatoes) to slow cooker; stir well. Cover and cook on HIGH for 8 hours.
3. Heat remaining 1 tablespoon oil in a large skillet over medium-high heat. Add squash; sauté 5 minutes. Add squash to slow cooker. Cover and cook on HIGH for 1 hour; stir in peas. Divide couscous among 8 bowls. Ladle chili over couscous. Serve with lime wedges and cilantro. Yield: 8 servings (serving size: 1 cup chili, ¾ cup couscous, 1 lime wedge, and 1½ teaspoons cilantro).

CALORIES 382; FAT 7.6g (sat 0.9g, mono 4.1g, poly 0.8g); PROTEIN 12.9g; CARB 69.4g; FIBER 8.6g; CHOL 0mg; IRON 4mg; SODIUM 790mg; CALC 133mg

Vegetable and Chickpea Curry

Aromatic Indian spices mingle with chickpeas, green beans, and potatoes. Coconut milk provides a creamy finish to the cooked curry. A squeeze of lemon over each serving adds a bright, fresh contrast to the spicy flavors of the dish.

1 tablespoon olive oil
1¹/₂ cups chopped onion
1 cup (¹/₄-inch-thick) slices carrot
1 tablespoon curry powder
1 teaspoon brown sugar
1 teaspoon grated peeled fresh ginger
2 garlic cloves, minced
1 serrano chile, seeded and minced
3 cups cooked chickpeas (garbanzo beans)
   or 2 (15¹/₂-ounce) cans chickpeas,
   rinsed and drained

1¹/₂ cups cubed peeled baking potato
1 cup diced green bell pepper
1 cup (1-inch) cut green beans
¹/₂ teaspoon salt
¹/₄ teaspoon freshly ground black pepper
¹/₈ teaspoon ground red pepper
1 (14.5-ounce) can diced tomatoes, undrained
1 (14-ounce) can vegetable broth
3 cups fresh baby spinach
1 cup light coconut milk
6 lemon wedges

1. Heat oil in a large nonstick skillet over medium heat. Add onion and carrot; cover and cook 5 minutes or until tender. Add curry powder, sugar, ginger, garlic, and chile; cook 1 minute, stirring constantly.

2. Place onion mixture in an electric slow cooker. Stir in chickpeas and next 8 ingredients (through broth). Cover and cook on HIGH for 6 hours or until vegetables are tender. Add spinach and coconut milk; stir until spinach wilts. Serve with lemon wedges. Yield: 6 servings (serving size: 1⅓ cups vegetable mixture and 1 lemon wedge).

CALORIES 276; **FAT** 7.2g (sat 1.9g, mono 2.3g, poly 1.3g); **PROTEIN** 10.9g; **CARB** 44.7g; **FIBER** 10.6g; **CHOL** 0mg; **IRON** 4.3mg; **SODIUM** 623mg; **CALC** 107mg

Pinto Bean Chili with Corn and Winter Squash

The subtle sweetness of corn and winter squash complements the spiciness of this light yet satisfying chili. Queso fresco is a crumbly, slightly salty Mexican cheese. If you can't find it, substitute crumbled feta or farmer cheese. For a heartier vegetarian chili, add 1 cup thawed frozen meatless crumbles.

1 tablespoon olive oil
1½ cups chopped onion
1½ cups chopped red bell pepper
1 garlic clove, minced
2 tablespoons chili powder
½ teaspoon ground cumin
4 cups (½-inch) cubed peeled butternut squash (about 1 pound)
1½ cups water
1 cup frozen whole-kernel corn

1 teaspoon salt
2 (16-ounce) cans pinto beans, rinsed and drained
1 (14.5-ounce) can crushed tomatoes, undrained
1 (4.5-ounce) can chopped green chiles, undrained
¾ cup (3 ounces) crumbled queso fresco
6 lime wedges

1. Heat oil in a large nonstick skillet over medium heat. Add onion, bell pepper, and garlic to pan; cover and cook 5 minutes or until tender. Add chili powder and cumin; cook 1 minute, stirring constantly.
2. Place onion mixture in an electric slow cooker. Stir in squash and next 6 ingredients (through chiles). Cover and cook on LOW for 8 hours or until vegetables are tender and chili is thick.
3. Ladle chili into soup bowls; top each serving with cheese. Serve with lime wedges. Yield: 6 servings (serving size: 1½ cups chili, 2 tablespoons cheese, and 1 lime wedge).

CALORIES 296; **FAT** 6.5g (sat 2.2g, mono 2.7g, poly 1g); **PROTEIN** 15.1g; **CARB** 49.6g; **FIBER** 13.3g; **CHOL** 10mg; **IRON** 4.8mg; **SODIUM** 835mg; **CALC** 206mg

Cuban Beans and Rice

Dried beans are inexpensive and a convenient choice for economical meals. They also lend themselves well to slow cooking because, unlike on the stovetop, there is no risk of burning during the long simmering period.

1 pound dried black beans
2 cups water
2 cups organic vegetable broth
2 cups chopped onion
1½ cups chopped red bell pepper
1 cup chopped green bell pepper
2 tablespoons olive oil
3 teaspoons salt
2 teaspoons fennel seeds, crushed
2 teaspoons ground coriander
2 teaspoons ground cumin
2 teaspoons dried oregano
2 tablespoons sherry or red wine vinegar
2 (10-ounce) cans diced tomatoes and green chiles, drained
5 cups hot cooked rice
Hot sauce (optional)

1. Sort and wash beans; place in a large bowl. Cover with water to 2 inches above beans; cover and let stand 8 hours. Drain beans.

2. Place beans, 2 cups water, and next 10 ingredients (through oregano) in an electric slow cooker; stir well. Cover and cook on HIGH for 5 hours or until beans are tender. Stir in vinegar and tomatoes. Serve over rice. Sprinkle with hot sauce, if desired. Yield: 10 servings (serving size: 1 cup bean mixture and ½ cup rice).

CALORIES 314; **FAT** 3.3g (sat 0.4g, mono 2g, poly 0.5g); **PROTEIN** 12.1g; **CARB** 58.3g; **FIBER** 6g; **CHOL** 0mg; **IRON** 3.7mg; **SODIUM** 816mg; **CALC** 24mg

STORAGE TIP: This meatless entrée reheats well the next day for lunch. Store leftover bean mixture and rice in separate containers in the refrigerator.

Pesto Lasagna with Spinach and Mushrooms

No-boil lasagna noodles are perfect for this recipe, as they absorb all the juices that accumulate in the cooker. Use 2 (10-ounce) packages of frozen chopped spinach, thawed, drained, and squeezed dry, in place of fresh, if you prefer. Also, any variety of fresh mushroom will work.

4 cups torn spinach
2 cups sliced cremini mushrooms
½ cup commercial pesto
¾ cup (3 ounces) shredded part-skim
   mozzarella cheese
¾ cup (3 ounces) shredded provolone cheese
1 (15-ounce) carton fat-free ricotta cheese
1 large egg, lightly beaten

¾ cup (3 ounces) grated fresh Parmesan
   cheese, divided
1 (25-ounce) jar low-sodium, fat-free
   tomato-basil pasta sauce
1 (8-ounce) can no-salt-added tomato sauce
Cooking spray
1 (8-ounce) package no-boil lasagna noodles
   (12 noodles)

1. Arrange spinach in a vegetable steamer; steam, covered, 3 minutes or until spinach wilts. Drain, squeeze dry, and coarsely chop. Combine spinach, mushrooms, and pesto in a medium bowl. Stir well.
2. Combine mozzarella, provolone, ricotta, and beaten egg in a medium bowl, stirring well. Stir in ¼ cup Parmesan; set aside. Combine pasta sauce and tomato sauce in a medium bowl.
3. Coat a 6-quart electric slow cooker with cooking spray. Spread 1 cup pasta sauce mixture in bottom of slow cooker. Arrange 3 noodles over pasta sauce mixture; top with 1 cup cheese mixture and 1 cup spinach mixture. Repeat layers, ending with spinach mixture. Arrange 3 noodles over spinach mixture; top with remaining 1 cup cheese mixture and 1 cup pasta sauce mixture. Place remaining 3 noodles over sauce mixture, and spread remaining sauce mixture over noodles. Sprinkle with remaining ½ cup Parmesan. Cover and cook on LOW for 5 hours or until done. Yield: 8 servings (serving size: 1 piece).

CALORIES 405; FAT 18.1g (sat 7.9g, mono 5.3g, poly 3.5g); PROTEIN 21.9g; CARB 37.6g; FIBER 2.4g; CHOL 56mg; IRON 2.9mg; SODIUM 705mg; CALC 442mg

Barley-Stuffed Cabbage Rolls with Pine Nuts and Currants

This dish works well assembled the night before, giving you a head start on the next day's dinner. Trimming away part of the thick center vein from the cabbage leaves makes them more pliable and easier to roll up.

1 large head green cabbage, cored
1 tablespoon olive oil
1½ cups finely chopped onion
3 cups cooked pearl barley
¾ cup (3 ounces) crumbled feta cheese
½ cup dried currants
2 tablespoons pine nuts, toasted
2 tablespoons chopped fresh parsley

½ teaspoon salt, divided
¼ teaspoon freshly ground black pepper, divided
½ cup apple juice
1 tablespoon cider vinegar
1 (14.5-ounce) can crushed tomatoes, undrained

1. Steam cabbage head 8 minutes; cool slightly. Remove 16 leaves from cabbage head; discard remaining cabbage. Cut off raised portion of the center vein of each cabbage leaf (do not cut out vein); set trimmed cabbage leaves aside.

2. Heat oil in a large nonstick skillet over medium heat. Add chopped onion; cover and cook 6 minutes or until tender. Remove from heat; stir in barley, feta cheese, currants, pine nuts, and parsley. Stir in ¼ teaspoon salt and ⅛ teaspoon pepper.

3. Place cabbage leaves on a flat surface; spoon about ⅓ cup barley mixture into center of each cabbage leaf. Fold in edges of leaves over barley mixture; roll up. Arrange cabbage rolls in bottom of an electric slow cooker.

4. Combine remaining ¼ teaspoon salt, remaining ⅛ teaspoon pepper, apple juice, vinegar, and tomatoes; pour evenly over cabbage rolls. Cover and cook on HIGH for 2 hours or until thoroughly heated. Yield: 4 servings (serving size: 4 cabbage rolls and 2 tablespoons sauce).

CALORIES 402; FAT 11.3g (sat 4.2g, mono 4.4g, poly 1.9g); PROTEIN 11.3g; CARB 70.1g; FIBER 11.3g; CHOL 19mg; IRON 5mg; SODIUM 693mg; CALC 234mg

Slow-Simmered Meat Sauce

Mafaldine is a flat noodle with ruffled edges. You can substitute spaghetti, if you like.

1 tablespoon olive oil
2 cups chopped onion
1 cup chopped carrot
6 garlic cloves, minced
2 (4-ounce) links hot Italian sausage, casings removed
1 pound ground sirloin
½ cup kalamata olives, pitted and sliced
¼ cup no-salt-added tomato paste
1½ teaspoons sugar
1 teaspoon kosher salt
½ teaspoon crushed red pepper
1 (28-ounce) can no-salt-added crushed tomatoes, undrained
1 cup no-salt-added tomato sauce
1 tablespoon chopped fresh oregano
16 ounces uncooked mafaldine pasta
½ cup torn fresh basil
3 ounces shaved fresh Parmigiano-Reggiano cheese

1. Heat oil in a large skillet over medium-high heat. Add onion and carrot to pan; cook 4 minutes, stirring occasionally. Add garlic; sauté 1 minute. Place vegetable mixture in a 6-quart electric slow cooker. Add sausage and beef to skillet; cook 6 minutes or until browned, stirring to crumble. Remove beef mixture from pan using a slotted spoon. Place beef mixture on a double layer of paper towels; drain. Add beef mixture to slow cooker. Stir olives and next 6 ingredients (through tomato sauce) into beef mixture in slow cooker. Cover and cook on LOW for 8 hours. Stir in oregano.
2. Prepare pasta according to package directions, omitting salt and fat. Serve sauce with hot cooked pasta; top with basil and cheese. Yield: 8 servings (serving size: 1 cup pasta, 1 cup sauce, 1 tablespoon basil, and 2 tablespoons cheese).

CALORIES 503; **FAT** 16.7g (sat 5.7g, mono 8g, poly 2g); **PROTEIN** 26.3g; **CARB** 59.7g; **FIBER** 5.6g; **CHOL** 48mg; **IRON** 4.8mg; **SODIUM** 766mg; **CALC** 198mg

Chunky Minestrone with Beef

1 pound lean beef stew meat, trimmed
1 cup chopped onion
½ cup chopped carrot
2 (14.5-ounce) cans no-salt-added diced
   tomatoes with roasted garlic, undrained
2 (14-ounce) cans fat-free, lower-sodium
   chicken broth
1 teaspoon dried Italian seasoning
½ teaspoon salt

¼ teaspoon freshly ground black pepper
2 cups chopped cabbage
1 cup thinly sliced yellow squash
1 (15½-ounce) can chickpeas
   (garbanzo beans), rinsed and drained
2 cups cooked seashell pasta
6 tablespoons (1½ ounces) grated
   Parmesan cheese

1. Place first 8 ingredients (through pepper) in an electric slow cooker; stir well. Cover and cook on HIGH for 1 hour.

2. Reduce heat to LOW, and cook an additional 5 hours or until meat is tender.

3. Stir in cabbage, squash, and chickpeas. Cook on HIGH for 45 minutes or until vegetables are tender. Stir in cooked pasta. Top each serving with cheese. Yield: 6 servings (serving size: 1½ cups soup and 1 tablespoon cheese).

CALORIES 253; FAT 8.2g (sat 3.2g, mono 2.3g, poly 0.3g); PROTEIN 22.1g; CARB 21.8g; FIBER 3.7g; CHOL 53mg; IRON 3.1mg; SODIUM 590mg; CALC 136mg

All-American Beef Stew

A few minutes of effortless prep yield this flavorful classic.

2 tablespoons uncooked granulated tapioca
1 tablespoon sugar
1 tablespoon garlic powder
1 teaspoon salt
3 (5.5-ounce) cans tomato juice

4 cups chopped onion
3 cups chopped celery
2½ cups (¼-inch-thick) slices carrot
2 (8-ounce) packages presliced mushrooms
2 pounds lean beef stew meat, trimmed

1. Place tapioca, sugar, garlic powder, salt, and tomato juice in a blender; process until smooth.

2. Place onion, celery, carrot, mushrooms, and beef in an electric slow cooker; stir well. Add juice mixture, stirring well. Cover and cook on HIGH for 5 hours or until beef is tender. Yield: 6 servings (serving size: about 1¾ cups).

CALORIES 345; **FAT** 11.1g (sat 4g, mono 4.7g, poly 0.7g); **PROTEIN** 34.1g; **CARB** 28.8g; **FIBER** 5.9g; **CHOL** 95mg; **IRON** 5.3mg; **SODIUM** 811mg; **CALC** 81mg

PREP TIP: Using a blender is the quickest and easiest way to dissolve the tapioca completely.

Beef Burgundy with Egg Noodles

This dish tastes even better made a day or two in advance and reheated.

2 pounds lean beef stew meat, trimmed
6 tablespoons all-purpose flour
   (about 1³/₄ ounces)
2 cups (1-inch-thick) slices carrot
1 (16-ounce) package frozen pearl
   onions, thawed
1 (8-ounce) package mushrooms,
   stems removed
2 garlic cloves, minced

³/₄ cup fat-free, lower-sodium beef broth
¹/₂ cup dry red wine
¹/₄ cup tomato paste
1¹/₂ teaspoons salt
¹/₂ teaspoon dried rosemary
¹/₄ teaspoon dried thyme
¹/₂ teaspoon freshly ground black pepper
8 ounces uncooked egg noodles
¹/₄ cup chopped fresh thyme

1. Sprinkle beef with flour in a large bowl, tossing well to coat. Place beef mixture, carrot, onions, mushrooms, and garlic in an electric slow cooker; stir well. Combine beef broth and next 6 ingredients (through pepper); stir into beef mixture. Cover and cook on LOW for 8 hours.

2. Cook noodles according to package directions, omitting salt and fat. Serve beef mixture over noodles; sprinkle with thyme. Yield: 8 servings (serving size: about 1¼ cups beef mixture, ½ cup egg noodles, and 1½ teaspoons thyme).

CALORIES 357; FAT 9.3g (sat 3.3g, mono 3.8g, poly 0.7g); PROTEIN 28.4g; CARB 38.9g; FIBER 2.5g; CHOL 94mg; IRON 4.7mg; SODIUM 637mg; CALC 53mg

WINE NOTE: When choosing a dry red wine for this recipe, consider a Chianti or zinfandel. Either is a good choice.

Beef Pot Roast with Turnip Greens

Cipollini onions are small, flat Italian onions. If you can't find them, substitute pearl onions. Other large, full-flavored greens like mustard greens or kale will work as well.

3.4 ounces all-purpose flour (about ¾ cup)
1 (3-pound) boneless chuck roast, trimmed
1 teaspoon kosher salt
½ teaspoon freshly ground black pepper
1 tablespoon olive oil
1 pound fresh turnip greens, trimmed and
   coarsely chopped
3 cups (2-inch) diagonally cut parsnips
   (about 1 pound)
3 cups cubed peeled Yukon gold potatoes
   (about 1 pound)

2 cups cipollini onions, peeled and quartered
2 tablespoons tomato paste
1 cup dry red wine
1 (14-ounce) can fat-free, lower-sodium
   beef broth
1 tablespoon black peppercorns
4 thyme sprigs
3 garlic cloves, crushed
2 bay leaves
1 bunch fresh flat-leaf parsley
Thyme sprigs (optional)

1. Place flour in a shallow dish. Sprinkle beef evenly with salt and pepper; dredge in flour. Heat oil in a large skillet over medium-high heat. Add beef; cook 10 minutes, turning to brown on all sides. Place turnip greens in a 6-quart electric slow cooker; top with parsnips, potatoes, and onions. Transfer beef to slow cooker. Add tomato paste to skillet; cook 30 seconds, stirring constantly. Stir in wine and broth; bring to a boil, scraping pan to loosen browned bits. Cook 1 minute, stirring constantly. Pour broth mixture into slow cooker.
2. Place peppercorns and next 4 ingredients (through parsley) on a double layer of cheese-cloth. Gather edges of cheesecloth together; secure with twine. Add cheesecloth bundle to slow cooker. Cover and cook on LOW for 8 hours or until beef and vegetables are tender. Discard cheesecloth bundle. Remove roast from slow cooker; slice. Serve with vegetable mixture and cooking liquid. Garnish with thyme sprigs, if desired. Yield: 12 servings (serving size: 3 ounces beef, ¾ cup vegetable mixture, and ⅓ cup sauce).

CALORIES 424; **FAT** 21.3g (sat 8.1g, mono 9.4g, poly 0.9g); **PROTEIN** 33g; **CARB** 23.5g; **FIBER** 2.9g; **CHOL** 99mg; **IRON** 3.8mg; **SODIUM** 348mg; **CALC** 90mg

Provençal Beef Daube

If niçoise olives aren't available, use another meaty variety, such as kalamata or gaeta.

1 (2-pound) boneless chuck roast, trimmed and cut into chunks
1 tablespoon extra-virgin olive oil
6 garlic cloves, minced
½ cup boiling water
½ ounce dried porcini mushrooms
¾ teaspoon salt, divided
Cooking spray
½ cup red wine
¼ cup fat-free, lower-sodium beef broth
⅓ cup pitted niçoise olives
½ teaspoon freshly ground black pepper
2 large carrots, peeled and diagonally cut

1 large onion, chopped
1 celery stalk, diagonally cut
1 (15-ounce) can whole tomatoes, drained and crushed
1 teaspoon black peppercorns
3 flat-leaf parsley sprigs
3 thyme sprigs
1 bay leaf
1 (1-inch) strip orange rind
1 tablespoon water
1 teaspoon cornstarch
1½ tablespoons fresh flat-leaf parsley leaves

1. Combine first 3 ingredients in a large zip-top plastic bag. Seal and marinate at room temperature 30 minutes, turning bag occasionally.
2. Combine ½ cup boiling water and mushrooms; cover and let stand 30 minutes. Drain through a sieve over a bowl, reserving mushrooms and ¼ cup soaking liquid. Chop mushrooms.
3. Heat a large skillet over medium-high heat. Sprinkle beef mixture with ¼ teaspoon salt. Coat pan with cooking spray. Add half of beef mixture to pan; cook 5 minutes, turning to brown on all sides. Place browned beef mixture in a 6-quart electric slow cooker. Repeat procedure with cooking spray and remaining beef mixture. Add wine and broth to skillet; bring to a boil, scraping pan to loosen browned bits. Pour wine mixture into slow cooker. Stir mushrooms, reserved ¼ cup soaking liquid, remaining ½ teaspoon salt, olives, and next 5 ingredients (through tomatoes) into beef mixture in cooker. Place peppercorns, parsley sprigs, thyme sprigs, bay leaf, and orange rind on a double layer of cheesecloth. Gather edges of cheesecloth together; secure with twine. Add cheesecloth bundle to slow cooker. Cover and cook on LOW for 6 hours or until beef and vegetables are tender. Discard cheesecloth bundle.
4. Combine 1 tablespoon water and cornstarch in a small bowl, stirring until smooth. Add cornstarch mixture to slow cooker; cook 20 minutes or until slightly thick, stirring occasionally. Sprinkle with parsley leaves. Yield: 8 servings (serving size: about ¾ cup).

CALORIES 360; **FAT** 22.5g (sat 8g, mono 10.6g, poly 1.1g); **PROTEIN** 30.2g; **CARB** 7.8g; **FIBER** 2.2g; **CHOL** 94mg; **IRON** 3.5mg; **SODIUM** 516mg; **CALC** 53mg

Brazilian Feijoada

Feijoada (pronounced fay-ZWAH-da) is a delicious stew of pork and black beans that's traditionally served over rice with fresh orange slices. In Brazil, this dish is often reserved for special occasions, but preparing the recipe in a slow cooker makes it possible to serve on the busiest weeknights.

2 cups dried black beans
4 applewood-smoked bacon slices
1 pound boneless pork shoulder (Boston butt), trimmed and cut into ½-inch cubes
¾ teaspoon salt, divided
½ teaspoon freshly ground black pepper, divided
3 bone-in beef short ribs, trimmed (about 2 pounds)

3 cups finely chopped onion (about 2 medium)
1¼ cups fat-free, lower-sodium chicken broth
4 garlic cloves, minced
1 (9-ounce) smoked ham hock
1 tablespoon white vinegar
8 orange wedges

1. Place beans in a small saucepan; cover with cold water. Bring to a boil; cook 2 minutes. Remove from heat; cover and let stand 1 hour. Drain.

2. Cook bacon in a large skillet over medium heat until crisp. Remove bacon from pan; crumble. Sprinkle pork evenly with ⅛ teaspoon salt and ¼ teaspoon pepper. Increase heat to medium-high. Add pork to drippings in skillet; cook 8 minutes, turning to brown on all sides. Transfer pork to a 6-quart electric slow cooker. Sprinkle ribs evenly with ⅛ teaspoon salt and remaining ¼ teaspoon pepper. Add ribs to skillet; cook 3 minutes on each side or until browned. Place ribs in slow cooker. Add drained beans, remaining ½ teaspoon salt, onion, and next 3 ingredients (through ham hock) to slow cooker, stirring to combine. Cover and cook on LOW for 8 hours or until beans and meat are tender.

3. Remove ribs from slow cooker; let stand 15 minutes. Remove meat from bones; shred meat with 2 forks. Discard bones. Discard ham hock. Return beef to slow cooker. Stir in vinegar and crumbled bacon. Serve with orange wedges. Yield: 8 servings (serving size: about 1¼ cups bean mixture and 1 orange wedge).

CALORIES 458; **FAT** 17.4g (sat 6.8g, mono 6.7g, poly 1.1g); **PROTEIN** 39.5g; **CARB** 35.8g; **FIBER** 11.6g; **CHOL** 96mg; **IRON** 6.4mg; **SODIUM** 533mg; **CALC** 102mg

Company Pot Roast *(Pictured on page 298)*

You may substitute dried shiitake mushrooms for the morels. Leftover meat and gravy make great hot roast beef sandwiches on Kaiser rolls the next day.

1 (2-pound) boneless chuck roast, trimmed and cut in half
¼ cup lower-sodium soy sauce
2 garlic cloves, minced
1 cup beef broth
1 (0.35-ounce) package dried morels
1 tablespoon cracked black pepper
3 tablespoons sun-dried tomato paste
2 medium onions (about ¾ pound), quartered

1 (16-ounce) package carrots, cut into 2-inch pieces
16 small red potatoes (about 2 pounds), halved
1 tablespoon canola oil
1½ tablespoons all-purpose flour
3 tablespoons water
Fresh parsley leaves (optional)

1. Combine roast, soy sauce, and garlic in a large zip-top plastic bag; seal bag, and marinate in refrigerator at least 8 hours, turning bag occasionally.
2. Bring broth to a boil in a small saucepan, and add mushrooms. Remove from heat; cover and let stand 20 minutes. Drain mushrooms through a cheesecloth-lined colander over a small bowl, reserving mushroom broth mixture.
3. Remove roast from bag, reserving marinade. Sprinkle roast with pepper, gently pressing pepper into roast. Combine reserved roast marinade, reserved mushroom broth mixture, and tomato paste; stir well, and set aside.
4. Place mushrooms, onions, carrots, and potatoes in a 6-quart electric slow cooker; toss gently.
5. Heat oil in a large skillet over medium-high heat. Add roast, browning well on all sides. Place roast over vegetables in slow cooker. Pour tomato paste mixture into pan, scraping pan to loosen browned bits. Pour tomato paste mixture over roast and vegetables. Cover and cook on HIGH for 1 hour. Reduce heat to LOW, and cook 8 hours or until roast is tender. Place roast and vegetables on a serving platter; keep warm. Reserve liquid in slow cooker, and increase heat to HIGH.
6. Place flour in a small bowl. Gradually add 3 tablespoons water, stirring with a whisk until well blended. Add flour mixture to liquid in slow cooker. Cook, uncovered, 15 minutes or until gravy is slightly thick, stirring frequently. Serve gravy with roast and vegetables. Garnish with parsley, if desired. Yield: 8 servings (serving size: 3 ounces roast, 1 onion wedge, about 3 carrot pieces, 4 potato halves, and about ¼ cup gravy).

CALORIES 318; **FAT** 6.8g (sat 1.6g, mono 2.7g, poly 0.8g); **PROTEIN** 30.5g; **CARB** 33.1g; **FIBER** 5.2g; **CHOL** 40mg; **IRON** 3.9mg; **SODIUM** 552mg; **CALC** 70mg

Pork with Apricots, Dried Plums, and Sauerkraut

Sauerkraut balances the sweetness of the apricot preserves and orange juice. Slow cooking nicely tenderizes the pork and dried fruit.

1 (2-pound) pork tenderloin, trimmed
1 cup chopped onion (about 1 medium)
³⁄₄ cup apricot preserves
¹⁄₂ cup dried apricots
¹⁄₂ cup pitted dried plums
¹⁄₄ cup fat-free, lower-sodium chicken broth
¹⁄₄ cup orange juice

2 tablespoons cornstarch
1 teaspoon salt
¹⁄₂ teaspoon dried thyme
¹⁄₄ teaspoon freshly ground black pepper
1 (10-ounce) package refrigerated sauerkraut

1. Place pork in an electric slow cooker. Combine onion and remaining ingredients in a large bowl, and stir well; pour sauerkraut mixture over pork. Cover and cook on LOW for 7 hours. Remove pork from slow cooker. Let stand 10 minutes. Cut pork into ¼-inch-thick slices. Serve sliced pork with sauerkraut mixture. Yield: 8 servings (serving size: 3 ounces pork and about ½ cup sauerkraut mixture).

CALORIES 313; **FAT** 6.6g (sat 2.2g, mono 3g, poly 0.7g); **PROTEIN** 25.4g; **CARB** 38.3g; **FIBER** 2.5g; **CHOL** 67mg; **IRON** 1.7mg; **SODIUM** 41mg; **CALC** 594mg

Tuscan Chicken Soup

This recipe uses many common pantry staples and refrigerator ingredients. All you have to pick up at the supermarket is fresh spinach and chicken thighs.

1 cup chopped onion
2 tablespoons tomato paste
$\frac{1}{4}$ teaspoon salt
$\frac{1}{4}$ teaspoon freshly ground black pepper
1 (15-ounce) can cannellini beans, rinsed and drained
1 (14-ounce) can fat-free, lower-sodium chicken broth

1 (7-ounce) bottle roasted red bell peppers, rinsed, drained, and cut into $\frac{1}{2}$-inch pieces
1 pound skinless, boneless chicken thighs, cut into 1-inch pieces
3 garlic cloves, minced
$\frac{1}{2}$ teaspoon chopped fresh rosemary
1 (6-ounce) package fresh baby spinach
8 teaspoons grated fresh Parmesan cheese

1. Place first 9 ingredients (through garlic) in an electric slow cooker; stir well. Cover and cook on HIGH for 1 hour; reduce heat to LOW, and cook an additional 3 hours. Stir in rosemary and spinach; cook on LOW for 10 minutes. Ladle soup into shallow bowls; top each serving with Parmesan cheese. Yield: 4 servings (serving size: 1½ cups soup and 2 teaspoons cheese).

CALORIES 239; FAT 5.8g (sat 1.8g, mono 1.7g, poly 1.4g); PROTEIN 28.6g; CARB 16.3g; FIBER 4.6g; CHOL 97mg; IRON 3.9mg; SODIUM 768mg; CALC 126mg

Chicken and Shrimp Jambalaya

Try this dish when you're serving a crowd. Garnish with fresh flat-leaf parsley sprigs, if desired.

1 tablespoon canola oil

1 pound skinless, boneless chicken breast, cut into 1-inch pieces

³/₄ pound skinless, boneless chicken thighs, cut into 1-inch pieces

2 cups chopped onion

1 cup chopped green bell pepper

1 cup chopped celery

2 garlic cloves, minced

4 ounces turkey kielbasa, halved and cut into ¹/₄-inch-thick slices

2 teaspoons salt-free Cajun seasoning

¹/₂ teaspoon dried thyme

¹/₄ teaspoon Spanish smoked paprika (optional)

2 (14¹/₂-ounce) cans diced tomatoes with onion, celery, and green peppers

1 (14-ounce) can fat-free, lower-sodium chicken broth

2 (3¹/₂-ounce) bags boil-in-bag long-grain rice

1 pound medium shrimp, peeled and deveined

2 tablespoons chopped fresh flat-leaf parsley

1 tablespoon hot sauce

1. Heat oil in a large skillet over high heat. Add chicken; cook 4 minutes, stirring occasionally. Spoon chicken into an electric slow cooker.

2. Add onion, bell pepper, celery, and garlic to pan; sauté 4 minutes or until tender. Stir onion mixture, turkey kielbasa, and next 5 ingredients (through chicken broth) into chicken in slow cooker. Cover and cook on LOW for 5 hours.

3. Cook rice according to package directions. Add cooked rice and remaining ingredients to slow cooker. Cover and cook on HIGH for 15 minutes or until shrimp are done. Yield: 8 servings (serving size: 1¼ cups).

CALORIES 364; **FAT** 6.3g (sat 1.4g, mono 2g, poly 1.6g); **PROTEIN** 39.5g; **CARB** 34.8g; **FIBER** 3.5g; **CHOL** 157mg; **IRON** 4.8mg; **SODIUM** 727mg; **CALC** 110mg

White Chicken Chili

Chili lovers who enjoy less-spicy food can add this to their slow-cooker recipe collection.

1 cup fat-free, lower-sodium chicken broth
1 cup chopped onion (about 1 medium)
2 tablespoons all-purpose flour
2 teaspoons chili powder
1 teaspoon ground cumin
$^1/_2$ teaspoon salt
$^1/_2$ teaspoon hot sauce
$^1/_8$ teaspoon freshly ground black pepper
1 pound skinless, boneless chicken breast, cut into bite-sized pieces
3 (19-ounce) cans cannellini beans, rinsed and drained
1 (15.5-ounce) can no-salt-added whole-kernel corn, drained
1 (4.5-ounce) can chopped green chiles, drained
2 garlic cloves, minced
6 tablespoons (1$^1/_2$ ounces) preshredded reduced-fat Mexican blend or cheddar cheese
6 tablespoons reduced-fat sour cream
2 tablespoons chopped fresh cilantro
Baked tortilla chips (optional)

1. Place first 13 ingredients (through garlic) in an electric slow cooker; stir well. Cover and cook on HIGH for 1 hour; reduce heat to LOW, and cook 4 hours.
2. Ladle chili into soup bowls; top each serving with cheese, sour cream, and cilantro. Garnish with tortilla chips, if desired. Yield: 6 servings (serving size: 1 cup chili, 1 tablespoon cheese, 1 tablespoon sour cream, and 1 teaspoon cilantro).

CALORIES 232; FAT 5.9g (sat 3.1g, mono 0.6g, poly 0.6g); PROTEIN 22.3g; CARB 22.3g; FIBER 3.7g; CHOL 55mg; IRON 1.8mg; SODIUM 443mg; CALC 113mg

Sweet and Sour Chicken

Pork tenderloin can be used in place of chicken thighs.

1 cup chopped onion (about 1 medium)
⅓ cup sugar
⅓ cup ketchup
¼ cup orange juice
3 tablespoons cornstarch
3 tablespoons cider vinegar
2 tablespoons lower-sodium soy sauce
1 tablespoon grated peeled fresh ginger
1 pound skinless, boneless chicken thighs, cut into 1-inch pieces

2 (8-ounce) cans pineapple chunks in juice, drained
1 large green bell pepper, cut into ¾-inch pieces
1 large red bell pepper, cut into ¾-inch pieces
3 cups hot cooked white rice

1. Place first 12 ingredients (through red bell pepper) in an electric slow cooker; stir well. Cover and cook on LOW for 6 hours or HIGH for 4 hours. Serve over rice. Yield: 6 servings (serving size: ⅔ cup chicken mixture and ½ cup rice).

CALORIES 381; **FAT** 8.7g (sat 2.3g, mono 3.2g, poly 2g); **PROTEIN** 23.2g; **CARB** 51.9g; **FIBER** 2.1g; **CHOL** 72mg; **IRON** 2.5mg; **SODIUM** 396mg; **CALC** 29mg

Autumn Apple, Pear, and Cheddar Salad with Pecans, page 343

extras

Roasted Red Pepper Hummus

Enjoy this tasty appetizer with pita chips or raw vegetables while soup simmers on the stovetop or a casserole bakes in the oven.

⅓ cup tahini (roasted sesame seed paste)
¼ cup water
¼ cup chopped bottled roasted red bell
    peppers, rinsed and drained
2 tablespoons fresh lemon juice

¼ teaspoon salt
1 garlic clove, minced
1 (15½-ounce) can chickpeas (garbanzo
    beans), rinsed and drained

1. Place all ingredients in a food processor; process until smooth. Yield: 8 servings (serving size: ¼ cup).

CALORIES 102; **FAT** 5.7g (sat 0.8g, mono 2.1g, poly 2.5g); **PROTEIN** 3.5g; **CARB** 10.5g; **FIBER** 2g; **CHOL** 0mg; **IRON** 1mg; **SODIUM** 199mg; **CALC** 26mg

Artichoke, Spinach, and White Bean Dip

If you can't find baby artichoke hearts, use quartered artichoke hearts and chop them.

¼ cup (1 ounce) grated fresh pecorino
 Romano cheese
¼ cup canola mayonnaise
1 teaspoon fresh lemon juice
¼ teaspoon salt
¼ teaspoon freshly ground black pepper
⅛ teaspoon ground red pepper
2 garlic cloves, minced
1 (15-ounce) can organic white beans, rinsed
 and drained

1 (14-ounce) can baby artichoke hearts,
 drained and quartered
1 (9-ounce) package frozen chopped spinach,
 thawed, drained, and squeezed dry
Cooking spray
½ cup (2 ounces) shredded part-skim
 mozzarella cheese

1. Preheat oven to 350°.
2. Place first 8 ingredients in a food processor, and process until smooth. Spoon into a medium bowl. Stir in artichokes and spinach. Spoon mixture into a 1-quart glass or ceramic baking dish coated with cooking spray. Sprinkle with mozzarella. Bake at 350° for 20 minutes or until bubbly and brown. Yield: 12 servings (serving size: ¼ cup).

CALORIES 87; FAT 5.4g (sat 1.4g, mono 2.3g, poly 1g); PROTEIN 3.7g; CARB 4.9g; FIBER 1g; CHOL 6mg; IRON 0.7mg; SODIUM 232mg; CALC 91mg

> **MENU IDEA:** Serve with homemade pita chips or toasted baguette slices.

Black-Eyed Pea and Tomato Salsa

Adding the inner veins and seeds from the chile will increase the heat in this salsa.

1 cup chopped tomato
1/4 cup prechopped red onion
3 tablespoons chopped poblano chile
2 tablespoons chopped fresh cilantro
2 1/2 tablespoons fresh lime juice
1/4 teaspoon minced garlic

1/8 teaspoon salt
1/8 teaspoon ground cumin
1/8 teaspoon freshly ground black pepper
1 (15.8-ounce) can black-eyed peas, rinsed and drained

1. Place all ingredients in a large bowl, and toss to combine. Yield: 8 servings (serving size: about 1/3 cup).

CALORIES 35; FAT 0.3g (sat 0.1g, mono 0g, poly 0.1g); PROTEIN 1.9g; CARB 6.6g; FIBER 1.5g; CHOL 0mg; IRON 0.4mg; SODIUM 139mg; CALC 11mg

> **FYI:** This is a great appetizer to pair with a Mexican casserole.

Baked Mozzarella Bites

Serve as an alternative to fried cheese sticks.

⅓ cup panko (Japanese breadcrumbs)
3 (1-ounce) sticks part-skim mozzarella
  string cheese

3 tablespoons egg substitute
Cooking spray
¼ cup lower-sodium marinara sauce

1. Preheat oven to 425°.
2. Heat a medium skillet over medium heat. Add panko to pan, and cook 2 minutes or until toasted, stirring frequently. Remove from heat, and place panko in a shallow dish.
3. Cut mozzarella sticks into 1-inch pieces. Working with one piece at a time, dip cheese in egg substitute; dredge in panko. Place cheese on a baking sheet coated with cooking spray. Bake at 425° for 3 minutes or until cheese is softened and thoroughly heated.
4. Pour marinara sauce into a microwave-safe bowl. Microwave at HIGH 1 minute or until thoroughly heated, stirring after 30 seconds. Serve with mozzarella pieces. Yield: 4 servings (serving size: 3 mozzarella bites and 1 tablespoon sauce).

CALORIES 91; **FAT** 5.1g (sat 2.8g, mono 1.3g, poly 0.3g); **PROTEIN** 7.2g; **CARB** 6.7g; **FIBER** 0.1g; **CHOL** 12mg; **IRON** 0.3mg; **SODIUM** 162mg; **CALC** 162mg

Pecorino–Black Pepper Breadsticks

These breadsticks are quick and easy since the dough does not need to rise. You can also make them ahead. Cool completely, and store in an airtight container at room temperature for up to two days.

1.5 ounces all-purpose flour (about ⅓ cup)
1.2 ounces whole-wheat flour (about ¼ cup)
¼ cup (1 ounce) grated fresh pecorino Romano cheese
¾ teaspoon baking powder
½ teaspoon freshly ground black pepper
5 tablespoons water
1 teaspoon extra-virgin olive oil
Cooking spray

1. Preheat oven to 450°.
2. Weigh or lightly spoon flours into dry measuring cups; level with a knife. Combine flours, cheese, baking powder, and pepper in a medium bowl. Add 5 tablespoons water and oil; stir until a dough forms. Turn dough out onto a floured surface; knead lightly 4 or 5 times. Divide dough into 18 equal portions, shaping each portion into an 8-inch rope. Place ropes on a baking sheet coated with cooking spray.
3. Bake at 450° for 10 minutes or until bottoms are golden brown. Cool on a wire rack. Yield: 1½ dozen (serving size: 3 breadsticks).

CALORIES 64; **FAT** 1.9g (sat 0.7g, mono 0.8g, poly 0.7g); **PROTEIN** 2.7g; **CARB** 9.3g; **FIBER** 0.8g; **CHOL** 3mg; **IRON** 0.6mg; **SODIUM** 113mg; **CALC** 74mg

> **MENU IDEA:** Serve in place of crackers with a creamy dip or as an accompaniment to your meal. These go well with soups, stews, chili, and casseroles.

Fresh Thyme Popovers

Based on the Old English Yorkshire pudding, popovers are a quick bread typically paired with beef dishes. Make the popover batter up to two hours ahead, and refrigerate until 15 minutes before you plan to bake them. Popover cups are tall and narrow so the batter "pops over" the top as it bakes; you can find a popover pan at any kitchenware shop. Muffin cups will also do (with 5 minutes less time in the oven), though popovers won't puff quite as dramatically.

4.5 ounces all-purpose flour (about 1 cup)
2 teaspoons minced fresh thyme
½ teaspoon salt
1 cup 1% low-fat milk
2 large eggs

1 tablespoon butter, melted
Cooking spray
1 tablespoon finely grated Parmigiano-
 Reggiano cheese

1. Preheat oven to 375°.
2. Weigh or lightly spoon flour into a dry measuring cup; level with a knife. Combine flour, thyme, and salt, stirring with a whisk. Combine milk and eggs in a medium bowl, stirring with a whisk until blended; let stand 30 minutes. Gradually add flour mixture to milk mixture, stirring well with a whisk. Stir in melted butter.
3. Coat 8 popover cups with cooking spray; sprinkle Parmigiano-Reggiano cheese evenly among cups. Place cups in oven at 375° for 5 minutes. Divide batter evenly among prepared cups. Bake at 375° for 40 minutes or until golden. Serve immediately. Yield: 8 servings (serving size: 1 popover).

CALORIES 97; **FAT** 2.9g (sat 1.5g, mono 1g, poly 0.3g); **PROTEIN** 4.3g; **CARB** 12.4g; **FIBER** 0.4g; **CHOL** 51mg; **IRON** 1mg; **SODIUM** 200mg; **CALC** 52mg

Basic Beer-Cheese Bread

A quick bread that goes well with soup or chili, this is ideal for an open house or casual get-together.

1 tablespoon olive oil
½ cup finely chopped yellow onion
¼ teaspoon freshly ground black pepper
1 garlic clove, minced
13.5 ounces all-purpose flour (about 3 cups)
3 tablespoons sugar
2 teaspoons baking powder

1 teaspoon salt
1 cup (4 ounces) shredded Monterey Jack cheese
1 (12-ounce) bottle lager-style beer
Cooking spray
2 tablespoons melted butter, divided

1. Preheat oven to 375°.

2. Heat oil in a small skillet over medium-low heat. Add onion to pan; cook 10 minutes or until browned, stirring occasionally. Stir in pepper and garlic; cook 1 minute.

3. Weigh or lightly spoon flour into dry measuring cups; level with a knife. Combine flour, sugar, baking powder, and salt in a large bowl, stirring with a whisk; make a well in center of mixture. Add onion mixture, cheese, and beer to flour mixture, stirring just until moist.

4. Spoon batter into a 9 x 5–inch loaf pan coated with cooking spray. Drizzle 1 tablespoon butter over batter. Bake at 375° for 35 minutes. Drizzle remaining 1 tablespoon butter over batter. Bake an additional 25 minutes or until deep golden brown and a wooden pick inserted in center comes out clean. Cool in pan 5 minutes on a wire rack; remove from pan. Cool completely on wire rack. Yield: 16 servings (serving size: 1 slice).

CALORIES 144; **FAT** 4.4g (sat 2.4g, mono 1.6g, poly 0.2g); **PROTEIN** 4.3g; **CARB** 20.6g; **FIBER** 0.7g; **CHOL** 10mg; **IRON** 1.3mg; **SODIUM** 257mg; **CALC** 89mg

Flaky Buttermilk Biscuits

A light hand with the dough will help ensure tender biscuits. The method of folding the dough creates irresistible flaky layers.

9 ounces all-purpose flour (about 2 cups)
2½ teaspoons baking powder
½ teaspoon salt
5 tablespoons chilled butter, cut into small
  pieces

¾ cup nonfat buttermilk
3 tablespoons honey

1. Preheat oven to 400°.

2. Weigh or lightly spoon flour into dry measuring cups; level with a knife. Combine flour, baking powder, and salt in a large bowl; cut in butter with a pastry blender or 2 knives until mixture resembles coarse meal. Chill 10 minutes.

3. Combine buttermilk and honey, stirring with a whisk until well blended. Add buttermilk mixture to flour mixture; stir just until moist.

4. Turn dough out onto a lightly floured surface; knead lightly 4 times. Roll dough into a (½-inch-thick) 9 x 5–inch rectangle; dust top of dough with flour. Fold dough crosswise into thirds (as if folding a piece of paper to fit into an envelope). Reroll dough into a (½-inch-thick) 9 x 5–inch rectangle; dust top of dough with flour. Fold dough crosswise into thirds; gently roll or pat to a ¾-inch thickness. Cut dough with a 1¾-inch biscuit cutter to form 14 dough rounds. Place dough rounds 1 inch apart on a baking sheet lined with parchment paper. Bake at 400° for 12 minutes or until golden. Remove from pan; cool 2 minutes on wire racks. Serve warm. Yield: 14 servings (serving size: 1 biscuit).

CALORIES 121; **FAT** 4.2g (sat 2.6g, mono 1.1g, poly 0.2g); **PROTEIN** 2.4g; **CARB** 18.4g; **FIBER** 0.5g; **CHOL** 11mg; **IRON** 0.9mg; **SODIUM** 198mg; **CALC** 63mg

Cheddar-Bacon Drop Biscuits

A couple of slices of applewood-smoked bacon and sharp cheddar cheese boost the savory character of this quick bread. Serve warm to best harness the salty notes.

9 ounces all-purpose flour (about 2 cups)
½ teaspoon baking soda
¼ teaspoon kosher salt
3½ tablespoons chilled butter, cut into small pieces
⅓ cup (1½ ounces) finely shredded sharp cheddar cheese

2 applewood-smoked bacon slices, cooked and crumbled
¾ cup nonfat buttermilk
¼ cup water
Cooking spray

1. Preheat oven to 400°.
2. Weigh or lightly spoon flour into dry measuring cups; level with a knife. Combine flour, baking soda, and salt in a large bowl; stir with a whisk. Cut in butter with a pastry blender or 2 knives until mixture resembles coarse meal. Stir in cheese and bacon. Add milk and ¼ cup water, stirring just until moist. Drop dough by 2 level tablespoonfuls 1 inch apart onto a baking sheet coated with cooking spray. Bake at 400° for 11 minutes or until golden brown. Serve warm. Yield: 18 biscuits (serving size: 1 biscuit).

CALORIES 91; **FAT** 3.7g (sat 2.2g, mono 0.8g, poly 0.1g); **PROTEIN** 2.8g; **CARB** 11.5g; **FIBER** 0.4g; **CHOL** 10mg; **IRON** 0.7mg; **SODIUM** 127mg; **CALC** 32mg

Corn Bread Bites

This recipe also makes a dozen muffins in a standard-size muffin tin; bake them for 17 minutes or until golden brown. You also can double the recipe and freeze the extra muffins for up to one month. If you do this, prepare the muffins in two batches so the baking powder in the extra batter does not lose its effectiveness while the first batch bakes.

3 ounces all-purpose flour (about ²/₃ cup)
½ cup yellow cornmeal
1 tablespoon sugar
1½ teaspoons baking powder
¼ teaspoon salt
½ cup (2 ounces) shredded sharp cheddar cheese

½ cup reduced-fat sour cream
¼ cup thinly sliced green onions
1 (8¾-ounce) can cream-style corn
Dash of hot sauce
1 large egg, lightly beaten
Cooking spray

1. Preheat oven to 375°.
2. Weigh or lightly spoon flour into a dry measuring cup, and level with a knife. Combine flour, cornmeal, and next 3 ingredients (through salt) in a large bowl; stir with a whisk. Combine cheddar cheese and remaining ingredients except cooking spray in a small bowl; stir with a whisk. Add cheese mixture to flour mixture, and stir just until moistened.
3. Divide batter evenly among miniature muffin cups coated with cooking spray. Bake at 375° for 10 minutes or until golden brown. Cool in cups 2 minutes; remove from pans. Cool completely on wire racks. Yield: 12 servings (serving size: 3 muffins).

CALORIES 108; **FAT** 3.4g (sat 1.9g, mono 0.5g, poly 0.1g); **PROTEIN** 3.7g; **CARB** 15.5g; **FIBER** 0.8g; **CHOL** 28mg; **IRON** 0.8mg; **SODIUM** 221mg; **CALC** 89mg

Broccoli Slaw with Oranges and Crunchy Noodles

Slaw:
6 cups thinly sliced napa (Chinese) cabbage
1 cup diagonally sliced celery
1 cup finely chopped broccoli florets
½ cup grated carrot (1 medium)
¼ cup thinly sliced green onions
¼ cup unsalted sunflower seed kernels
1 (5-ounce) can whole water chestnuts, drained and chopped

Dressing:
¼ cup lower-sodium soy sauce
3 tablespoons rice vinegar

1 tablespoon fresh lime juice
1 tablespoon honey
1 teaspoon crushed red pepper
⅛ teaspoon ground ginger
1 garlic clove, crushed
⅓ cup canola oil

Remaining ingredients:
1 cup fresh orange sections
¼ cup sliced almonds, toasted
1 (3-ounce) package ramen noodles, crumbled and toasted (discard seasoning packet)

1. To prepare slaw, combine first 7 ingredients in a large bowl; toss well to combine.
2. To prepare dressing, combine soy sauce and next 6 ingredients (through garlic) in a small bowl, stirring with a whisk. Gradually add oil to soy sauce mixture, stirring constantly with a whisk. Drizzle dressing over slaw, tossing gently to coat. Top slaw with oranges, almonds, and noodles. Yield: 12 servings (serving size: ½ cup).

CALORIES 162; **FAT** 10.7g (sat 1.3g, mono 5.4g, poly 3.4g); **PROTEIN** 3.7g; **CARB** 15.2g; **FIBER** 3.6g; **CHOL** 0mg; **IRON** 1.2mg; **SODIUM** 308mg; **CALC** 51mg

NUTRITION TIP: The veggies, seeds, nuts, and fruit make this salad a powerhouse of vitamins, minerals, and antioxidants.

Fall Salad with Apples, Walnuts, and Stilton

The varied flavors in this upscale salad make it an ideal first course for a special meal.

1 tablespoon minced shallots
1½ tablespoons champagne or white wine
   vinegar
1 tablespoon fresh lemon juice
1 tablespoon honey
1 teaspoon Dijon mustard
1 dried apricot, finely chopped
3 tablespoons extra-virgin olive oil
¼ teaspoon salt

⅛ teaspoon freshly ground black pepper
2 cups torn green leaf lettuce
2 cups thinly sliced Belgian endive
   (about 2 heads)
¼ cup (1 ounce) Stilton cheese, thinly sliced
¼ cup walnuts, coarsely chopped
1 (5-ounce) package baby arugula
1 ounce very thin slices prosciutto, torn
1 Granny Smith apple, cored and thinly sliced

1. Place first 6 ingredients in a blender. With blender on, slowly add oil; process until well combined. Stir in salt and pepper.

2. Combine lettuce and remaining ingredients in a large bowl; add apricot mixture, tossing gently to coat. Yield: 4 servings (serving size: 2 cups).

CALORIES 294; **FAT** 18.4g (sat 3.6g, mono 8.9g, poly 5g); **PROTEIN** 9.2g; **CARB** 28g; **FIBER** 10.8g; **CHOL** 9.5mg; **IRON** 3.7mg; **SODIUM** 429mg; **CALC** 254mg

> **SIMPLE SUB:** Use crumbled goat cheese in place of Stilton, if you prefer a milder cheese.

Autumn Apple, Pear, and Cheddar Salad with Pecans *(Pictured on page 328)*

Serve this classic combination of fruit, cheese, and nuts with a chicken or pork dish.

1 cup apple juice
2 tablespoons cider vinegar
1 teaspoon extra-virgin olive oil
½ teaspoon salt
¼ teaspoon freshly ground black pepper
10 cups gourmet salad greens
  (about 10 ounces)
1 cup seedless red grapes, halved

1 medium McIntosh apple, cored and cut into
  18 wedges
1 medium Bartlett pear, cored and cut into
  18 wedges
¼ cup (1 ounce) shredded sharp cheddar
  cheese
3 tablespoons chopped pecans, toasted

1. Place apple juice in a small saucepan, and bring to a boil over medium-high heat. Cook until reduced to about 3 tablespoons (about 10 minutes). Combine reduced apple juice, vinegar, oil, salt, and pepper, stirring with a whisk.

2. Combine greens, grapes, apple, and pear in a large bowl. Drizzle with apple juice mixture; toss gently to coat. Sprinkle with cheese and nuts. Yield: 6 servings (serving size: about 1⅔ cups salad, 2 teaspoons cheese, and 1½ teaspoons nuts).

CALORIES 134; **FAT** 5.4g (sat 1.2g, mono 2.6g, poly 1.1g); **PROTEIN** 3.4g; **CARB** 21.1g; **FIBER** 4.1g; **CHOL** 5mg; **IRON** 1.5mg; **SODIUM** 255mg; **CALC** 93mg

Candied Walnut, Pear, and Leafy Green Salad

⅓ cup sugar

⅔ cup chopped walnuts, toasted

Cooking spray

½ teaspoon kosher salt, divided

2 tablespoons white balsamic vinegar

1½ teaspoons Dijon mustard

3 tablespoons extra-virgin olive oil

1 tablespoon capers, drained and chopped

4 cups torn green leaf lettuce

4 cups chopped romaine lettuce

4 cups chopped radicchio

1 ripe red Anjou pear, thinly sliced

¼ teaspoon freshly ground black pepper

1. Place sugar in a small, heavy saucepan over medium-high heat; cook until sugar dissolves, stirring gently as needed to dissolve sugar evenly (about 1 minute). Continue cooking 1 minute or until golden (do not stir). Remove from heat; carefully stir in nuts to coat evenly. Spread nuts on a baking sheet coated with cooking spray; separate nuts quickly. Sprinkle with ¼ teaspoon salt. Set aside until cool; break into small pieces.

2. Combine vinegar and mustard, stirring with a whisk. Gradually add oil, stirring constantly with a whisk. Stir in capers.

3. Combine lettuces and radicchio; top with pear and candied walnuts. Drizzle dressing evenly over salad; sprinkle with remaining ¼ teaspoon salt and pepper. Toss gently to combine. Yield: 8 servings (serving size: about 1 cup).

CALORIES 171; **FAT** 11.6g (sat 1.3g, mono 4.6g, poly 5.2g); **PROTEIN** 2.7g; **CARB** 16.3g; **FIBER** 2.6g; **CHOL** 0mg; **IRON** 1mg; **SODIUM** 177mg; **CALC** 37mg

Greens with Golden Raisins

Escarole's bitter, assertive flavor will complement Lamb Tagine (page 272).

2 tablespoons canola oil
1/2 cup golden raisins
**1 small white onion, halved and thinly sliced
   (about 2 cups)**

6 ounces chopped escarole
1 pound fresh baby spinach
1/2 teaspoon kosher salt
1/2 teaspoon garam masala

1. Heat oil in a large nonstick skillet over medium-high heat. Add raisins and onion to pan; cook 3 minutes or until onion is lightly browned. Add half of escarole to pan; cook 2 minutes or until greens wilt. Repeat with remaining escarole. Add a third of spinach to pan; cook 2 minutes or until spinach wilts. Repeat procedure 2 times with remaining spinach. Stir in salt and garam masala. Yield: 6 servings (serving size: about 1/2 cup).

CALORIES 136; **FAT** 4.9g (sat 0.4g, mono 3g, poly 1.4g); **PROTEIN** 3.2g; **CARB** 23.7g; **FIBER** 5.9g; **CHOL** 0mg; **IRON** 3.1mg; **SODIUM** 290mg; **CALC** 89mg

FYI: Literally translated as "warm mixture," garam masala is an aromatic North Indian spice blend. It's used in everything from flatbreads to soups.

Arugula and Pear Salad with Toasted Walnuts

Splurge on a high-quality olive oil, which enhances the ingredients.

1 tablespoon minced shallots
2 tablespoons extra-virgin olive oil
2 teaspoons white wine vinegar
¼ teaspoon salt
¼ teaspoon Dijon mustard

⅛ teaspoon freshly ground black pepper
6 cups baby arugula
2 Bosc pears, thinly sliced
¼ cup chopped walnuts, toasted

1. Combine first 6 ingredients in a large bowl; stir with a whisk. Add arugula and pears to bowl; toss to coat. Place about 1½ cups salad on each of 4 plates; sprinkle each serving with 1 tablespoon walnuts. Yield: 4 servings.

CALORIES 168; **FAT** 12.5g (sat 1.5g, mono 5.7g, poly 4.6g); **PROTEIN** 2.5g; **CARB** 15.1g; **FIBER** 3g; **CHOL** 0mg; **IRON** 0.7mg; **SODIUM** 164mg; **CALC** 106mg

Spinach Salad with Gorgonzola, Pistachios, and Pepper Jelly Vinaigrette

Red pepper jelly adds a snappy note to the vinaigrette that makes this simple salad memorable. You can prepare the vinaigrette (step one) earlier in the day and refrigerate; let it come to room temperature before tossing it with the spinach.

¼ cup red pepper jelly
2 tablespoons cider vinegar
1 tablespoon extra-virgin olive oil
⅛ teaspoon kosher salt
⅛ teaspoon freshly ground black pepper

8 cups fresh baby spinach
¼ cup (1 ounce) crumbled Gorgonzola
  cheese
¼ cup shelled dry-roasted pistachios

1. Place jelly in a 1-cup glass measure. Microwave at HIGH 30 seconds. Add cider vinegar, oil, salt, and black pepper, stirring with a whisk until blended. Cool to room temperature.
2. Combine spinach and cheese in a large bowl. Drizzle vinegar mixture over spinach mixture; toss well. Place 1 cup spinach mixture on each of 6 plates. Sprinkle each serving with 2 teaspoons nuts. Serve immediately. Yield: 6 servings.

CALORIES 101; **FAT** 6.1g (sat 1.6g, mono 3g, poly 1.1g); **PROTEIN** 2.9g; **CARB** 10.4g; **FIBER** 2.3g; **CHOL** 4mg; **IRON** 1.3mg; **SODIUM** 187mg; **CALC** 54mg

Arugula, Grape, and Sunflower Seed Salad

This salad's simple vinaigrette has a nice combination of sweet, tart, and pungent flavors to balance the peppery arugula and crisp grapes. The seeds add a nutty crunch to the mix.

3 tablespoons red wine vinegar
1 teaspoon honey
1 teaspoon maple syrup
½ teaspoon stone-ground mustard
2 teaspoons grapeseed or canola oil
7 cups loosely packed baby arugula

2 cups red grapes, halved
2 tablespoons toasted sunflower seed kernels
1 teaspoon chopped fresh thyme
¼ teaspoon salt
¼ teaspoon freshly ground black pepper

1. Combine first 4 ingredients in a small bowl. Gradually add oil, stirring with a whisk.
2. Combine arugula, grapes, seeds, and thyme in a large bowl. Drizzle vinegar mixture over arugula mixture; sprinkle with salt and pepper. Toss gently to coat. Yield: 6 servings (serving size: about 1 cup).

CALORIES 81; **FAT** 3.1g (sat 0.3g, mono 0.5g, poly 2g); **PROTEIN** 1.6g; **CARB** 13.1g; **FIBER** 1.2g; **CHOL** 0mg; **IRON** 0.7mg; **SODIUM** 124mg; **CALC** 47mg

Pesto Caesar Salad

3 ounces French bread baguette, cut into
 ½-inch cubes
1½ teaspoons extra-virgin olive oil
Cooking spray
2 ounces Parmigiano-Reggiano cheese
¼ cup organic canola mayonnaise
3 tablespoons commercial pesto
4 teaspoons water

2 teaspoons fresh lemon juice
1 teaspoon anchovy paste
½ teaspoon Worcestershire sauce
½ teaspoon Dijon mustard
⅛ teaspoon hot pepper sauce
1 garlic clove, minced
12 cups torn romaine lettuce

1. Preheat oven to 400°.

2. Toss bread with oil in a large bowl; arrange bread in a single layer on a baking sheet coated with cooking spray. Bake at 400° for 10 minutes or until golden, turning once.

3. Grate 2 tablespoons cheese. Shave remaining cheese; set aside.

4. Combine grated cheese, mayonnaise, and next 8 ingredients (through garlic) in a medium bowl; stir with a whisk. Combine croutons and lettuce in a large bowl. Drizzle mayonnaise mixture over salad; toss to coat. Place 1⅓ cups salad on each of 6 plates. Top each serving with 1 tablespoon shaved cheese. Yield: 6 servings.

CALORIES 202; FAT 14.3g (sat 2.3g, mono 6.2g, poly 5.4g); PROTEIN 6.2g; CARB 13.6g; FIBER 2.9g; CHOL 15mg; IRON 1.9mg; SODIUM 331mg; CALC 131mg

Winter Salad

This colorful salad complements a variety of dishes. It makes attractive individual salads for a family supper or a buffet offering on a platter at a party.

¼ cup fresh lemon juice
½ teaspoon salt
¼ teaspoon freshly ground black pepper
1 garlic clove, minced
2 tablespoons extra-virgin olive oil
2 cups thinly sliced fennel

½ cup diagonally sliced celery
4 cups torn romaine lettuce
2 cups grapefruit sections
1 cup pomegranate seeds
½ cup chopped peeled avocado
2 tablespoons pine nuts, toasted

1. Combine first 4 ingredients in a small bowl. Gradually add olive oil, stirring with a whisk until well blended.

2. Combine 1 tablespoon dressing, fennel, and celery in a bowl; cover and refrigerate 2 hours. Set aside remaining dressing.

3. Arrange ½ cup lettuce on each of 8 plates. Top each serving with ⅓ cup fennel mixture, ¼ cup grapefruit, 2 tablespoons pomegranate seeds, 1 tablespoon avocado, and ¾ teaspoon pine nuts. Drizzle each serving with about 2¼ teaspoons reserved dressing. Yield: 8 servings.

CALORIES 105; FAT 6.6g (sat 0.9g, mono 3.8g, poly 1.5g); PROTEIN 1.7g; CARB 12.2g; FIBER 2.7g; CHOL 0mg; IRON 0.8mg; SODIUM 169mg; CALC 33mg

**Sesame-Miso
Cucumber Salad**

Sesame-Miso Cucumber Salad

Miso is a thick soybean paste with a salty, slightly sweet flavor. Look for it in the refrigerated part of the produce section or with the dairy products.

1½ tablespoons sesame seeds, toasted
2 tablespoons white miso (soybean paste) or lower-sodium soy sauce
1 tablespoon rice vinegar
1 tablespoon honey

1 tablespoon hot water
1 teaspoon crushed red pepper
2 teaspoons dark sesame oil
4 cups thinly sliced seeded cucumber

1. Combine first 7 ingredients in a large bowl, stirring with a whisk. Add cucumber; toss to coat. Yield: 6 servings (serving size: ¾ cup).

CALORIES 60; **FAT** 2.7g (sat 0.2g, mono 0.6g, poly 0.7g); **PROTEIN** 1.9g; **CARB** 7.2g; **FIBER** 1.6g; **CHOL** 0mg; **IRON** 3.8mg; **SODIUM** 182mg; **CALC** 12mg

---

MENU IDEA: Serve with an Asian stir-fry, fried rice, or a curry dish.

Haricots Verts, Radish, and Watercress Salad

Haricots verts are short, slim, tender green beans. If you substitute regular green beans, cook them a little longer. The recipe is easily cut in half.

3 pounds haricots verts, trimmed
4 cups trimmed watercress (about 4 ounces)
1 cup sliced radishes
2 tablespoons extra-virgin olive oil
1 tablespoon white wine vinegar

1 tablespoon water
1 tablespoon Dijon mustard
1 teaspoon salt
¼ teaspoon freshly ground black pepper

1. Steam beans, covered, 6 minutes or until crisp-tender. Rinse beans with cold water; drain. Chill.
2. Combine beans, watercress, and radishes in a large bowl; toss gently. Combine oil and remaining ingredients in a small bowl, stirring well with a whisk. Drizzle over watercress mixture; toss gently. Serve immediately. Yield: 12 servings (serving size: 1 cup).

CALORIES 51; **FAT** 2.4g (sat 0.3g, mono 1.7g, poly 0.3g); **PROTEIN** 1.8g; **CARB** 7.4g; **FIBER** 4.2g; **CHOL** 0mg; **IRON** 0.6mg; **SODIUM** 235mg; **CALC** 72mg

Green Beans with Toasted Garl

Green Beans with Toasted Garlic

1 pound green beans, trimmed
2 teaspoons butter
1 teaspoon olive oil

4 garlic cloves, thinly sliced
¼ teaspoon salt
¼ teaspoon freshly ground black pepper

1. Bring a large saucepan of water to a boil. Add beans; cook 5 minutes. Plunge beans into ice water; drain.

2. Heat butter and oil in a large skillet over medium-high heat. Add garlic; sauté 30 seconds. Remove garlic; set aside. Add beans to pan; sprinkle with salt and pepper. Cook 2 minutes, tossing frequently. Top with garlic. Yield: 4 servings (serving size: about 1 cup).

CALORIES 67; **FAT** 3.2g (sat 1.4g, mono 1.3g, poly 0.3g); **PROTEIN** 2.3g; **CARB** 9.2g; **FIBER** 4g; **CHOL** 5mg; **IRON** 1.3mg; **SODIUM** 169mg; **CALC** 49mg

Green Beans with Toasted Hazelnut–Lemon Butter

Stir together the butter up to three weeks in advance, and store in the freezer. Prepare extra butter to serve with bread or baked potatoes.

1½ tablespoons butter, softened
3 tablespoons finely chopped hazelnuts, toasted
1½ teaspoons grated lemon rind

2¼ teaspoons salt, divided
8 cups water
1½ pounds green beans, trimmed

1. Combine butter, hazelnuts, lemon rind, and ½ teaspoon salt in a small bowl; stir with a fork until well blended.

2. Bring 8 cups water and remaining 1¾ teaspoons salt to a boil in a large saucepan. Add green beans; cook 3 minutes. Drain. Return pan to medium heat. Add beans and butter mixture; cook 3 minutes or until butter mixture melts. Toss gently to coat. Yield: 6 servings (serving size: 1⅓ cups).

CALORIES 54; **FAT** 3.1g (sat 0.8g, mono 1.9g, poly 0.3g); **PROTEIN** 1.7g; **CARB** 6.4g; **FIBER** 3.8g; **CHOL** 3mg; **IRON** 0.6mg; **SODIUM** 400mg; **CALC** 51mg

Spinach with Garlic Vinaigrette

Spinach with Garlic Vinaigrette

1½ tablespoons extra-virgin olive oil
1 tablespoon white wine vinegar
½ teaspoon Dijon mustard
¼ teaspoon freshly ground black pepper
⅛ teaspoon salt
2 garlic cloves, minced
6 cups baby spinach leaves (about 6 ounces)
¼ cup vertically sliced red onion

1. Combine first 6 ingredients in a large bowl, stirring well with a whisk. Add 6 cups spinach and red onion; toss to coat. Yield: 4 servings (serving size: 1¾ cups).

CALORIES 66; FAT 5.1g (sat 0.7g, mono 3.7g, poly 0.5g); PROTEIN 1.1g; CARB 5.2g; FIBER 1.9g; CHOL 0mg; IRON 1.3mg; SODIUM 147mg; CALC 31mg

Spinach with Raisins and Pine Nuts

This dish complements a pasta-and-cheese casserole. Have your ingredients prepped; cook just before you're ready to serve.

¼ cup raisins
1 teaspoon olive oil
1 cup chopped onion
2 pounds bagged prewashed spinach
¼ cup pine nuts, toasted
½ teaspoon salt
¼ teaspoon freshly ground black pepper

1. Place raisins in a small bowl; cover with hot water. Let stand 5 minutes or until plump; drain.
2. Heat oil in a Dutch oven over medium heat. Add onion to pan; cook 10 minutes or until tender, stirring occasionally. Add about one-fourth of spinach to pan; cook 3 minutes or until spinach wilts, stirring occasionally. Repeat procedure 3 times with remaining spinach. Stir in raisins, nuts, salt, and pepper. Yield: 10 servings (serving size: ½ cup).

CALORIES 68; FAT 3g (sat 0.6g, mono 1g, poly 1.2g); PROTEIN 3.5g; CARB 8.4g; FIBER 2.8g; CHOL 0mg; IRON 2.8mg; SODIUM 193mg; CALC 96mg

Asparagus with Balsamic Tomatoes

Asparagus with Balsamic Tomatoes

1 pound asparagus, trimmed
2 teaspoons extra-virgin olive oil
1½ cups halved grape tomatoes
½ teaspoon minced garlic

2 tablespoons balsamic vinegar
¼ teaspoon salt
3 tablespoons crumbled goat cheese
½ teaspoon freshly ground black pepper

1. Cook asparagus in boiling water 2 minutes or until crisp-tender. Drain.
2. Heat olive oil in a large skillet over medium-high heat. Add tomatoes and garlic; cook 5 minutes. Stir in vinegar; cook 3 minutes. Stir in salt. Arrange asparagus on a platter; top with tomato mixture. Sprinkle with cheese and pepper. Yield: 4 servings.

CALORIES 69; **FAT** 3.9g (sat 1.4g, mono 2g, poly 0.3g); **PROTEIN** 3g; **CARB** 6.5g; **FIBER** 2.1g; **CHOL** 4mg; **IRON** 1.6mg; **SODIUM** 181mg; **CALC** 45mg

Roasted Chile-Garlic Broccoli

The bold flavors of chile paste and sesame oil call for pairing with a robust entrée such as Almost-Classic Pork Fried Rice (page 149).

6 cups broccoli florets
2 tablespoons dark sesame oil
2 teaspoons sambal oelek (ground fresh
  chile paste)

½ teaspoon salt
⅛ teaspoon sugar
6 large garlic cloves, coarsely chopped

1. Place a small roasting pan in oven. Preheat oven to 450°.
2. Place broccoli in a large bowl; drizzle with oil. Toss to coat. Add sambal oelek, salt, and sugar to broccoli mixture; toss. Add broccoli mixture to hot roasting pan; toss. Bake at 450° for 5 minutes; remove from oven. Add garlic to pan; stir. Bake an additional 5 minutes or until broccoli is lightly browned. Yield: 4 servings (serving size: 1¼ cups).

CALORIES 99; **FAT** 7.2g (sat 1g, mono 2.7g, poly 3g); **PROTEIN** 3.5g; **CARB** 7.7g; **FIBER** 3.2g; **CHOL** 0mg; **IRON** 1mg; **SODIUM** 252mg; **CALC** 59mg

> **FLAVOR HIT:** Roasting broccoli adds a new flavor dimension.

Carrots Roasted with Smoked Paprika

Smoky paprika balances the sweet carrots.

2 tablespoons olive oil
1½ teaspoons Spanish smoked paprika
1 teaspoon kosher salt
½ teaspoon freshly ground black pepper

2½ pounds medium carrots, peeled and halved lengthwise
2 tablespoons finely chopped fresh cilantro

1. Place a jelly-roll pan on bottom oven rack. Preheat oven to 450°.
2. Combine first 5 ingredients in a large bowl; toss well. Arrange carrot mixture in a single layer on preheated pan. Bake at 450° for 25 minutes or until tender, stirring after 12 minutes. Sprinkle with cilantro. Yield: 10 servings (serving size: about ⅓ cup).

CALORIES 72; **FAT** 3g (sat 0.4g, mono 2g, poly 0.4g); **PROTEIN** 1.1g; **CARB** 11.1g; **FIBER** 3.3g; **CHOL** 0mg; **IRON** 0.4mg; **SODIUM** 267mg; **CALC** 39mg

Curried Cauliflower with Capers

Look for olive-sized caperberries—the immature fruit of the caper bush—at gourmet grocers or specialty stores.

6 cups cauliflower florets (about 1 large head)
1/4 cup extra-virgin olive oil, divided
2 teaspoons grated lemon rind
2 tablespoons fresh lemon juice
1/4 teaspoon salt

1/2 teaspoon curry powder
1/4 teaspoon freshly ground black pepper
1/3 cup caperberries, thinly sliced
1/4 cup chopped fresh flat-leaf parsley
1/4 cup capers, drained

1. Preheat oven to 450°.

2. Combine cauliflower and 1 tablespoon oil on a jelly-roll pan, tossing to coat. Bake at 450° for 30 minutes or until browned, turning once.

3. Combine remaining 3 tablespoons oil, lemon rind, and next 4 ingredients (through black pepper) in a large bowl; stir with a whisk. Add roasted cauliflower, caperberries, parsley, and capers to bowl; toss mixture well to combine. Yield: 6 servings (servings size: about 1 cup).

CALORIES 107; **FAT** 9.5g (sat 1.3g, mono 6.6g, poly 1.2g); **PROTEIN** 2.1g; **CARB** 5.3g; **FIBER** 2.6g; **CHOL** 0mg; **IRON** 0.7mg; **SODIUM** 348mg; **CALC** 24mg

Nutritional Analysis

How to Use It and Why

Glance at the end of any *Cooking Light* recipe, and you'll see how committed we are to helping you make the best of today's light cooking. With chefs, registered dietitians, home economists, and a computer system that analyzes every ingredient we use, *Cooking Light* gives you authoritative dietary detail like no other magazine. We go to such lengths so you can see how our recipes fit into your healthful eating plan. If you're trying to lose weight, the calorie and fat figures will probably help most. But if you're keeping a close eye on the sodium, cholesterol, and saturated fat in your diet, we provide those numbers, too. And because many women don't get enough iron or calcium, we can help there, as well. Finally, there's a fiber analysis for those of us who don't get enough roughage.

Here's a helpful guide to put our nutritional analysis numbers into perspective. Remember, one size doesn't fit all, so take your lifestyle, age, and circumstances into consideration when determining your nutrition needs. For example, pregnant or breast-feeding women need more protein, calories, and calcium. And women older than 50 need 1,200mg of calcium daily, 200mg more than the amount recommended for younger women.

In Our Nutritional Analysis, We Use These Abbreviations

sat saturated fat

mono monounsaturated fat

poly polyunsaturated fat

CARB carbohydrates

CHOL cholesterol

CALC calcium

g gram

mg milligram

Daily Nutrition Guide

	Women ages 25 to 50	Women over 50	Men ages 25 to 50	Men over 50
Calories	2,000	2,000*	2,700	2,500
Protein	50g	50g	63g	60g
Fat	65g*	65g*	88g*	83g*
Saturated Fat	20g*	20g*	27g*	25g*
Carbohydrates	304g	304g	410g	375g
Fiber	25g to 35g	25g to 35g	25g to 35g	25g to 35g
Cholesterol	300mg*	300mg*	300mg*	300mg*
Iron	18mg	8mg	8mg	8mg
Sodium	2,300mg*	1,500mg*	2,300mg*	1,500mg*
Calcium	1,000mg	1,200mg	1,000mg	1,000mg

The nutritional values used in our calculations either come from The Food Processor, Version 8.9 (ESHA Research), or are provided by food manufacturers. *Or less, for optimal health.

Metric Equivalents

The information in the following charts is provided to help cooks outside the United States successfully use the recipes in this book. All equivalents are approximate.

Cooking/Oven Temperatures

	Fahrenheit	Celsius	Gas Mark
Freeze Water	32° F	0° C	
Room Temperature	68° F	20° C	
Boil Water	212° F	100° C	
Bake	325° F	160° C	3
	350° F	180° C	4
	375° F	190° C	5
	400° F	200° C	6
	425° F	220° C	7
	450° F	230° C	8
Broil			Grill

Liquid Ingredients by Volume

¼ tsp					=	1 ml
½ tsp					=	2 ml
1 tsp					=	5 ml
3 tsp	= 1 tbl		= ½ fl oz	=	15 ml
	2 tbls	= ⅛ cup	= 1 fl oz	=	30 ml
	4 tbls	= ¼ cup	= 2 fl oz	=	60 ml
	5⅓ tbls	= ⅓ cup	= 3 fl oz	=	80 ml
	8 tbls	= ½ cup	= 4 fl oz	=	120 ml
	10⅔ tbls	= ⅔ cup	= 5 fl oz	=	160 ml
	12 tbls	= ¾ cup	= 6 fl oz	=	180 ml
	16 tbls	= 1 cup	= 8 fl oz	=	240 ml
	1 pt	= 2 cups	= 16 fl oz	=	480 ml
	1 qt	= 4 cups	= 32 fl oz	=	960 ml
			33 fl oz	=	1000 ml = 1l

Dry Ingredients by Weight

(To convert ounces to grams, multiply the number of ounces by 30.)

1 oz	=	1/16 lb	=	30 g
4 oz	=	¼ lb	=	120 g
8 oz	=	½ lb	=	240 g
12 oz	=	¾ lb	=	360 g
16 oz	=	1 lb	=	480 g

Length

(To convert inches to centimeters, multiply the number of inches by 2.5.)

1 in	=			2.5 cm
6 in	=	½ ft	=	15 cm
12 in	=	1 ft	=	30 cm
36 in	=	3 ft	=	1 yd =	90 cm
40 in	=			100 cm	= 1m

Equivalents for Different Types of Ingredients

Standard Cup	Fine Powder (ex. flour)	Grain (ex. rice)	Granular (ex. sugar)	Liquid Solids (ex. butter)	Liquid (ex. milk)
1	140 g	150 g	190 g	200 g	240 ml
¾	105 g	113 g	143 g	150 g	180 ml
⅔	93 g	100 g	125 g	133 g	160 ml
½	70 g	75 g	95 g	100 g	120 ml
⅓	47 g	50 g	63 g	67 g	80 ml
¼	35 g	38 g	48 g	50 g	60 ml
⅛	18 g	19 g	24 g	25 g	30 ml

index